Job Stress:
From Theory to Suggestion

Job Stress: From Theory to Suggestion

John M. Ivancevich and Daniel C. Ganster
Editors

The Haworth Press
New York • London

Job Stress: From Theory to Suggestion has also been published as *Journal of Organizational Behavior Management*, Volume 8, Number 2, Fall/Winter 1986.

The Haworth Press, Inc., 12 West 32 Street, New York, NY 10001
EUROSPAN/Haworth, 3 Henrietta Street, London WC2E 8LU England

Library of Congress Cataloging-in-Publication Data

Job stress.

"Has also been published as Journal of organizational behavior management, volume 8, number 2, fall/winter 1986-87/9D/ – T.p. verso.
Includes bibliographies.
1. Job stress. I. Ivancevich, John M. II. Ganster, Daniel C. [DNLM: 1. Job Satisfaction. 2. Stress, Psychological. W1 J0804L v.8 no.2/WM 172 J62]
HF5548.85.J65   1987   658.3'82   87-8568
ISBN 0-86656-630-9

Job Stress:
From Theory to Suggestion

Journal of Organizational Behavior Management
Volume 8, Number 2

CONTENTS

Stress: Theory, Research, and Suggestions

What is stress? If you asked 100 people, you would probably receive 100 different definitions. There is no specific definition that has been universally accepted as the final view of what stress entails. An optimist might state that we are coming closer to a generally accepted interpretation of what stress is. On the other hand, a realist knows that theorists, researchers, and practitioners are no closer today to a general definition than we were two decades ago.

In preparing this volume, we decided that since no universal definition or ideal starting point existed it would be more informative and insightful to invite individuals from diverse backgrounds to prepare papers for the *Journal of Organizational Behavior Management*. We felt the diversity of our selected authors would show agreement, disagreement, and interests of theorists and researchers who are engaged in studying and accumulating knowledge on stress. Our expectations were met by the authors who worked hard to prepare papers that were (1) clearly written for the *Journal of Organizational Behavior Management* (*JOBM*) audience; (2) focused on a topic that would be of interest to *JOBM* readers; (3) current and relevant; (4) representative of the type of topics currently being covered in the numerous outlets reporting on stress; and (5) practical in terms of offering suggestions and directions for individuals interested in applying organizational behavior management principles.

In developing this volume, we looked closely at the OBM literature to determine if a body of stress research and/or conceptual work was available. There was no such body of work. There are available a few studies that use OBM principles in stress management intervention programs. However, for the most part, these studies did not cover the type of general topics that the highly visible stress community of theorists and researchers were examining. Also, the number of studies were limited and offered no systematic pattern of accumulated knowledge. Thus, we decided to invite writers who have been engaged in specific and multiple stress related projects and not to search for the handful of OBM oriented scholars and researchers who have been involved in a single project or have prepared a single paper. Certainly, our decision undoubtedly excluded some outstanding OBM authors, but hopefully the breadth offered by the writers of this volume's papers will make up for some of this deficiency.

THE ORGANIZATION OF THE SPECIAL ISSUE

The excitement of preparing a general and descriptive paper for a predominantly OBM audience resulted in fourteen well crafted, succinct papers. The result of the work of the author team for this volume is a six-part series of papers. *Part I: Introduction* contains three papers: Terry A. Beehr and Thomas M. Franz tackle the very difficult problem of interpreting what is meant by stress. Next, Jonathan D. Quick, Rebecca S. Horn, and James C. Quick discuss some health consequences associated with stress. The final article in Part I by Jeffrey H. Greenhaus and Saroj Parasuraman examines the interaction of work and non-work conditions as they impact stress.

Part II: Individual Differences examines two of the many potentially significant moderators of the stress-outcome-consequence linkage, namely Type A behavior and social support. Daniel C. Ganster examines studies of Type A behavior in terms of a causal model. Susan Gore discusses current research approaches that focus on social support processes.

Part III: Stress Measurement includes three papers. Lisa R. Balick and J. Alan Herd present a view of selected physiological indices of job stress. The second paper by India Fleming and Andrew Baum discusses a multidimensional approach to stress measurement. Next, a paper by David Watson, James W. Pennebaker, and Robert Folger introduces a pervasive personality dimension— negative affectivity—that they propose should be considered when assessing stress via self-report measurement.

Part IV: Organizational Studies of Stress contains three papers. Joseph J. Hurrell, Jr. and Michael J. Colligan examine machine-paced work and shiftwork in terms of job stress type consequences. Steven P. Glowinkowski and Cary L. Cooper report research evidence on managers and professionals in business/industrial settings. Cynthia Lee discusses research involving various professional medical occupations.

Part V: Stress Management Interventions includes two papers. Lawrence R. Murphy presents a review of methodological considerations of organizational stress management research. John M. Ivancevich and Michael T. Matteson provide a model, review, and recommendations on organizational level stress management interventions.

Part VI: Conclusion presents the closing paper by Ronald J. Burke. He presents, in a realistic manner, the current state of stress research. It is his belief that our understanding of stress phenomena will continue to be a slow process of accumulation and knowledge gain.

A FINAL VIEW

This special volume is intended to stimulate more OBM research and conceptual work in the stress area. We would like to see these papers open up new thinking and stimulate more applied research using OBM principles. As editors we would like to thank the authors for their help and cooperation in developing this special issue. We would also like to thank Thomas C. Mawhinney, who considered stress an important topic for *JOBM* readers to review in their journal.

John M. Ivancevich
Daniel C. Ganster

PART I: INTRODUCTION

The Current Debate About the Meaning of Job Stress

Terry A. Beehr
Thomas M. Franz

SUMMARY. There is currently a great deal of disagreement about the meaning of job stress. This probably has happened in part because the topic has its roots in several diverse fields, including medicine, clinical psychology, engineering psychology, and organizational psychology. The differences among these fields in their interpretations of job stress are seen in both their choices of labels and in the substance of their theories and approaches to treatments. There are many specific controversies in the field, of which four are especially central to the meaning of job stress: the existence and nature of first mediators, awareness as a necessary component of stress, the possibility and effects of "good" stress, and acute versus chronic stressors.

Stress, including job or occupational stress, is currently both an object of massive scientific research and a term so loosely defined that there have been recommendations that the use of the term be

Terry A. Beehr, PhD in organizational psychology, University of Michigan, is Professor and Director of the Doctoral Program in Industrial/Organizational Psychology at Central Michigan University. Thomas M. Franz is a doctoral student in Industrial/Organizational Psychology at Central Michigan University. Both can be contacted at Psychology Department, Central Michigan University, Mt. Pleasant, MI 48859. C. Merle Johnson provided helpful comments on earlier drafts of the manuscript.

abandoned altogether. Ivancevich and Matteson (1980) have even compared stress with sin, as both topics are considered important by many people even though different people are not always talking about the same thing when they use the word.

Stress has commonly been defined in one of three ways: as an environmental stimulus often described as a force applied to the individual, as an individual's psychological or physical response to such an environmental force, or as the interaction between these two events (Ivancevich & Matteson, 1980; Mason, 1975a). These differences in the use of the word have been discussed so often in recent literature that they will not be discussed at length here.

There are more important controversies in this topic area than the choice of labels or terms, however, and journal space is better used on them. What can be agreed upon is that the term stressor, when it is used, refers to the environmental stimulus (e.g., Beehr, 1984; Beehr & Bhagat, 1985; Fried, Rowland & Ferris, 1984; McLean, 1979; Selye, 1975; Sharit & Salvendy, 1982), and that the term strain, when it is used usually refers to the individual response (e.g., Beehr, 1984; Caplan, Cobb, French, Harrison & Pinneau, 1975; Kahn & Quinn, 1970). Strains can be physical, psychological or behavioral, but they are by definition indicators of ill health and/ or well-being of the individual. A job stressor is an environmental condition or event in the workplace that causes strain. When the words stressor and strain are used in the literature, they are nearly always used in these ways, making these definitions easily understood by most people. The word stress is not used for one of these specific elements but is reserved as a general term referring to an area of work or study that includes stressors and strains.

SELECTED EARLY WORKS
ON STRESS IN GENERAL

The physiologist, Walter Cannon (1914), in his work on homeostasis, had used the term stress to describe emotional states that had possible detrimental physical results on organisms. In 1935, Cannon (c.f., Mason, 1975a) modified the use of the term to describe physical stimuli and used the term strain to mean the organism's response.

Cannon's contributions to the understanding of stress lay almost dormant for decades, until Selye began working in this area. In the classic, *The Stress of Life*, Hans Selye (1956) described efforts to isolate a new sex hormone. The hormone was not found, but a phenomenon he labeled the General Adaptation Syndrome was observed. It was described as the bodily response to prolonged debilitating circumstances. The responses or symptoms resulted from injections of purified hormones, X-rays, forced exercise, cold, etc. In fact, Selye "could find no noxious agent that did not produce the syndrome" (p. 35). Initially Selye yielded to the opinions of others and refrained from using the term stress in discussion of the GAS. The term stress at that time was equated with "nervous strain" and implied a psychological rather than a physical state.

SELECTED HISTORICAL WORKS
ON JOB STRESS IN PARTICULAR

Although Selye and even Cannon occasionally referred to occupational or work-related stress, their actual research never focused on it; indeed, much of their ground-breaking work was done with animals. A major source of the current interest in occupational stress probably can be traced instead to a book reporting research results from non-experimental studies done with American workers in the early 1960s (Kahn, Wolfe, Quinn, Snoek & Rosenthal, 1964). Using survey methods, these social and organizational psychology researchers estimated one-third or more of the employees in their national sample were experiencing some occupational stress.

A totally different approach to occupational stress, meanwhile, had already been initiated by researchers from an experimental and engineering psychology point of view. Here, physical stressors such as noise were studied for their effects on job performance or on performance of laboratory tasks (e.g., Broadbent, 1954). In addition to job performance as a criterion, physiological responses were also studied as outcomes. Often, however, this was done on the grounds that these physiological responses would be related to performance.

FOUR APPROACHES TO JOB STRESS

These different historical antecedents to today's job stress theories and practices have no doubt contributed to the current state of confusion about the topic. Even if everyone used the terms the same way, there would still be observable differences in approaches to the topic. There are currently at least four identifiable approaches to studying and treating occupational stress, and these are outlined in Table 1. For convenience these four approaches have been labeled by the profession in which they have their strongest historical roots. Today's practitioners and researchers in these disciplines — as there are people in each of these fields today who work in a multidisciplinary fashion.

The table indicates the type of stressors and strains (or other outcomes, such as job performance) on which each approach typically focuses, and in addition, it indicates something about the type of treatment that each approach is prone to recommend for alleviating problems due to job stress. The primary target of treatment refers to the element in the job stress process (usually stressor or strain) that the professional tries to alter directly. Two categories of primary target are used: individual targets and organizational targets. Individual-target treatments indicate that there is an attempt to change some characteristic or response of the individual directly. Most of these types of treatments are aimed at changing the strains directly (e.g., administering biofeedback training for hypertension or traditional psychotherapy for depression). Organizational-target treatments are attempts to change some aspect of the organization or the

Table 1

Four Approaches to Occupational Stress

Approach	Typical Stressor	Typical Outcome	Typical Primary Target of Treatment
Medical	Physical	Physical Strain	Individual
Clinical/Counseling Psychology	Psychological	Psychological Strain	Individual
Engineering Psychology	Physical	Job Performance	Organization
Organizational Psychology	Psychological	Psychological Strain	Organization

individual's immediate work environment, usually the stressors (e.g., reducing conflict or noise levels in the workplace).

The approach labeled "medical" clearly has its historical roots in the tradition of Cannon and Selye, described previously. The stressors and strains tend to be physical. The typical primary target of treatments for this approach is the individual, for example treatment of the person through application of medication. It is noteworthy for our purposes that this approach did not develop from a primary interest in occupations or the workplace, although it is occasionally applied to them.

One of the psychological approaches to occupational stress closely parallels the medical model approach, but it emphasizes psychological causes and consequences instead of physical ones. This is labeled the clinical/counseling psychology approach in Table 1. Most of the treatments are aimed directly at the individual, for example, treating depression or anxiety through counseling or psychotherapy. As with the medical approach, this approach was not developed specifically for dealing with workplace stress, but it has often been applied there. Treatments based on this approach have recently been recommended through Employee Assistance Programs (Winkelpleck, 1984).

The two approaches above the dotted line in the table, the medical and the clinical/counseling psychology approaches, have in common the fact that they tend to focus on the individual more than on the organization. The field sometimes known as medical psychology spans these two viewpoints by using treatments developed in psychology (e.g., variants of relaxation training) to treat what are conceived as physical strains (e.g., hypertension). This is a natural integration of these two approaches, since both focus on the individual more than on the organizational. These two do not as frequently overlap with the engineering or organizational psychology approaches, however.

As can be seen in Table 1, a third approach can be identified that has traditionally focused on physical characteristics of the work or workplace as stressors and on job performance as the primary outcome. With roots in the previously mentioned engineering and experimental psychology efforts, this has implications for the physical design of the work and workplace as treatments. It is a very different approach from any of the others in its preferred choice of outcome, since job performance does not fit the definition of strain usually offered by the other approaches. This approach has, however, often been applied specifically to the work setting.

Table 1 also outlines an organizational psychology approach in which psychological stressors are found to influence psychological strains, and the organizational or workplace characteristics are the indicated targets for direct treatment. This approach, receiving pioneering impetus from the 1964 book by Kahn et al., was developed with a specific interest in workplace stress.

The four views in the table obviously have different historical antecedents. The views indicate some of the typical approaches to job stress by people involved in the field, and the entries in the body of the table are intended to direct readers to categorize stressors, outcomes, and treatments in three particular ways: First whether stressors are physical or psychological characteristics of the work environment, second, whether the outcomes are strains (psychological or physical) on performance; and third, whether treatments are aimed at changing some aspect of the individual directly (usually at a strain response) or at changing some part of the organization (usually at something conceived as a stressor). People working in the job stress field from one of these perspectives often try to broaden their approaches to take into consideration important characteristics of job stress from other approaches, but they naturally remain focused on the areas in which they have the most expertise.

As a striking indication of the separate development of these approaches, the Kahn et al. (1964) book, identified as a classic from the organizational psychology approach, does not even reference Selye anywhere in its 400-odd pages; Selye, however, is often given credit as a pioneer in the medical and the clinical/counseling approaches (McLean, 1979; Mason, 1975a). The point is that these approaches have developed largely independently from each other. Therefore it should not be expected that they use terms in the same way or that they are even working on the same problems. Yet this assumption is commonly made, and this a major source of the current debates about the meaning of job stress.

CONTROVERSIAL ISSUES REGARDING JOB STRESS

There are many issues regarding job stress that have kindled disagreement in the literature or that have at least been studied with conflicting results. Four of those that seem most important to the topic of this article are discussed here.

First Mediators

In 1975 Selye and Mason debated in the *Journal of Human Stress* about the meaning of stress, and some of their issues regarding the meaning of the term have yet to be solved. One particular issue was the potential existence and the nature of something Selye had called "first mediators" of the stress process. Since stress could affect many different parts of the body through many different disease processes, Selye (1956) hypothesized that there must be some messengers in the body that are activated by stressors and that are capable of sending messages to different parts of the body activating illnesses or strains. Biochemical messages could be sent through the blood stream, for example, or electrical impulses through the nervous system. Selye never was able to determine what these "first mediators" of stress were, however, and Mason (1975b) proposed that this missing link in stress might simply be emotional arousal rather than a physiological response.

Obviously, this issue comes from the medical approach to stress and is not intimately tied to the setting with which this journal is concerned: human organizations. To tie it to organizational or job stress, however, we need only to look at the Beehr-Newman (1978) model (Figure 1) of occupational stress, which is general enough to be a framework for most approaches to and research on job stress. Briefly, the model gives a way of categorizing concepts related to job stress. The concepts discussed in this article all fit into some facet of the model. The process facet consists of psychological and physical processes that occur in stressful situations, and it would include the first mediators, whether they might be physical or psychological. Job stressors are parts of the environmental facet, relatively stable personal characteristics or traits are part of the personal facet, strains are part of the human consequences facet, job performance is a major part of the organizational consequences facet, and the "adaptive responses" are divided into individually and organizationally targeted treatments.

Although the controversy about the meaning of the word stress was dismissed earlier in the paper, it comes into play again on this issue. If a first mediator that is common to all stress were found,

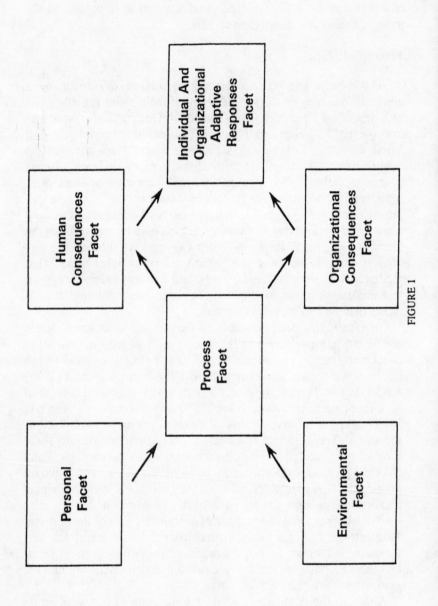

FIGURE 1

12

this might be defined as stress, and if present in an organizational member might be evidence of a stressful situation.

Awareness as a Necessary Component of Stress

A second issue in need of clarification is whether awareness is a necessary component of occupational stress. Phrased as a question, is it possible to experience stress without realizing it? As with the previously discussed issue, this issue is also concerned primarily with the process facet in Figure 1. Behavioral assessment paradigms often include motor, physiological, and cognitive responses (Nelson & Hayes, 1979). The individual's appraisal of an environmental situation as stressful would be a cognitive process.

Examination of the works of some well-known researchers can be used to illustrate this issue. Lazarus (e.g., 1966; Lazarus & Launier, 1978) has argued that an appraisal process occurs in which the individual evaluates the situation as one that is or is not threatening (stressful). *"For threat to occur, an evaluation must be made of the situation to the effect that a harm is signified"* (Lazarus, 1966, p. 44). On the other hand, Selye's (e.g., 1956) work describes stressors that were discovered with laboratory animals for whom we do not know about awareness. In fact, Selye's early work included the investigation of many physical stressors, including exposure to x-rays. It seems especially unlikely that the animals knew they had been exposed to x-rays. Therefore, it is not clear that awareness is a necessary condition for the existence of stress in all of its forms.

Both of these examples come from the approaches in the upper half of Table 1 and focus primarily on the individual. In the organizational psychology realm, however, some researchers (e.g., Barnes, Potter & Fiedler, 1983; Potter & Fiedler, 1981) have used the stress concept and employed measures of stress that require the individual to be aware of stress. The questionnaire item, "rate your present job on how much overall stress it places on you," assumes that people are aware of their stress (Potter & Fiedler, 1981). Assumed awareness does not seem to be a necessary function of the use of self rating methods, however, since other organizational psychology researchers used questionnaires to measure perceived job characteristics and to correlate them with strains in order to see whether the characteristics were in fact stressful—without ever asking employees directly whether they think they have experienced "stress" (e.g., Beehr, 1976). This approach seems to assume that people do not necessarily know what is stressful but that stressors are best determined by seeing whether they have a (presumed causal) relationship with strains.

If awareness of stressors is the issue, there are some reputed organizational stressors of which people are usually aware (e.g., role conflict) and some of which they typically are not (e.g., x-rays). There may also be some individual strains of which people are aware (e.g., anxiety) and some of which they typically are not (e.g., hypertension). In addition, if stress is evidenced by a relationship between stressors and strains, it is plausible that employees may be or may not be aware of the relationship. Questionnaire items (e.g., see Kahn, Wolfe, Quinn, Snoek, Rosenthal, 1964) asking the extent to which employees experience psychological reactions (strains) due to role ambiguity or conflict (stressors) assume that people are aware of a causal relationship; yet if employees can be unaware of some job stressors and some individual strains, it is unlikely that they could be aware of all relationships between stressors and strains.

It may be that Lazarus' notion of the necessity of this type of awareness is driven by his particular interest in the coping process. It makes sense that individuals might not engage in coping processes until they are aware of some sort of problem. At any rate, it is a debatable issue whether people need to be aware of stress in order for it to result in strains or poor performance. Is it possible, for example, for people to believe they thrive on situations that are actually stressful and even to seek out such situations (e.g., Type A people; Friedman & Rosenman, 1974)? These types of people might do little to protect themselves from the potentially harmful effects of the strains.

Acute and Chronic Stressors

A third issue concerns the nature of stressors. The life events tradition (e.g., Holmes & Rahe, 1967; Sarason, et al., 1978) focuses on acute stressors, that is events usually occurring in a short period of time such as the death of a spouse. Typical research on stress in the workplace, however, consistent with Kahn et al. (1964), has focused on chronic stressors such as the long-term existence of role ambiguity and role conflict. Some important exceptions to this focus include the findings that (1) an impending tax deadline affected physiological strain among tax accountants

(Friedman, Rosenman & Carroll, 1958), (2) an impending computer shutdown affected psychological strains and heart rates among college students (Caplan & Jones, 1975), and (3) the first experience at providing comprehensive patient care affected both psychological and physiological strains among nursing students (Eden, 1982).

The controversy, which has not yet been discussed much in the occupational literature, is whether the most important types of occupational stress are chronic or acute. It is also possible that the frequent occurrence of acute stressors could in some way speed the development of chronic stressors. The relative importance of and the relationships between these two types of job stressors remains to be discovered.

The Stress of "Good" Situations

The fourth issue is also one regarding a type of evaluation of the potentially stressful situation, and it therefore also concerns the process facet in Figure 1. The issue is whether ostensibly good events or situations are stressful and/or whether they are as stressful as ostensibly bad situations or events. The best known life stress scale (The Social Readjustment Rating Scale; Holmes & Rahe, 1967) includes both good and bad events (e.g., getting a pay raise might be a good event and getting fired might be a bad event) as potential stressors.

The life events literature is probably closest to the approaches in the upper half of Table 1, and the items in life events scales refer primarily to nonwork-related events. Some researchers working primarily in the organizational psychology tradition, however, have advocated similar positions. It has been proposed, for example (e.g., Beehr & Schuler, 1982; Schuler, 1980), that one kind of work-related stress is "opportunity stress," the chance to do something the individual desires to do. As one would expect, most of the identifiable stressors in the workplace are events or situations that are intuitively "bad" to most people, however.

Some research (e.g., Sarason, Johnson & Siegel, 1978) in the life stress area has indicated that negative events are more predictive of individual strains than positive events, which seems to challenge the idea that positive and negative events are likely to be equally stressful. More work needs to be done on this topic in both the work and nonwork stress areas.

RECOMMENDATIONS FOR FUTURE RESEARCH

Five topics or questions for future research derive directly from this discussion of the controversies regarding the meaning of stress. First, how are the different approaches to organizational stress (Table 1) related empirically? It would help to *know* the extent to which the different types of job stressors and outcomes are related to each other instead of *assuming* they are related, as is often done now. Second, are there physiological first mediators of stress, as Selye has often assumed? If researchers in physiology settle the question for their approach, (e.g., if they were to decide that adrenaline-related hormones are first mediators), the question remains whether these are related to the stressors and outcomes that the organizational approaches have been studying. Third, is awareness of stressors a prerequisite for the experience of stress? Alternatively, is such awareness necessary for coping to take place? Fourth, the relative effects of acute and chronic workplace stressors need to be determined, and possible relationships between them need to be examined. The potential for acute stressors, while getting a great deal of attention in the life stress literature, has been almost neglected in the area of organizational stress. Fifth and finally, how do the presumed stresses of positive and negative events or states in the workplace compare? While several writers have claimed that either positive or negative events can be stressful, this claim has not led to much research in the workplace. If positive events are stressful, the connection between the positive and negative stressors would need to be examined. It may be, for example, that they each have the element of uncertainty or unpredictability in them, a characteristic central to many types of stress according to recent reviews and theoretical developments (e.g., Sharit & Salvendy, 1982; Beehr & Bhagat, 1985).

This fifth issue can be used to illustrate the use of field methods to study occupational stress controversies. First, a long list of potentially positive and negative work-related states or events could be generated by experts and/or employees. Second, a sample of employees would rate the importance (without regard to positive or negative sign) of each of these potential stressors in order to allow comparison of positive and negative stressors presumed to be of equal intensity. Then, measures of these potential stressors could be administered to a sample of employees who are similar to the first sample (i.e., similar on most demographic and work-setting variables) along with measures of potential strains. A key comparison would be the percentage of variance of the strains for which stressors of equal importance but opposite signs (positive or negative) account. This would be a non-experimental field study with a cross-sectional design. A stronger (but more time-consuming and expensive) non-experimental field method would be to measure the occurrence of stressors and strains of a sample of employees over a period of time in order to make a stronger inference about causation of the stressor-strain relationships. This inference would be based on the temporal ordering of the occurrence of stressors and strains.

Occupational stress has become a hotbed of research in several psychological- and medical-related fields during the last two decades, and no signs of abatement appear in this activity. Partly due to research being directed from several different approaches, the research results and theories do not always fit together neatly. In fact, there is little agreement regarding the definition of stress among many researchers, theorists, and practitioners. The recommendations presented here are intended to direct us all toward developing a more integrated field of workplace stress.

REFERENCES

Barnes, V., Potter, E. H., III & Fiedler, F. E. (1983). Effect of interpersonal stress on the prediction of academic performance. *Journal of Applied Psychology, 68*, (pp. 686-697).

Beehr, T. A. (1976). Perceived situational moderators of the relationship between subjective role ambiguity and role strain. *Journal of Applied Psychology, 61*, 35-40.

Beehr, T. A. (1984). Stress coping research: Methodological issues. In A. S. Sethi & R. S. Schuler (Eds.), *Handbook of organizational stress coping strategies*. Cambridge, MA: Ballinger Publishing Company.

Beehr, T. A. (1984). *The themes of social psychological stress in work organizations: From roles to goals*. Paper for the Seventh Annual Symposia on Applied Behavioral Science, Virginia Polytechnic Institute and State University, Blacksburg, Virginia, Nov.

Beehr, T. A. & Bhagat, R. S. (1985). Introduction to human stress and cognition in organizations. In T. A. Beehr & R. S. Bhagat (Eds.), *Human Stress and Cognition in Organizations: An Integrated Perspective*, (pp. 3-19). New York: John Wiley & Sons.

Beehr, T. A. & Newman, J. E. (1978). Job stress, employee health, and organizational effectiveness: A facet analysis, model and literature review. *Personnel Psychology, 31*, 665-699.

Beehr, T. A. & Schuler, R. S. (1982). Stress in organizations. In K. M. Rowland & G. R. Ferris (Eds.), *Personnel Management* (pp. 390-419). Boston: Allyn & Bacon.

Broadbent, D. E. (1954). Some effects of noise on visual performance. *Quarterly Journal of Experimental Psychology, 6*, 1-5.

Cannon, W. B. (1914). The interrelations of emotions as suggested by recent physiological researches. *American Journal of Psychology, 25*, 256-282.

Cannon, W. B. (1935). Stresses and strains of homeostasis. *American Journal of Medical Science, 189*, 1–14.

Caplan, R. D. & Jones, K. W. (1975). Effects of work load, role ambiguity, and type A personality on anxiety, depression, and heart rate. *Journal of Applied Psychology, 60*, 713–719.

Caplan, R. D., Cobb, S. & French, J. R. P. (1975). Relationships of cessation of smoking with job stress, personality and support. *Journal of Applied Psychology, 60*, 211–219.

Eden, D. (1982). Critical job events, acute stress, and strain: A multiple interrupted time series. *Organizational Behavior and Human Performance, 30*, 312–319.

Fried, Y., Rowland, K. M., Ferris, Gerald R. (1984). The physiological measurement of work stress: A critique. *Personnel Psychology, 37*, 583–615.

Friedman, M. & Rosenman, R. H. (1974). *Type A behavior and your heart.* New York: Knopf.

Friedman, M., Rosenman, R. H. & Carroll, V. (1958). Changes in serum cholesterol and blood clotting time in men subjected to cyclic variation of occupational stress. *Circulation, 17*, 852–861.

Holmes, T. H. & Rahe, R. H. (1967). Social readjustment rating scale. *Journal of Psychosomatic Research, 11*, 213–218.

Ivancevich, J. M. & Matteson, M. T. (1980). *Stress and Work: A managerial perspective.* Glenview, IL: Scott, Foresman and Company.

Kahn, R. L. & Quinn, R. P. (1970). Role stress: A framework for analysis. In A. McLean (Ed.), *Occupational mental health.* New York: Wiley.

Kahn, R. L., Wolfe, D. M., Quinn, R. P., Snock, J. D. & Rosenthal, R. A. (1964). *Organizational stress: Studies in role conflict and ambiguity.* New York: Wiley.

Lazarus, R. H. & Launier, R. (1978). Stress related transactions between person and environment. In L. A. Pervin and M. Lewis (Eds.), *Internal and external determinants of behavior.* New York: Plenum.

Lazarus, R. S. (1966). *Psychological stress and the coping process.* New York: McGraw-Hill.

Mason, J. W. (1975a). A historical view of the stress field: Part 1. *Journal of Human Stress, 1*, (March) 6–12.

Mason, J. W. (1975b). A historical view of the stress field: Part 2. *Journal of Human Stress, 1*, (June) 22–35.

McLean, A. (1974). *Occupational Stress.* Springfield, IL: Thomas.

McLean, A. A. (1979). *Work Stress.* Reading, MA: Addison-Wesley.

Nelson, R. D. & Hayes, S. C. (1979). Some current dimensions of behavioral assessments. *Behavioral Assessment, 1*, 1–16.

Potter, E. H. III & Fiedler, F. E. (1981). The utilization of staff member intelligence and experience under high and low stress. *Academy of Management Journal, 24*, 361–376.

Sarason, I. G., Johnson, James H. & Siegel, J. M. (1978). Assessing the impact of life changes: Development of the Life Experiences Survey. *Journal of Consulting and Clinical Psychology, 46*, 932–946.

Schuler, R. S. (1980). Definition and conceptualization of stress in organizations. *Organizational Behavior and Human Performance, 25*, 184–215.

Selye, H. (1956). *The stress of life.* New York: McGraw-Hill.

Selye, H. (1975). Confusion and controversy in the stress field. *Journal of Human Stress,* (June), 37–44.

Sharit, J. & Salvendy, G. (1982). Occupational stress: Review and reappraisal. *Human Factors, 24*, 129–162.

Stone, G. S. (1980). (Ed). *Health Psychology.* San Francisco: Jossey-Bass.

Winkelpleck, J. M. (1984). Directions EAP's move: Evolvement toward organizational methods. *EAP Digest, 4*(5), 18–21.

Health Consequences of Stress

Jonathan D. Quick
Rebecca S. Horn
James Campbell Quick

SUMMARY. Stress is the naturally occurring mind-body response to demanding and/or emergency situations, either of a chronic or episodic nature. Properly monitored and managed, the stress response contributes to a state of optimum health and well being. When improperly managed, the stress response may lead to a variety of medical, psychological, and behavioral health problems. These problems range from cigarette smoking, alcohol and drug abuse, violence, and family conflict to insomnia, cardiovascular diseases, cancer, and ulcers. However, there are several stressful activities, including aerobic exercise, weight training, and flexibility training, which contribute to a number of health benefits. There are some individual differences in personality dimensions, sex, etc., which moderate the stress-health relationship.

The nature of the stress response was first studied at the beginning of the century by Walter Cannon and in the mid-1920s by Hans Selye. These two physicians have made significant contributions to our understanding of the stress response and the effects of its mismanagement. More recently, there has been an important focus on the health consequences of stress in the workplace, both out of concern for individuals and for organizations. This concern is founded on the idea that the intense or persistent stimulation of the stress response without sufficient rest or recovery can result in a host of health problems.

Stressful events are inevitable, but the destructive or distressful effects of these events are not inevitable. Stress is a naturally occur-

---

Jonathan D. Quick, MD, Rebecca S. Horn, RN, and James Campbell Quick, PhD are all affiliated with Management Sciences for Health, The University of Texas at Arlington.

ring experience essential to our growth, change development and performance both at work and at home. Depending on the way in which stress is managed, it may have a detrimental effect on our well-being and health — or it may have a beneficial effect.

In this article we review research findings on three questions related to stress and health. First, what is the sequence of events which links demanding situations, the stress response, and individual health? Second, what are the individual health problems and health benefits which have been associated with stress? Third, what are the moderating factors which are the linkages between stressful events and health?

PREVENTIVE STRESS MANAGEMENT

Health is frequently thought of as freedom from disease. In addition, it is *freedom from risk of* or *preconditions that lead to* disease (WHO, 1948). Figure 1 presents a framework for examining health, preventive stress management, and the medical model for the development of most chronic illnesses (Morris, 1955; Quick & Quick, 1984). The key sequence here is (1) demanding or stressful situation, (2) the stress response, and (3) distressful consequences or health problems. There is no way to avoid all stressful situations or risk factors in life. When subject to organizational demands or health risk factors, such as work layoff or habitual smoking, a person is vulnerable to a variety of health problems. This does not mean that the vulnerability will turn into a specific health problem. The prevention activities included in the model are discussed more thoroughly elsewhere (Quick & Quick, 1984: 151–158) and in the articles by Ivancevich and Murphy in this issue.

The stress response is the immediate, unconscious, patterned mobilization of energy and resources when faced with any demand (Asterita, 1985; Quick & Quick, 1984). The response consists of four basic mind-body changes:

1. increase in the sense of alertness;
2. redirection of blood to the muscles and brain;
3. release of glucose and fatty acids from their storage sites into the blood stream; and
4. reduction of less emergent activities and the immune systems.

Figure 1: The Preventive Stress Management Model

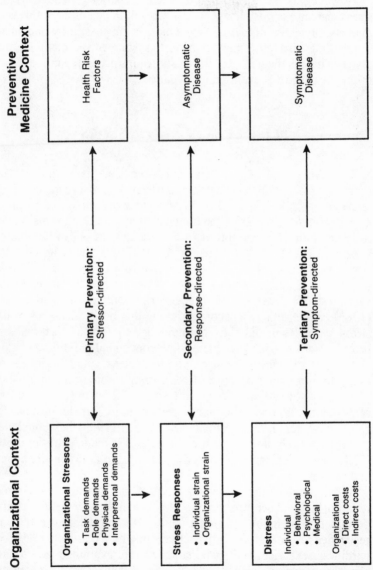

Organizational Context

Preventive Medicine Context

Organizational Stressors	**Primary Prevention:** Stressor-directed
• Task demands	
• Role demands	→ Health Risk Factors
• Physical demands	
• Interpersonal demands	

Stress Responses	**Secondary Prevention:** Response-directed
• Individual strain	
• Organizational strain	→ Asymptomatic Disease

Distress	**Tertiary Prevention:** Symptom-directed
Individual	
• Behavioral	
• Psychological	→ Symptomatic Disease
• Medical	
Organizational	
• Direct costs	
• Indirect costs	

In and of itself, the stress response is not a problem.

However, as we see in Figure 1, if the energy generated by the stress response is mismanaged, it may result in one of three forms of distress, or health problems. While there is the possibility of achieving healing through a number of tertiary prevention methods, our concern here is the nature of the relationships presented in the figure in the absence of preventive intervention.

LIFE EVENTS AS STRESSORS

The source of stress is a demand of some sort, be it an organizational stressor, health risk factor, or a life event (see Figure 1). Much stress research has focused on life events as precursors to physical or psychological disease. The underlying assumption in this line of research is that the amount of environmental stress can be reliably measured (Creed, 1985). Lazarus et al. (1985) have argued that stress is a reciprocal person-environment rubric in which it is fruitless to work on developing better measures of "the independent variable" (i.e., stressor or life event). Dohrenwend and Shrout (1985) counter this perspective, arguing that better measures of life stress variables avoid the confounding inherent in Lazarus' approach. Both perspectives have some conceptual validity.

In terms of empirical research on life events, much has been retrospective in nature because of the variety of environmental stressors measured. As an alternative, single life events, such as bereavement and unemployment provide more fertile ground for prospective research. In either case, Creed (1985) has concluded that the research base in the life events area is inadequate for drawing firm conclusions regarding the relationship between life events and physical illness.

While much of the life events research has focused on the direct relationship between life events and physical illness, there is an important line of inquiry which examines the moderating effects of resistance resources. In a prospective study by Kobasa et al. (1985), hardiness, exercise, and social support were examined as three resistance resources. Their findings suggest that resistance resources are effective defenses against illness, especially in the case of hardiness as a resource. These findings support the efficacy of the model in Figure 1 with regard to points of preventive intervention.

HEALTH PROBLEMS AND DISTRESS

When health is taken in its broader meaning, as "complete physical, mental and social well-being and not merely the absence of disease" (WHO, 1948), it is apparent that the health consequences of stress can be numerous. Distress resulting from mismanaged stress can manifest itself in behavioral, psychological, or medical problems. We will consider these problems before turning to the health benefits of stress.

Behavioral Consequences

Behavioral changes are among the earliest and most overt signs of rising levels of stress. Increased cigarette smoking, greater alcohol and drug abuse, accident proneness, and violence are among the changes which research has associated with increased stress.

Cigarette consumption may serve as pleasure smoking, social smoking, or stress smoking. Russek (1965) surveyed 12,000 professional men in fourteen occupational categories and used 32 expert judges to categorize the occupations as high-stress or low-stress. He found 46 percent of men in high-stress occupations to be smokers compared with 32 percent in low-stress occupations. Both stress and cigarette consumption were related to the incidence of heart disease. Similarly, Conway and colleagues (1981), in a study of U.S. Navy petty officers, found a significant correlation between occupational stress and cigarette smoking. In an attempt to address the cause-effect relationship, studies by Lindenthal and associates (1972) and Hillier (1981) demonstrate that increases in smoking under stress are proportional to the number of stressors within a given period of time. This suggests a dose-effect of stress on smoking behavior.

Increased levels of stress also appear to lead to increased alcohol consumption and drug abuse. About 10 million Americans and up to 10 percent of the work force are alcoholics. Alcohol consumption is a major factor in one-half of this country's homicides and motor vehicle fatalities, one-third of reported suicides, the majority of the nation's 30,000 annual deaths from liver cirrhosis, and a substantial number of serious birth defects (Trice & Roman, 1981). The economic cost of alcoholism is equally staggering: an estimated national cost of $43 billion in 1975, including about $20 billion in lost production.

Occupation is highly associated with drinking habits and consequent alcohol-related problems (Ojesjo, 1980). Various explanations have been offered for this relationship, including differences in social pressures and social controls which allow or encourage drinking within some groups; recruitment and selection trends which attract alcoholism-prone individuals to certain careers; and variations in occupational stress (Cosper, 1979; Plant, 1979). Not all alcohol consumption is destructive, however. Recent research indicates that, with the exception of catastrophic events, moderate and occasional alcohol consumption may have a beneficial buffering effect (Neff, 1985).

A subtler, but still potentially lethal effect of stress is to predispose the individual to industrial, automobile, and other forms of accidents. The role of stress in industrial accidents has long been suspected, but the classic studies of accident proneness were conducted in the mid-1960s by two Cleveland psychiatrists who reviewed about 300 cases of industrial accidents leading to disability (Hirschfeld & Behan, 1963; 1966). They found that stress not only contributed significantly to the occurrence of an accident, but it also was found to slow the recovery process and prolong disability. Violence on the part of the stressed individual is one of the more extreme, but often less visible manifestations of individual distress. Incidents of family violence, including spouse and child abuse, are increasing. As a result of public concern about becoming victims of violence, the U.S. Public Health Service recently expanded its health promotion and disease prevention objectives of the nation to include the control of stress and violent behaviors (Silver, Goldston & Silver, 1985).

Psychological Consequences

As Figure 1 points out, individual distress may take the form of specific psychological or psychiatric problems, including family problems, sleep disturbances, sexual dysfunction, depression, psychogenic disability, and burnout. In the medical context, these are classified as symptomatic disease. The relationship between life events and mental illness has been most extensively reviewed by Rahe (1979). (As seen earlier, more recent life events research has looked at physical illness as the dependent variable.)

Marital discord and family conflict result from a variety of sources; the combination of home and work stress appears to have been a particularly significant factor in the last several decades. Burke, Weir, and DuWors (1979) examined the view of women married to men who exhibited unbalanced professional striving and competitive overdrive. The wives of men with such characteristics reported greater levels of depression, less satisfaction, fewer friends and less contact with those friends, and more feelings of tension, anxiety, isolation, worthlessness, and guilt. Handy (1978), studying the marriages of 23 successful mid-career executives, found four principal marital patterns, as defined by the attitudes and values of each spouse. Certain patterns were associated with resentment and discontent, while other patterns were associated with low stress and supportive relationships. The data suggest that the impact of organizational stress on a marital relationship is in part determined by the structure of the relationship.

Insomnia each year affects up to 30 percent of the general population. Worries over promotion, conflict at work, and project deadlines frequently cause difficulty in falling asleep. Evidence on alcohol metabolism indicates that this common home remedy for insomnia may actually contribute to the problem. The initial depressant effect of the alcohol helps a person to fall asleep, but also disrupts sleep cycles because of increased adrenalin in the middle of the night. However, individual differences play a role in understanding the mechanisms for these effects (Scrima, Broudy, Nay & Cohn, 1982).

Medical Consequences

While the interrelations are not explicitly depicted in Figure 1, distress of a behavioral and psychological nature may become transformed into even more devastating and irreversible medical problems. When these are at the asymptomatic stage (see Figure 1), they often go undetected. This can be particularly frightening in the case of CHD because the first symptom may be sudden death.

Numerous studies reviewed elsewhere have associated work overload, job dissatisfaction, job insecurity, role conflict, interpersonal demands, and a variety of other work stressors with classic "stress symptoms" such as headache, heartburn, backache, SKM conditions, and generalized fatigue (Quick & Quick, 1984). Table 1 summarizes information on the ten leading causes of mortality in

Table 1

Work Stress and Mortality

Rank	Cause of Death	1985 Number of Deaths	Findings Related to Workstress	Reference
1	Heart disease	975,660	For a controlled study of 453 male post-myocardial infarction patients, a stress reduction program led to a decreased incidence of death.	Frasure-Smith & Prince, 1985
2	Cancer	457,200	A prospective study of 208 female breast cancer patients showed that higher levels of objective stress was associated with decreased survival rates in the 61 and older age group, and higher levels of subjective stress was associated with decreased survival of the 15 to 45 age group.	Funch & Marshall, 1983
3	Stroke	153,330	There is a positive correlation between stressful events and hypertension but further research is needed to determine the exact physiologic etiology of essential hypertension which will eventually lead to methods of prevention of stroke caused by hypertension.	Julius, 1984
4	Accidents and adverse effects	91,690	According to insurance industry data, 75-85% of accidents at work are stress-related.	Jones, 1984

Table 1 (continued)

Rank	Cause of Death	1985 Number of Deaths	Findings Related to Workstress	Reference
5	Chronic obstructive lung disease	73,430	In a review of over 90 references, cigarette smoking is described as being positively correlated to both work stress and health problems such as chronic obstructive pulmonary disease and lung cancer.	Schilling, Gilchrest, & Schinke, 1985
6	Pneumonia and influenza	65,230	In a study of 114 healthy people, those with reported high life change stress levels had low natural killer cell activity levels, suggesting that symptoms associated with stress may negatively affect immunity.	Locke, Krause, Leserman, Hurst, Heisel, & Williams, 1984
7	Diabetes	37,640	In a study of 66 insulin dependent diabetics, 75% had clinical symptoms or abnormally high blood sugars following stressful events.	Kisch, 1985
8	Suicide	27,350	In an analysis of U.S. mortality data, there was a pattern of stress-induced self-destructive behaviors in seven stress related causes of death: suicide, homicide, hypertension, liver cirrhosis, arteriosclerotic heart disease, stomach ulcers, and hypertensive cardiovascular disease.	Karcher & Linden, 1982

Table 1 (continued)

Rank	Cause of Death	1985 Number of Deaths	Findings Related to Workstress	Reference
9	Liver cirrhosis	26,740	In a screening program of 7948 males involved in a preventive medical program, mortality data were compared to the non-participant population, and the death rate due to alcohol-related diseases was five times higher in the non-participant group.	Trell, Kristenson, & Peterson, 1985
10	Homicide	19,310	Among 148 former mental patients and 245 respondents from the general population, self reports of frequency of life stress events was positively correlated with increased frequency of four types of aggressive behavior ranging from arguments to assaults with weapons.	Steadman & Ribner, 1982

Source: Monthly Vital Statistics Report, Vol. 34, No. 9 (December 16, 1985), National Center for Health Statistics. Figures are for the annual period September 1984 through August 1985.

the United States during 1985. Although genetics, biological development, and many other factors influence the appearance and course of these conditions, there is a growing body of empirical evidence suggesting that stress plays a role in hastening the appearance of disease and in worsening the impact of the disease.

Each year over 900,000 men and women in the United States die from heart disease and strokes (see Table 1). The most important factors contributing to these deaths are family history of cardiovascular disease, smoking, hypertension, blood lipids (cholesterol and triglycerides), Type A personality, and diabetes. Lack of exercise and poor diet are also contributing factors. With the exception of family history, there is evidence relating each of these factors to stress, in general, and in several cases to work stress, in particular.

The relationship between work stress and smoking was noted above. The onset or worsening of high blood pressure or hypertension has also been associated with psychological stress (Henry, 1976). Recent studies have re-emphasized the role of cholesterol levels in the development of heart disease and these levels appear to be related to stress. Friedman and associates (1958) in one of the earliest studies of this relationship, found that among tax accountants cholesterol levels increased as the deadline for filing federal income tax returns approached.

A growing body of evidence indicates that perhaps one-half of all cardiac deaths result not from a blockage of coronary arteries, as is the case of a heart attack, but from a condition known as "sudden cardiac death," in which death is believed to result from sudden and serious cardiac rhythm disturbances. Current evidence directly linking work stress to sudden death is largely anecdotal and retrospective studies of the relationship between life stresses and sudden death have been inconclusive (Binik, 1985). However, there are several studies demonstrating a significant relationship between potentially dangerous heart rhythm disturbances and psychological tasks (Lown, De Silva & Lenson, 1978). Such work stresses as public speaking have been found to stimulate abnormal heartbeats in one-quarter of normal patients and prolific abnormal beats in nearly three-quarters of CAD patients (Taggart, Carruthers & Somerville, 1973).

The Type A behavior pattern is a controversial risk factor linking work stress to heart disease. Studies reviewed by Dorion and Taylor (1984) indicate that Type A individuals have higher blood pressure and cholesterol levels, are more frequently smokers, more likely to be heavy drinkers, have less interest in exercise, and demonstrate other chemical and physiological alternatives related to the development of arteriosclerosis. Compared to Type B individuals, Type A individuals show greater cardiovascular reactivity in daily activities, including greater elevations of serum norepinephrine, heart rate and blood pressure under stressful circumstances. These effects have been found among Type A women as well as Type A men (Lawler, Rixse & Allen, 1983).

A more recent, large controlled study (Multiple Risk Factor Intervention Trial, 1982) found no significant relationship between Type A behavior and smoking, cholesterol, or the incidence of cardiovascular disease. In addition, recent studies of survival after acute heart attack have also failed to find an association between Type A behavior and long-term outcome (Case, Heller, Case & Moss, 1985). It may be only specific components of the Type A behavior pattern, for example, hostility and cynicism, which contribute to risk for heart attack. Jenkins (1982) has suggested that it is the sisyphean pattern (striving without joy or satisfaction) that leads Type A individuals to develop coronary heart disease. It is the combination of work overload and sustained dissatisfaction or depression which appear to put the Type A at risk. Thus, the relationship between Type A behavior pattern and cardiovascular disease is a complicated one.

The commonest sites of fatal cancers in the U.S. are lung, breast, colon and rectum, and prostate. An estimated three-quarters of lung cancers are attributable to smoking. To the extent that organizational stress increases smoking behavior, it will increase lung cancer and other tobacco-related cancers such as bladder cancer, stomach cancer, and cancer of the mouth, throat and larynx. The impact of increased smoking among women is just beginning to be reflected in rising lung cancer among women.

Several books on the subject of stress and cancer review evidence suggesting that stressful life events are associated with the appearance of a variety of cancers, including breast cancer, uterine cancer and lung cancer (Tache, Selye & Day, 1979; Cooper, 1984). Stress appears to have a direct effect on decreasing the immune response which might otherwise control a small cancer (McClelland, 1985).

Pneumonia, influenza and other acute respiratory infections are together the fifth leading cause of death in the U.S. and a leading cause of lost workdays and work-related disability. Most of this disability is due to disease from specific chemical and physical irritants. However, evidence from some of the earliest studies of recent life events indicate that stress in personal, financial, social or work areas is associated with increased incidence of acute respiratory illness as well as chronic respiratory diseases such as tuberculosis (Holmes, Hawkins, Bowerman, Clark & Joffee, 1957).

Musculoskeletal conditions—including arthritis, low back pain, and displaced intervertebral discs ("slipped discs")—are another leading cause of lost workdays and disability. While much of this disability is related to work injuries and non-work stress, increased work stress has also been associated with increases in acute and chronic musculoskeletal problems.

Ulceration of the stomach and first part of the small intestine represents the classic psychosomatic illness. This description is due to the early work of H. G. Wolff (1953), a neurologist and pioneer in psychosomatic medicine. Wolff found that during times of prolonged emotional stress, the stomach lining became engorged with blood, acid production increased, and eventually bleeding erosions developed. Subsequent studies have documented a higher incidence of chronic stress in ulcer patients compared to control subjects, increased acid production triggered by stressful events, and a more prolonged course with poorer prognosis among patients with chronic severe anxiety.

HEALTH BENEFITS OF STRESS

While work stress is a necessity, it does not have to inevitably lead to the health problems just discussed. Milsum (1984) has explored the positive aspects of optimal or well balanced stress. Recent evidence also indicates that stress can markedly increase blood levels of *endorphins*, naturally occurring morphine-like hormones associated with pain relief and feelings of well being (McCubbin, Surwit & Williams, 1985).

Exercise and Flexibility

There are three stressful activities found to be beneficial in either specific or general circumstances. The first of these is aerobic fitness. The benefits of aerobic fitness are primarily in improved cardiovascular functioning. These benefits include a lower heart rate, greater stroke volume, greater efficiency in returning to rest after stressful events, and decreased reactivity to stressful events. Roth and Holmes (1985) found that the physical health of aerobically fit individuals was not adversely affected by life stress while the physical health of less fit individuals was. Similar results were found concerning psychological depression.

The second stressful activity of benefit is weight training. The U.S. Air Force has found that pilots on weight training programs are significantly more able to sustain high G-forces without loss of consciousness than are aerobically fit pilots or a control group of pilots (Aerospace Medicine Division, 1985). This suggests that weight training, designed to strengthen the body, can have specific, specialized benefits when it comes to extreme physical environments.

The third stressful activity of benefit is flexibility training. The process of improving flexibility, along with strength, in specific muscle groups leads to stresses on these muscle groups. However, this improved flexibility enables improved body posture, a key issue in considering the physical stresses imposed on the body during the normal course of living.

Moderators of the Stress-Health Relationship

There is not a simple relationship between stress and health. Why do some individuals develop recurrent stomach ulcers, while others do not? Selye (1976) suggests that there may be individual moderating factors which influence the body's response to stress. These factors include "internal conditioning factors," such as family patterns of stress response, past experiences, age, sex, and personality, as well as "external conditioning factors," such as diet, climate, drugs, and social setting.

One important part of the explanation for different patterns of stress response lies in the "Achilles heel," or "organ inferiority" hypothesis developed through the work of Harold Wolff (1953). He hypothesized that an individual reacts to stress with a particular psychophysiologic pattern that is specific to that individual. Medical research provides support for this hypothesis.

Several personality dimensions appear to influence the impact of stressful events on the individual. In addition to the Type A behavior pattern discussed earlier, locus of control is another personality dimension which may have a moderating influence as demonstrated by Anderson and Cohen (1977) in a study of 102 owner-managers of small businesses in a Pennsylvania community extensively damaged by a flood. Following the flood, the internally oriented managers responded in a more task-oriented way and demonstrated less stress. Self-esteem may be a third important moderator of the response to stress (Mueller, 1965). A study by Kasl and Cobb (1970) indicated that coronary heart disease risk factors rise as self-esteem declined. Finally, a recent study by Flannery (1984) suggests that one's work ethic may be a moderator between life stress and physical illness.

Sex, age, ethnicity, social support, peer group, and diet may all play somewhat of a moderating role in the relationship between stress and health (Nelson & Quick, 1985; Quick & Quick, 1984; Sorenson, Pirie, Folsom, Leupker, Jacobs & Gillum, 1985). Therefore, it is often essential to identify stress-health relationships for the specific individual case as opposed to operating with generalizations alone.

CONCLUSION

The sequence of events linking demanding situations, the stress response, and individual health has been examined by a number of researchers. Reasonably good evidence exists to link stress to specific health problems and benefits, but these linkages are, in many cases, complicated. While stress is an inevitable fact of work and personal life, the health problems which often result are not inevitable. Heart disease, alcohol or smoking related diseases, and cancer are just some examples of health problems associated with stress that can be altered by moderators of stress.

The preventive stress management model (Figure 1) suggests four areas of stress research. The first two of these deal with the organizational context portion of the model. Further research is needed to explore the relationship among organizational stressors, psychophysiological aspects of the stress response, and health consequences (or distress) of the individual organization. Either longitudinal or prospective studies could possibly reveal how multiple health consequences are related to a specific stressor, such as loss of employment. On the other hand, research is also needed to demonstrate the link between multiple personal and professional demands and the incidence of specific events, such as the violent behaviors of child abuse or suicide.

A third and more complex research area involves both stressors and individualor organizational distress as they are affected by stress modifiers. Research is needed to study the interactions between personal and professional demands and a person's personality and other individual factors that makes this person vulnerable or resistent to stress. These interactive effects may lead to health problems that result from the demand/vulnerability interaction. Chemical dependency is just one health consequence that could be considered in this area of research.

A last area of possible research involves the preventive medicine context of the model (Figure 1). This broader arena of stress research deals with the discovery of effective stress prevention and intervention methods that need to be developed so that positive health consequences occur at both the individual and organizational levels.

REFERENCES

Aerospace Medicine Division. (1985). G-induced loss of consciousness. USAF: Brooks Air Force Base.

Anderson, Col. J. L. & Cohen, M. (1977). *The West Point fitness and diet book.* New York: Avon.

Asterita, M. F. (1985). *The physiology of stress.* New York: Human Sciences Press.

Binik, Y. M. (1985). Psychosocial predictor of sudden death: A review and critique. *Social Science Medicine, 20(7),* 667–680.

Burke, R. J., Weir, T. & DuWors, Jr., R. E. (1979). Type A behavior of administrators and wives' reports of marital satisfaction and well-being. *Journal of Applied Psychology, 64,* 57–65.

Case, R. D., Heller, S. S., Case, N. B., Moss, A. J. & Multicenter Post-Infarction Research Group. Type A behavior and survival after acute myocardial infarction. *The New England Journal of Medicine, 312(12),* 737–741.

Conway, T. L., Vickers, Jr., R. R., Ward, H. W. & Rahe, R. H. (1981). Occupational stress and variation in cigarette, coffee, and alcohol consumption. *Journal of Health and Social Behavior, 22(2),* 155–165.

Cooper, C. L. (Ed.). (1984). *Psychosocial stress and cancer.* New York: John Wiley & Sons.

Cosper, R. (1979). Drinking as conformity: A critique of sociological literature on occupational differences in drinking. *Journal of Studies on Alcohol, 40(9),* 868–891.

Creed, F. (1985). Life events and physical illness. *Journal of Psychosomatic Research, 29(2),* 113–123.

Dohrenwend, B. P. & Shrout, P. E. (1985). "Hassles" in the conceptualization and measurement of life stress variables. *American Psychologist, 40(7),* 780–785.

Dorian, D. & Taylor, C. B. (1984). Stress factors in the development of coronary artery disease. *Journal of Occupational Medicine, 26(10),* 747–756.

Flannery, R. B., Jr. (1984). The work ethic as moderator variable of life stress: Preliminary inquiry. *Psychological Reports, 55,* 361–362.

Frasure-Smith, N. & Prince, R. (1985). The Ischemic heart disease life stress monitoring program: Impact on mortality. *Psychosomatic Medicine, 47(5),* 431–445.

Friedman, M., Rosenman, R. H. & Carroll, V. (1958). Changes in serum cholesterol and blood clotting time in men subjected to cyclic variations of occupational stress. *Circulation, 17*, 852–861.

Funch, D. P. & Marshall, J. (1983). The role of stress, social support, and age in survival from breast cancer. *Journal of Psychosomatic Research, 27(1)*, 77–83.

Handy, C. (1978). The family: Help or hindrance. In C. L. Cooper and R. Payne (Eds.). *Stress at work* (pp. 107–123). New York: John Wiley & Sons.

Henry, J. P. (1976). Understanding the early pathophysiology of essential hypertension. *Geriatrics, 31*, 59–72.

Hillier, S. (1981). Stresses, strains and smoking. *Nursing Mirror, 152*, 26–30.

Hirschfield, A. H. & Behan, R. C. (1963). The accident process: I. Etiological considerations of industrial injuries. *The Journal of the American Medical Association, 186*, 193–199.

Hirschfield, A. H. & Behan, R. C. (1966). The accident process: III. Disability: Acceptable and unacceptable. *The Journal of the American Medical Association, 197(2)*, 125–129.

Holmes, T. H., Hawkins, N. G., Bowerman, C. E., Clark, Jr., E. R. & Joffee, J. R. (1957). Psychosocial and psychophysiological studies of tuberculosis. *Psychosomatic Medicine, 19*, 134–143.

Jenkins, C. D. (1982). Psychosocial risk factors for coronary heart disease. *Acta Med Scand Suppl, 660*, 123–136.

Jones, J. W. (1984). Managing stress to prevent accidents. *National Underwriter, 88*, 18–19.

Julius, S. (1984). Implications for hypertension. In N. I. H., *Stress reactivity and cardiovascular disease: Proceedings of the working conference* (pp. 63–71). Washington, DC: U.S. Department of Health and Human Services.

Karcher, C. J. & Linden, L. L. (1982). Is work conducive to self destruction? *Suicide and Life Threatening Behavior, 12(5)*, 151–157 (in *Suicide Abstracts, 32*, 1983, 386).

Kasl, S. V. & Cobb, S. (1970). Blood pressure changes in men undergoing job loss: A preliminary report. *Psychosomatic Medicine, 32*, 19–38.

Kisch, E. S. (1985). Stressful events and the onset of diabetes mellitus. *Israeli Journal of Medical Sciences, 21*, 356–358 (from *Practical Stress Management, 3*, 1985, 3).

Kobasa, S. C. O., Maddi, S. R.; Puccetti, M. C. & Zola, M. A. (1985). Effectiveness of hardiness, exercise, and social support as resources against illness. *Journal of Psychosomatic Research, 29(5)*, 525–533.

Lawler, K. A., Rixse, A. & Allen, M. T. (1983). Type A behavior and psychological responses in adult women. *Psychophysiology, 20(3)*, 343.

Lazarus, R. S., DeLongis, A., Folkman, S. & Gruen, R. (1985). Stress and adaptational outcomes: The problem of confounded measures. *American Psychologist, 40(2)*, 770–779.

Lindenthal, J. J., Myers, J. K. & Pepper, M. P. (1972). Smoking, psychological status, and stress. *Social Science Medicine, 6*, 583–591.

Locke, S. E., Kraus, L., Leserman, J., Hurst, M. W., Heisel, J. S. & Williams, R. M. (1984). Life change stress, psychiatric symptoms, and natural killer cell activity. *Psychosomatic Medicine, 46(5)*, 441–453.

Lown, P., DeSilva, R. A. & Lenson, R. (1978). Roles of psychologic stress and autonomic nervous system changes in provocation of ventricular premature complexes. *American Journal of Cardiology, 41*, 979–985.

McClelland, D. C. & Benson, H. (1985, March). The placebo effect, the faith factor, and alternative healing techniques. Paper presented to Behavioral Medicine Conference, Boston, Massachusetts.

McCubbin, J. A., Surwit, R. S. & Williams, R. B. (1985). Endogenous opiate peptides, stress reactivity, and risk for hypertension. *Hypertension, 7*, 808–811.

Milsum, J. H. (1984). *Health, stress and illness: A systems approach.* New York: Praeger Publications.

Morris, J. N. (1955). The uses of epidemiology. *British Medical Journal, 2*, 395–401.

Mueller, E. F. (1965). *Psychological and physiological correlates of work overload among university professors*. Unpublished doctoral dissertation, University of Michigan, Ann Arbor.

Multiple Risk Factor Intervention Trial. (1982). Risk factor changes and mortality results. *JAMA, 248*, 1465–1477.

Neff, J. A. (1985). Evaluating the stress-suffering role of alcohol consumption: Variation by types of event and type of symptom. *Alcohol and Alcoholism, 20(4)*, 391–401.

Nelson, D. L. & Quick, J. C. (1985). Professional women: Are distress and disease inevitable? *Academy of Management Review, 10(2)*, 206–218.

Ojesjo, L. (1980). The relationship to alcoholism of occupation, class, and employment. *Journal of Occupational Medicine, 22(10)*, 657–666.

Plant, M. A. (1979). Occupational, drinking patterns and alcohol-related problems: Conclusions from a follow-up study. *British Journal of Addiction, 74(3)*, 267–273.

Quick, J. C. & Quick, J. D. (1984). *Organizational stress and preventive management*. New York: McGraw-Hill, Inc.

Rahe, R. A. (1979). Life change events and mental illness: An overview. *Journal of Human Stress, 5*, 2–9.

Roth, D. L. & Holmes, D. S. (1985). Influence of physical fitness in determining the impact of stressful life events on physical and psychological health. *Psychosomatic Medicine, 47(2)*, 164–173.

Russek, H. (1965). Stress, tobacco, and coronary heart disease in North American professional groups. *Journal of American Medical Association, 192*, 189–194.

Schilling, R. F., Gilchrist, L. D. & Schinke, S. P. (1985). Smoking in the workplace: Review of the critical issues. *Public Health Reports, 100(5)*, 473–479.

Scrima, L., Broudy, M., Nay, K. N. & Cohn, M. A. (1982). Increased severity of obstructive sleep apnea after bedtime alcohol ingestion: Diagnostic potential and proposed mechanism of action. *Sleep, 5(4)*, 318–328.

Selye, H. (1976). *The stress of life*. 2nd Ed. New York: McGraw-Hill.

Silver, B. J., Goldston, S. E. & Silver, L. B. (1985). The 1990 objectives for the nation for control of stress and violent behavior: Progress report. *Public Health Reports, 100*, 374.

Sorensen, G., Pirie, P., Folsom, A., Luepker, R., Jacobs, D. & Gillum, R. (1985). Sex differences in the relationship between work and health: The Minnesota heart survey. *Journal of Health and Social Behavior, 26*, 379–394.

Steadman, H. J. & Ribner, S. A. (1982). Life stress and violence among ex-mental patients. *Social Science Medicine, 16(18)*, 1641–1647.

Tache, J., Selye, H. & Day, S. B. (Eds.). (1979). *Cancer, stress, and death*. New York: Plenum Medical Book Company.

Taggart, P., Carruthers, M. & Somerville, W. (1973). Electrocardiogram, plasma catecholamines and lipids, and their modification by oxprenolol when speaking before an audience. *Lancet, 2*, 341–346.

Trell, E., Kristenson, H. & Petersson, B. (1985). A risk factor approach to the alcohol-related diseases. *Alcohol and Alcoholism, 20(3)*, 333–345.

Trice, H. & Roman, P. (1981). Perspectives on job-based programs for alcohol and drug problems. *Journal of Drug Issues, 11*, 167–169.

Wolff, H. G. (1953). *Stress and disease*. Springfield, IL: Charles C Thomas.

World Health Organization. (1948). *Constitution of the world health organization*. Geneva.

A Work-Nonwork Interactive Perspective of Stress and Its Consequences

Jeffrey H. Greenhaus
Saroj Parasuraman

SUMMARY. This paper examines the intersection of work and nonwork roles as related to stress, and proposes an integrative framework for understanding the relationships among stressors, stress, and strains in the work and nonwork domains. The sources and consequences of work-nonwork stress are reviewed, individual and organizational strategies for effective management of work-nonwork stress are delineated, and directions for future research are identified.

Stress research in the organizational and behavioral sciences reflects two distinct streams of inquiry. The dominant focus in a large number of studies has been investigation of stressors in the work domain and associated emotional, behavioral, and health outcomes (Brief, Schuler & Van Sell, 1981; Cooper & Marshall, 1976; Ivancevich & Matteson, 1980). A second area of emphasis has been examination of nonwork sources of stress, notably stressful life events, and their effects on individuals' psychological and physiological health and well-being (Holmes & Rahe, 1967; Johnson & Sarason, 1979; Thoits, 1983).

While these independent streams of research have provided valuable insights into the sources, mediators, and consequences of stress *within* the work and nonwork spheres of life, much less is known about the interplay of stressors and stress reactions *between* the two

---

Jeffrey H. Greenhaus and Saroj Parasuraman are affiliated with Drexel University.

The authors contributed equally to the preparation of this article and their names are listed in alphabetical order. Correspondence can be directed to either author at the Department of Management and Organizational Sciences, Drexel University, Philadelphia, PA 19104.

life domains. For example, what is the influence of work-generated stressors on nonwork outcomes? Conversely, what effects do non-work stressors have on job attitudes and behavior? Do multiple stressors in the two domains have additive or interactive effects on individuals' physical and mental health and other outcomes? What is the relationship between coping resources in one area of life space and strain experienced in the other?

Answers to these and related issues call for a holistic, open systems approach to examining stressors at the work-nonwork interface and their consequences. It is only recently that researchers have crossed the boundaries of the two life domains, and explored inter-relationships between work and nonwork stressors and their individual and joint effects on various outcomes (Bhagat, McQuaid, Lindholm & Segovis, 1985; Greenhaus & Beutell, 1985; Hendrix, Ovalle & Troxler, 1985).

This paper seeks to integrate the different strands of research on work and nonwork stress, map the areas of work-nonwork intersection as related to stress, and develop a framework for understanding the relationships between stressors and their outcomes in the two domains. Such an understanding will facilitate the determination of appropriate individual and organizational strategies for effective management of the aversive consequences of stress.

THE MEANING OF STRESS

Consistent with recent conceptualizations (e.g., Beehr & Bhagat, 1985; Schuler, 1980), stress denotes the psychological state experienced by an individual when faced with demands, constraints, and/or opportunities that have important but uncertain outcomes. Stressors are environmental situations or events potentially capable of producing the state of stress, strains are the symptoms or indices of stress, and outcomes refer to consequences of strain that have implications for the work and nonwork domains.

Figure 1 summarizes the relationships among stressors, stress, strains, and outcomes. Note that stress can be produced by stressors that arise in the work domain (e.g., work overload), the nonwork domain (e.g., family tensions), and at the interface of the work and nonwork domains (e.g., work-nonwork time conflicts). However, people who are exposed to environmental stressors may not neces-

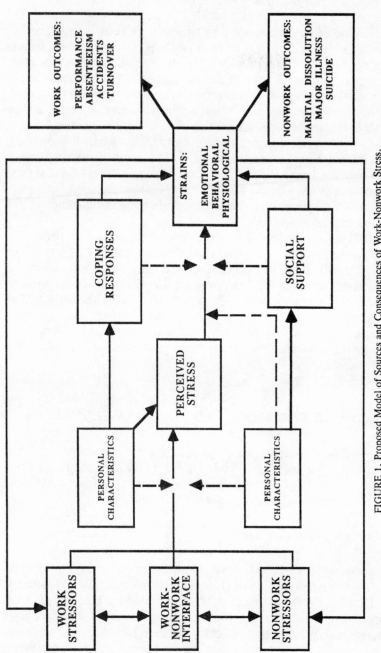

FIGURE 1. Proposed Model of Sources and Consequences of Work-Nonwork Stress.

39

sarily perceive the situation as stressful. Personal characteristics, such as high self-esteem, an internal locus of control, and a feeling of personal hardiness, can affect the way people interpret the environment and thereby determine the degree of stress that is experienced. Extensive stress is generally expected to produce emotional, behavioral, and/or physiological strain. However, effective coping (for example, by modifying the stressful environment) and the utilization of social support (informational, instrumental, appraisal, and/or emotional support; House, 1981) from the work or nonwork domain can lessen the aversive consequences of stress on strain and can also directly improve well-being. Finally, the model proposes that extensive strain can produce dysfunctional outcomes in the work and nonwork domains.

Having provided a brief overview of the model of stress presented in Figure 1, we will discuss the components of the model in more detail. First, we will examine the research on work stressors, nonwork stressors, and stressors produced by the intersection of work and nonwork roles. We will then examine the influence of coping, social support, and personal characteristics on work-nonwork stress, and will conclude with a discussion of individual and organizational interventions relevant to a work-nonwork perspective of stress.

WORK STRESSORS AND THEIR CONSEQUENCES

In this section, we will highlight some of the more consistent findings on work stress. Following Eden (1982), among others, we will distinguish ongoing, chronic work stressors from acute, episodic events that occur in the work domain.

Chronic Work Stressors

Models of work stress have identified several categories of stressors as pervasive in the work domain (Brief et al., 1981; Cooper & Marshall, 1976; Ivancevich & Matteson, 1980). These include roles in the organization (e.g., role conflict, role ambiguity); job characteristics (e.g., quantitative and qualitative overload; responsibility for people); interpersonal relationships (e.g., peers, supervisors, subordinates); organizational structure (e.g., lack of participation;

hours of work); career development (e.g., career success or frustration); and the physical environment (e.g., noise, temperature, safety hazards).

Chronic work stressors have been found to be related to various psychological symptoms including job dissatisfaction, tension, anxiety, depression, boredom, psychological fatigue, self-esteem, and alienation. Major behavioral and outcome correlates of work stress include smoking, drug use, escapist drinking, performance decrements, absenteeism, and turnover. The health consequences of work stress documented in the literature include diastolic blood pressure, serum cholesterol level, heart rate, gastrointestinal disorders, and cardiovascular disease (Brief et al., 1981; Cooper & Marshall, 1976; Ivancevich & Matteson, 1980).

Acute Work Stressors

In its preoccupation with chronic stressors, research has generally neglected acute sources of work stress, although exceptions include some studies of stressful organizational and job change events (Bhagat et al., 1985; Eden, 1982). Recent attention has also been directed toward career transitions as sources of stress that require adaptation to important and uncertain outcomes. As Louis (1980) indicated, a career transition is a period in which a person changes career roles (interrole transition) or changes orientation to his or her current role (intrarole transition). Career transitions, such as job changes, transfers, and layoffs, are likely to be most stressful when they are undesirable, coerced, extensive, unexpected, accompanied by other life stresses, and experienced by people with inadequate psychological or social resources (Bhagat et al., 1985; Louis, 1980; Schlossberg & Leibowitz, 1980).

NONWORK STRESSORS AND THEIR CONSEQUENCES

The nonwork domain is composed of a number of life domains including family (which itself could be further divided), leisure/recreational, community/social, and religious roles (Parasuraman, Zammuto & Outcalt, 1984). In this section, we will briefly review sources of stress that arise in the nonwork domain, drawing a distinction again between acute stressors and chronic stressors.

Acute Nonwork Stressors: Stressful Life Events

Research on the nonwork domain has focused extensively on life events or changes as a dominant source of stress. The conceptual logic underlying this perspective is that such events require significant social readjustment and adaptation, and as such constitute potential stressors. Stressors in this category include events such as death of a spouse, serious illness of family members, marriage, separation and divorce, loss of job, and change of residence. Since the large majority of life events included in such studies are not directly related to the work role, we consider this body of research relevant to nonwork sources of stress. Total life stress as assessed by the Holmes-Rahe (1967) Schedule of Recent Experiences (SRE) scale has been found to be related to anxiety, depression, and psychiatric disorders as well as assorted health-related problems and illnesses (Johnson & Sarason, 1979; Thoits, 1983).

Recent studies of life stress have distinguished between positive or desirable events (e.g., marriage) and those that are negative or undesirable (e.g., death of a spouse), and have produced a new measure, the Life Experiences Survey (LES), to assess positive and negative life changes separately (Johnson & Sarason, 1979). The appropriateness of this distinction is demonstrated by findings that negative life changes have a greater impact than positive life changes on various indices of psychological distress (Johnson & Sarason, 1979; Vinokur & Selzer, 1975).

Chronic Nonwork Stressors

In contrast to the extensive research on chronic stressors in the work domain, relatively little attention has been devoted to chronic nonwork stressors and their consequences. This gap has recently been addressed in studies of "daily hassles" (DeLongis, Coyne, Dakof, Folkman & Lazarus, 1982) and the development of an instrument, the Hassles Scale, to measure eight types of daily hassles: household; health; time pressure; inner concerns; environmental; financial responsibility; work; and future security. These eight types of hassles have been found to be related to psychological symptomatology and somatic illness.

Research in family dynamics also indicates that ongoing stressors within the family domain may produce a variety of strain symptoms. In their study of recently relocated U.S. army families, Lavee, McCubbin, and Patterson (1985) reported that high levels of family distress (e.g., emotional and legal problems) were associated with low levels of personal well-being. Moreover, dissatisfaction with leisure (perhaps indicative of stressful conditions within the leisure role) can detract from one's overall quality of life (London, Crandall & Seals, 1977).

WORK-NONWORK STRESSORS AND THEIR CONSEQUENCES

We will now consider how work and nonwork forces combine to produce stress and its consequences. We envision three categories of linkages between stress and strain at the intersection of work and nonwork domains: (a) additive effects of stressors in the two domains; (b) spillover effects of stressors and strain across the work and nonwork domains; and (c) interactive effects of work-nonwork conflicts.

Work-Nonwork Additivity

Models of work-nonwork stress (e.g., Bhagat et al., 1985) posit that the total amount of stress and strain experienced by a person is a function of both work *and* nonwork stressors. As Beehr and Bhagat (1985) indicate, this is the simplest way to view work-nonwork influences on stress. This approach assumes that, all other things being equal, the greater the number of stressful domains encountered, and the more extensive the stressors within each domain, the greater the degree of stress and strain experienced. Results supportive of this perspective are reported by Bhagat et al. (1985) who found total negative life stress to be a stronger predictor of satisfaction with work than either negative personal life stress or negative job stress alone. Sekaran's (1985) findings that job satisfaction and life satisfaction jointly mediate the effects of work and nonwork factors on the mental health of male partners in dual-career families are also consistent with the additive approach, as are findings that employees undergoing a job loss experience more strain when they simultaneously experience severe nonwork changes (Schlossberg & Leibowitz, 1980).

Work-Nonwork Spillover

Work-nonwork spillover occurs when the strain produced by stressors in one domain provokes stressful situations in another domain. Greenhaus and Beutell (1985) identified this process as strain-based interrole conflict and observed that the original stress can arise from either the work role or a nonwork role.

Spillover from Work to Nonwork

In this type of spillover, the strain produced by stressful work situations is transferred to the nonwork domain through "emotional interference" that ultimately maintains or increases the stress experience. The feedback loop from strain to nonwork stressors in Figure 1 illustrates the way in which work-produced strain spills over into the nonwork domain.

For example, Kanter (1977) observed that employees who experience "interaction fatigue" at work may withdraw from personal contact at home. Presumably such withdrawal behavior within the family role can introduce additional stress and strain into one's life. Similarly, Bartolome and Evans (1980) reported that male managers often experience "negative emotional spillover" from work to family. Such work stressors as a recent job change, lack of person-job fit, and career disappointments generate feelings of fatigue and emotional tension that can produce aggressive or withdrawal behavior in the family domain. "One loses one's temper with the children. One explodes in fury if one's wife makes a minor mistake. Such aggression is visible and painful, but withdrawal is equally damaging to family relationships" (Bartolome & Evans, 1980, p. 139).

Further evidence of the negative consequences of work stress on family functioning is provided by Jackson and Maslach (1982) who found that police officers who experienced high levels of job burnout tended to come home angry, exhausted, and tense, complain a great deal about work, have difficulty sleeping at night, spend off-hours away from the family, and become uninvolved in family matters. In another study examining the transfer of negative job reactions to the family domain, Jackson, Zedeck, and Summers (1985) reported that emotional interference was significantly related to decreased quality of family life and increased spouse dissatisfaction with the employee's job.

A variety of career transitions can also affect relationships outside work. Louis (1980) suggested that an "extrarole adjustment" is often required when changes in one role (e.g., work) impinge on other life roles. Consistent with this notion, difficulties associated with job transfers have been associated with family stress (Lavee et al., 1985), while job loss can also severely disrupt family relationships (DeFrank & Ivancevich, 1986; Kaufman, 1982). One theme that consistently emerges from this research is that events and stressors that originate in the work domain are capable of producing stressful experiences in the nonwork domain.

Spillover from Nonwork to Work

Despite the inclusion of nonwork factors (e.g., family relations, financial difficulties, race and class problems) as potential stressors in some models of work stress (Cooper & Marshall, 1976; Ivancevich & Matteson, 1980), only a few empirical studies have investigated the relationships of nonwork stressors to job stress and other outcomes in the work domain. Researchers have found negative life stress to be associated with decreased job satisfaction and organizational commitment, and with increased job strain, job alienation, and turnover intentions (Bhagat et al., 1985; Sarason & Johnson, 1979). In a recent path analytic study of the antecedents and consequences of stress, Hendrix et al. (1985) found that home-family relationships had indirect effects on job stress through their impact on life stress. Similarly, Cooke and Rousseau's (1984) results indicate that the effect of family role expectations on strain is mediated by interrole conflict. Crouter's (1984) study provides rich illustrations of women with young children being "at risk" and experiencing negative spillover from family responsibilities to work, as reflected in tardiness and absenteeism, inattention and inefficiency, and inability to accept new responsibilities at work.

According to Levinson, Darrow, Klein, Levinson, and McKee (1978), stressors at the midlife transition (ages 40-45) can induce a crisis-like reaction to one's work accomplishments/failures and force a reappraisal of one's original "Dream." Moreover, among some executives, "workaholism" may be an escapist response to a negative family situation and an inability to confront marital conflicts (Bartolome, 1983). The studies cited in this section generally suggest that the strains produced by nonwork factors can cycle back, as in Figure 1, and produce stress within the work domain.

Work-Nonwork Conflicts

Pressures that arise in one domain may be exacerbated by the *simultaneous* occurrence of pressures in the other domain. In such cases, represented as the work-nonwork interface in Figure 1, the antecedent conditions in the work and nonwork domains may or may not be highly stressful in and of themselves but their joint occurrence is likely to produce stress. For example, neither a Saturday work meeting nor a Saturday outing with the family is in itself a stressful event, but the simultaneous role demands are likely to arouse conflict and stress due to the inability to satisfy the expectations of both work and family role senders.

Work-nonwork conflicts due to multiple role pressures have been associated with such strain symptoms as job dissatisfaction, life dissatisfaction, and low mental health (Kopelman, Greenhaus & Connolly, 1983; Pleck, Staines & Lang, 1980; Sekaran, 1985), and may be particularly disruptive to women in two-career families (Sekaran, 1985). Role characteristics that produce work-nonwork conflict of this type include long and irregular work hours, inflexible work schedules, extensive travel, marriage, parenthood, primary responsibility for childcare, and one's spouse's career pursuits. Each of these environmental variables can place extensive time demands on the focal person to participate in activities within that domain that can conflict with simultaneous demands to participate extensively in the other domain (Greenhaus & Beutell, 1985).

The perceived intensity (and hence stressfulness) of work-nonwork conflicts is partly contingent upon the relative importance or salience of work and nonwork roles. The more equally an individual is committed to his or her work *and* nonwork roles and responsibilities, the more the self-imposed demands to be competent in each role, and the greater the psychological conflict experienced as a result of incompatible demands from the two domains. Moreover, strong negative sanctions for noncompliance with role demands (from work or nonwork) can also heighten conflict and stress because of the loss of flexibility in scheduling work and nonwork role activities (Greenhaus & Beutell, 1985). An interesting perspective on conflicts and strain engendered by multiple roles has been provided by Marks (1977), who argued that individuals often find the time and energy to meet the requirements of "over-committed" interests, but that scarcity of time and energy are invoked to camouflage under-commitment to particular roles or interests.

Work-Nonwork Stress and the Two-Career Family

The magnitude and consequences of work-nonwork stress are likely to be particularly severe for members of two-career relationships. With expanded work and family responsibilities for both partners, the likelihood of work-nonwork time conflicts increases, the stressors in the work and nonwork domains can easily cumulate, and the resultant strains may spill over into other life roles.

In addition to the usual stressors working men and women encounter in their work and nonwork roles, two types of interindividual (between partner) stressors have been identified as unique to two-career couples (Gupta & Jenkins, 1985): (a) interindividual work role stressors arising from interactions of the work roles of the two partners, e.g., career comparisons, competitiveness, status inconsistency, administrative attitudes and policies toward career wives; and (b) interindividual interrole stressors which arise from the interplay of the work and family roles of the two partners, e.g., role coordination, barriers to social and organizational assimilation, difficulties in dual job searches and transfers, and lack of auxiliary career support from the partner. While these unique stressors appear to have little effect on the work productivity and marital adjustment of two-career couples, a potential negative consequence is retarded career advancement, particularly for the female partner (Gupta & Jenkins, 1985).

Evidence regarding the health outcomes of interrole conflict on two-career partners is mixed. Some studies have reported that overall, working men and women enjoy better health than full-time housewives (Bird, 1979), and that two-career couples are energetic, active, and in good health, although they may experience periods of complete physical exhaustion (St. John-Parsons, 1978). Sekaran (1985) reported results indicating that multiple role pressures and the number of children in the family have direct adverse consequences on the mental health of women in dual career families, but not men.

PERSONAL AND SOCIAL INFLUENCES ON WORK-NONWORK STRESS

As Figure 1 indicates, three mechanisms influence the perception and interpretation of environmental stressors and moderate their effects on perceived stress and strain: (a) personal characteristics; (b) coping responses; and (c) social support. In this section we will examine the roles played by these variables in the management of stress and its consequences by the focal individual.

Personal Characteristics

The mere exposure to environmental stressors will not necessarily lead to perceptions of stress and subsequent strain symptoms. Personal characteristics play an important role in the interpretation of situational demands, constraints, and/or opportunities as stressful, as well as in influencing the coping mechanisms evoked and social support sought to deal with environmental stressors. The most consistent results have been found with regard to the mediating role of age, trait anxiety, locus of control, and Type A behavior pattern (Brief et al., 1981; Cooper & Marshall, 1976; Johnson & Sarason, 1979; Parasuraman & Cleek, 1984). Thus, younger individuals who are highly anxious, perceive an external locus of control, and exhibit a Type A behavior pattern are more likely to interpret a given situation or event as stressful and experience symptoms of strain than their older, less anxious, internal, and Type B counterparts.

In contrast to the notion of vulnerability, personal characteristics have also been viewed as "psychological resources" that individuals can draw on to help withstand stressors in the work and nonwork environments. Self-esteem and mastery have been found to buffer individuals faced with financial and occupational strains (Pearlin & Schooler, 1978), and a significant stress resistance resource found to insulate individuals from the aversive consequences of stressful events is personal hardiness, a constellation of personality dispositions encompassing internal locus of control, commitment to self, and positive attitude toward challenge and change (Kobasa, Maddi & Kahn, 1980).

Personal characteristics serve an additional role in stressor-strain relationships through their influence on coping and social support. Thus variations in the type of coping mechanism used by individuals have been found to be related to age, gender, organizational tenure, trait anxiety, mastery, self-esteem, social and autonomy needs, and Type A behavior pattern (Fleishman, 1984; Folkman & Lazarus, 1980; Newton & Keenan, 1985; Osipow, Doty & Spokane, 1985; Parasuraman & Cleek, 1984). Moreover, Kobasa and Puccetti (1983) reported results demonstrating interactive effects of hardiness and family support in buffering executives from the illness-provoking effects of stress.

Coping with Work-Nonwork Stress

Although stress researchers have defined coping in a variety of ways, there appears to be general agreement that coping refers to the overt behavioral and cognitive responses made by individuals to master, reduce, manage, or tolerate stressful environmental and internal demands and conflicts that tax or exceed the individual's resources (Lazarus & Launier, 1978; Parasuraman & Cleek, 1984; Pearlin & Schooler, 1978). While many different typologies of coping strategies have been proposed (Kessler, Price & Wortman, 1985), they generally encompass three dimensions of coping. These include coping strategies to (a) modify the stressful situation (i.e., stressor) through direct action; (b) control the meaning of the stressful situation; and (c) manage the strain symptoms. The first two dimensions parallel two of Hall's (1972) three classes of coping with interrole conflicts, viz., structural role redefinition, and personal role reorientation.

Studies in the work and nonwork domains provide evidence that coping behaviors can have both direct effects on symptoms of strain and moderator effects on the stress-strain relationship (Kessler et al., 1985; Parasuraman & Cleek, 1984; Pearlin & Schooler, 1978) as indicated in Figure 1. Although it appears reasonable to expect that modification of the stressful environment will produce more satisfying and long-term amelioration of stress and attendant strains, it is unlikely that any specific coping strategy will be universally effective. Individual differences in coping behavior noted earlier and situational factors argue for a contingency approach to coping that utilizes a variety of approaches depending upon the nature of the stressor and individual's own psychological resources and repertoire of coping skills (Burke & Belcourt, 1974; Newton & Keenan, 1985; Pearlin & Schooler, 1978).

For example, Folkman and Lazarus (1980) found that in general, work contexts favored problem-focused coping whereas health contexts favored emotion-focused coping, but that individuals tended to use both forms of coping depending upon their appraisal of the situation. Other studies (e.g., Parasuraman & Cleek, 1984) have shown that emotional/defensive behaviors in dealing with role stressors may tend to exacerbate felt stress and thus may be maladaptive.

Social Support

The establishment of supportive relationships with other people plays two roles in the stress process (Cohen & Wills, 1985). First, support may foster well-being independent of the presence or magnitude of the stress, the "main effect" approach represented by the solid arrows from the support variable in Figure 1. Second, the buffering approach proposes that support attenuates the relationship between stress and strain, represented by the dashed arrows in Figure 1.

Since another article in this issue (Gore, 1986) examines the role of social support in considerable detail, we will simply note that support can come from either the work or nonwork domain and can be applied to stressors in either domain. The capability of social support to enhance broadly useful coping abilities (Cohen & Wills, 1985) strongly suggests that supportive relationships are particularly relevant to employees confronted with multiple stressors from work and nonwork roles.

INDIVIDUAL INTERVENTIONS RELEVANT TO WORK-NONWORK STRESS

Since stress is ultimately based on the focal person's perception and interpretation of the environment, individual actions are often required to manage stress and the resultant strain. The multiple sources of work-nonwork stress suggest the need for the selective use of diverse coping responses and sources of social support. Schein's (1978) coping cycle — diagnosis, self-assessment, coping response, and feedback — is consistent with such a contingency approach and reinforces the importance of understanding the interdependence of work and nonwork domains.

In addressing stressors and strain arising from the intersection of work and nonwork roles, coping strategies could be directed toward elements of the work domain and/or the nonwork domain. The three-fold categorization of coping described earlier is used as a framework for proposing a variety of individual interventions designed to manage stress.

Problem-solving strategies designed to change the work environment include attempts to obtain: a clarification of job duties and performance level; more (or less) autonomy, responsibility, and challenge; an elimination of the burdensome parts of the job; a more flexible work schedule or place of work; a change of occupation, career path, or employer; and an increased level of instrumental or informational support (Cooper & Marshall, 1977; Greenhaus, in press; House, 1981; Newman & Beehr, 1979). Parallel problem-solving strategies in the nonwork domain could take the form of seeking an effective division of labor in the family domain; eliminating burdensome nonwork roles; making decisions about the presence, number, and timing of children; obtaining outside help for home and child care; and improving communications with role senders. It should be noted that individual efforts to modify the work or nonwork environment require negotiation with one or more role senders (Hall, 1972), a proactive approach to the environment, and effective problem-solving skills (Newton & Keenan, 1985).

Coping strategies aimed at changing the meaning of the work situation include a reexamination of the importance of "career success" and a redefinition of internal standards of performance. Recognizing the impossibility of being a "perfect" parent or spouse and reprioritizing family goals represent similar cognitive approaches to changing the meaning of the nonwork environment (Beutell & Greenhaus, 1986). Seeking emotional/appraisal support, career/personal counseling, and training in time management (Burke & Weir, 1980; Cooper & Marshall, 1977) represent additional approaches to changing the meaning of a work or nonwork situation.

The third set of proposed coping strategies encompasses varied approaches to managing strain symptoms produced by work-nonwork stressors. These include such self-care or self-management activities as physical exercise, recreation, relaxation through transcendental meditation, biofeedback, and yoga (Burke & Weir, 1980; Osipow et al., 1985). Table 1 summarizes the three types of coping strategies and social support mechanisms that may be used in managing work-nonwork stress. Since individual strategies may not be sufficiently effective in isolation, combinations of actions, such as problem-solving and strain management (Bruning & Frew, 1985), may be helpful in certain circumstances.

Table 1

Individual Strategies for Managing Work-Nonwork Stress

Target of Strategy

	Work Domain	Nonwork Domain
Modify the Stressful Environment	Seek clarity of job performance, job duties, and career prospects	Seek effective division of labor in family domain
	Seek reduced or more flexible work schedule, and flexibility in locus of workplace	Seek outside help for home and/ child care
	Seek change in occupation, career path, or organization	Make decisions about presence, number, and timing of children
	Seek more (or less) autonomy, responsibility, and challenge on job	Eliminate burdensome nonwork roles
		Improve problem-solving skills
	Eliminate burdensome parts of job through delegation or negotiation	Improve communication with role senders
	Seek instrumental/informational support	Seek instrumental/informational support
Change Meaning of Situation	Reexamine importance of "career success"	Recognize the impossibility of being a "perfect" parent, spouse, or friend
	Redefine one's internal standards of performance	Reprioritize family goals
	Seek emotional/appraisal support	Seek emotional/appraisal support
	Seek career counseling	Seek personal life counseling
	Develop time management skills	Develop time management skills
Manage Strain Symptoms	Relaxation Transcendental meditation Biofeedback Yoga Physical exercise Follow good diet and eating habits Recreation	

ORGANIZATIONAL INTERVENTIONS RELEVANT TO WORK-NONWORK STRESS

Pearlin and Schooler (1978) observed that chronic, organizationally generated stressors may be resistant to amelioration through personal coping efforts. At the same time, high levels of employee stress can be dysfunctional to an organization and detract from its ability to accomplish its goals. It is estimated that the costs of stress-related illness, accidents, poor decision making, turnover, and death in the U.S. may reach at least $75-$90 billion annually (Ivancevich & Matteson, 1980). State workers' compensation laws and recent court decisions that make employers liable for physical and psychological injuries resulting from continued stress on the job further emphasize the importance of organizational interventions designed to reduce employee stress to tolerable levels (Ivancevich, Matteson & Richards, 1985).

It is useful to classify organizational efforts according to the three types of individual coping strategies identified earlier, although any given program is likely to incorporate two or more of the strategies. Thus, organizations can attempt to: (a) modify the stressful environment (e.g., through the design of jobs that are in line with employees' capabilities and interests, or the elimination of aversive elements in the physical work environment); (b) help employees change their interpretation of the environment (through counseling or social support programs); or (c) help employees manage their strain symptoms more effectively (by providing facilities for relaxation, physical exercise, and medical treatment).

Because work-nonwork stress can be produced by emotional spillover or by competing time demands, organizational actions relevant to the work-nonwork interface should provide: (a) accurate information to employees; (b) greater flexibility within the work environment; and (c) support services for employees facing specific work-nonwork dilemmas (Beutell & Greenhaus, 1986; Greenhaus, in press).

Alternative career paths may differ substantially in the amount of time and emotion required and the amount of stress induced. Therefore, employees concerned about managing work-nonwork stress must come to appreciate the subtle yet crucial differences in lifestyle associated with the pursuit of different career options. A realistic career path preview, not unlike a realistic job preview for job candidates, can provide the necessary information for employees to make career decisions compatible with their involvements in multiple life roles. Accurate information can also reduce the strains associated with such career transitions as job transfers (Brett & Werbel, 1980), promotions (Leibowitz & Schlossberg, 1982), and terminations (Schlossberg & Leibowitz, 1980).

Accurate information should be supported by organizational flexibility in policies and practices. Obvious illustrations include the establishment of more flexible work schedules, part-time and job sharing opportunities, and parental leave programs. Moreover, permitting employees in selected jobs to conduct their work at home may reduce certain forms of work-family conflict, although the risks may include exacerbation of other stresses and strains, heightened social isolation, and barriers to career advancement (Shamir & Salomon, 1985).

Since career paths can differ in terms of their intrusion into the nonwork domain, organizations should provide employees with more flexibility in choosing among multiple career path opportunities (Evans & Bartolome, 1980). Organizations and individuals need to understand that there are many different ways for employees to contribute to the organization and experience "career success" and that some career paths are more compatible with a desired lifestyle than are others.

Organizations should examine the possibility of providing more flexibility in their demands for heavy work involvement. Employees in their early career may be particularly susceptible to work-nonwork stress because the extraordinary time and emotional demands required to establish oneself in a career often coincide with the extensive demands of rearing young children. Bailyn (1980) has proposed a "slow burn" approach to career development in which job challenge and time involvement start off at moderate levels during the early career and gradually increase over time as family demands subside. This approach, which flies in the face of conventional wisdom about career development, deserves serious consideration by organizations concerned about helping their employees manage work-nonwork stress.

Organizations can also provide support services to help employees deal with specific sources of work-nonwork stress. In addition to direct aid and support (such as the development or sponsorship of a childcare program), organizationally-sponsored support groups can provide opportunities for employees to develop problem solving and coping skills relevant to work-nonwork stress. For example,

Culbert and Renshaw's (1972) group problem solving intervention enabled husbands and wives to understand and cope with the stresses produced by the husbands' extensive job-related travel. Such groups could be formed to address a variety of work-nonwork issues including conflicting time demands, emotional spillover, and spouses' career priorities.

CONCLUSIONS AND DIRECTIONS FOR FUTURE RESEARCH

Our review of the sources and consequences of work-nonwork stress highlighted the permeability of work-nonwork boundaries and revealed a complex pattern of linkages among stressors, strains, and other outcomes in the two life domains. Three distinct categories of links are evident. First, there is growing support for the proposition that work and nonwork stressors have additive effects, such that the greater the extent of stressors encountered in the two spheres, the greater the resulting strains experienced by the focal individual. A second perspective is that stressors and strain generated within one domain can transfer or "spill over" into the other domain, thus creating additional sources of stress in the latter with potentially damaging consequences. The third, and potentially most stressful, link is that involving work-nonwork conflicts engendered by the intersection of simultaneous role pressures emanating from the two life domains. The concurrent role demands can greatly exacerbate the level of stress experienced and have dysfunctional work and nonwork consequences.

The exposure to work-nonwork stressors need not invariably have detrimental effects on individuals. Certain psychological resources associated with increased age and experience, internal locus of control, and personal "hardiness" can buffer individuals from the deleterious effects of stressful work-nonwork experiences. Based on evidence of both main and moderating effects of varied coping responses and social support on indices of strain and other outcomes, we proposed a proactive approach to dealing with environmental stressors, and identified a variety of individual strategies for managing stress and its consequences. The resistance of certain chronic organizationally-generated stressors to amelioration through individual coping efforts, and enlightened organizational self-interest in managing the high cost of stress emphasize the need for concomitant organizational interventions designed to reduce stress to tolerable levels as well as equip individuals to manage stress more effectively.

A critical examination of the literature indicates considerable progress in recent years. There seems to be an increasingly widespread adoption of a work-nonwork perspective of stress as evidenced by a steadily growing body of theory and empirical research. Moreover, a number of the empirical studies have incorporated work and nonwork variables in causal models of stress that have been tested with increasingly sophisticated statistical techniques. Furthermore, recent research on job, organizational, and career transitions has begun to fill a gap in our understanding of acute work stressors, just as research on daily hassles addresses our need to understand chronic, cumulative stressors in the nonwork domain.

Nevertheless, work-nonwork stress remains a fertile field for additional theory and research, especially in light of the pervasiveness of the phenomenon and the attention it has drawn in the popular press. Although we have proposed three types of linkages between work and nonwork sources of stress (additive, spillover, and conflict), this schema may not fully capture the manner in which work and nonwork domains intersect. In fact, a more complete understanding of work-nonwork stress requires a mapping of each role — work (supervisor, subordinate, peer) and nonwork (parent, spouse, member of community, religious participant) — into its component parts. In addition, although there is consistent evidence attesting to the significance of personal characteristics, coping behaviors, and social support in ameliorating stress arising from either the work or nonwork domain, only a few studies have tested the moderating effects of these variables on individual reactions to work-nonwork stressors.

From a methodological perspective, much of the effort in scale development has focused on measures of stressors, perceived stress, and strain symptoms. More effort should be devoted to the valid measurement of personal coping responses and social support, especially as they relate to work-nonwork stress. Moreover, since coping and social support are dynamic processes in which certain actions are used jointly or are discarded in favor of others, measures must reflect the concurrent and sequential nature of these variables. This argues for more longitudinal and qualitative research designs that are capable of detecting changes in coping and support resources over time. Furthermore, since work and nonwork pressures arise from diverse role senders, research in the area would be strengthened by the collection of data from key members of the focal individual's role set.

Finally, more research is required to determine the impact of organizational interventions on work-nonwork stress and its consequences. Although the recommendations presented in the previous section are generally rooted in conceptual and/or empirical analysis, specific interventions must be evaluated in the particular environment in which they are implemented. For example, despite convincing evidence that work schedule flexibility can directly or indirectly reduce work-nonwork conflicts (Pleck, Staines & Lang, 1980; Staines & Pleck, 1986), the effectiveness of a particular flexible work schedule program is likely to depend on a match between the characteristics of the specific program and the needs of different groups of employees (Bohen & Viveros-Long, 1981).

In conclusion, research has begun to shed light on the complex interactions between work and nonwork sources and consequences of stress. We hope that the integrative framework presented in this paper will stimulate additional conceptualization and empirical research.

REFERENCES

Bailyn, L. (1980). The slow-burn way to the top: Some thoughts on the early years of organizational careers. In C.B. Derr (Ed.), *Work, family, and the career* (pp. 94–105). New York: Praeger.

Bartolome, F. (1983). The work alibi: When it's harder to go home. *Harvard Business Review, 61*(2), 67–74.

Bartolome, F. & Evans, P.A.L. (1980). Must success cost so much? *Harvard Business Review, 58*(2), 137–148.

Beehr, T.A. & Bhagat, R.S. (1985). Introduction to human stress and cognition in organizations. In T.A. Beehr and R.S. Bhagat (Eds.), *Human stress and cognition in organizations* (pp. 3–19). New York: Wiley.

Beutell, N.J. & Greenhaus, J.H. (1986). Balancing acts: Work-family conflict and the dual-career couple. In L.L. Moore (Ed.), *Not as far as you think: The realities of working women* (pp. 149–162). Lexington, MA: Lexington Books.

Bhagat, R.S., Lindholm, H., McQuaid, S.J. & Segovis, J. (1985). Total life stress: A multimethod validation of the construct and its effects on organizationally valued outcomes and withdrawal behaviors. *Journal of Applied Psychology, 70*, 202–214.

Bird, C. (1970). *The two-paycheck marriage.* New York: Rawson Wade.

Bohen, H.C. & Viveros-Long, A. (1981). *Balancing jobs and family life: Do flexible work schedules help?* Philadelphia: Temple University Press.

Brett, J.M. & Werbel, J.D. (1980). *The effect of job transfer on employees and their families.* Washington, DC: Employee Relocation Council.

Brief, A.P., Schuler, R.S. & Van Sell, M. (1981). *Managing job stress*. Boston: Little, Brown and Company.

Bruning, N.S. & Frew, D.R. (1985). *The impact of various stress management training strategies: A longitudinal field experiment*. Unpublished manuscript.

Burke, R.J. & Belcourt, M.L. (1974). Managerial role stress and coping responses. *Journal of Business Administration, 5*(2), 55–68.

Burke, R.J. & Weir, T. (1980). Coping with the stress of managerial occupations. In C.L. Cooper & R. Payne (Eds.), *Current concerns in occupational stress* (pp. 299–335). New York: Wiley.

Cohen, S. & Wills, T.A. (1985). Stress, social support, and the buffering hypothesis. *Psychological Bulletin, 98*, 310–357.

Cooke, R.A. & Rousseau, D.M. (1984). Stress and strain from family roles and work-role expectations. *Journal of Applied Psychology, 69*, 252–26.

Cooper, C.L. & Marshall, J. (1976). Occupational sources of stress: A review of the literature relating to coronary heart disease and mental ill health. *Journal of Occupational Psychology, 49*, 11–28.

Crouter, A.C. (1984). Spillover from family to work: The neglected side of the work-family interface. *Human Relations, 37*, 425–442.

Culbert, S.A. & Renshaw, J.R. (1972). Coping with the stresses of travel as an opportunity for improving the quality of work and family life. *Family Process, 11*, 321–337.

DeFrank, R.S. & Ivancevich, J.M. (1986). Job loss: An individual level review and model. *Journal of Vocational Behavior, 28*, 1–20.

DeLongis, A., Coyne, J.C., Dakof, G., Folkman, S. & Lazarus, R.S. (1982). Relationship of daily hassles, uplifts, and major life events to health status. *Health Psychology, 1*, 119–136.

Eden, D. (1982). Critical job events, acute stress, and strain: A multiple interrupted time series. *Organizational Behavior and Human Performance, 30*, 312–329.

Evans, P.A.L. & Bartolome, F. (1980). *Must success cost so much?* New York: Basic Books.

Fleishman, J.A. (1984). Personality characteristics and coping patterns. *Journal of Health and Social Behavior, 25*, 229–244.

Folkman, S. & Lazarus, R.S. (1980). An analysis of coping in a middle-aged community sample. *Journal of Health and Social Behavior, 21*, 219–239.

Gore, S. (1987). Perspectives on Social Support and Research on Stress Moderating Processes. *Journal of Organizational Behavior Management, 8*(2), 87–103.

Greenhaus, J.H. (In Press). *Career management*. Hinsdale, IL: Dryden.

Greenhaus, J.H. & Beutell, N.J. (1985). Sources of conflict between work and family roles. *Academy of Management Review, 10*, 76–88.

Gupta, N. & Jenkins, D. (1985). Dual-career couples. In T.A. Beehr and R.S. Bhagat (Eds.), *Human Stress and Cognition in Organizations* (pp. 141–175). New York: Wiley.

Hall, D.T. (1972). A model of coping with role conflict: The role behavior of college-educated women. *Administrative Science Quarterly, 17*, 471–489.

Hendrix, W.H., Ovalle, N.K. & Troxler, R.G. (1985). Behavioral and physiological consequences of stress and its antecedent factors. *Journal of Applied Psychology, 70*, 188–201.

Holmes, T.H. & Rahe, R.H. (1967). The social readjustment rating scale. *Journal of Psychosomatic Research, 11*, 213–218.

House, J.S. (1981). *Work stress and social support*. Reading, MA: Addison-Wesley.

Ivancevich, J.M. & Matteson, M.T. (1980). *Stress and work: A managerial perspective*. Dallas: Scott, Foresman.

Ivancevich, J.M., Matteson, M.T. & Richards, E.P. (1985). Who's liable for stress on the job? *Harvard Business Review, 68*(2), 60–61, 66, 70–71.

Jackson, S.E. & Maslach, C. (1982). After-effects of job-related stress: Families as victims. *Journal of Occupational Behaviour, 3*, 63–77.

Jackson, S.E., Zedeck, S. & Summers, E. (1985). Family life disruptions: effects of job-induced structural and emotional interference. *Academy of Management Journal, 28*, 574–586.

Johnson, J.H. & Sarason, I.G. (1979). Recent developments in research on life stress. In V. Hamilton & D.M. Warburton (Eds.), *Human stress and cognition* (pp. 205–233). New York: Wiley.

Kanter, R.M. (1977). *Work and family in the United States*. New York: Russel Sage Foundation.

Kaufman, H.G. (1982). *Professionals in search of work: Coping with the stress of job loss and underemployment*. New York: Wiley.

Kessler, R.C., Price, R.H. & Wortman, C.B. (1985). Social factors in psychopathology: Stress, social support, and coping processes. *Annual Review of Psychology, 36*, 531–572.

Kobasa, S.C., Maddi, S.R. & Kahn, S. (1980). Hardiness and health: A prospective study. *Journal of Personality and Social Psychology, 42*, 168–177.

Kobasa, S.C. & Puccetti, M.C. (1983). Personality and social resources in stress resistance. *Journal of Personality and Social Psychology, 45*, 839–850.

Kopelman, R.E., Greenhaus, J.H. & Connolly, T.F. (1983). A model of work, family, and interrole conflict: A construct validation study. *Organizational Behavior and Human Performance, 32*, 198–215.

Lavee, Y., McCubbin, H.I. & Patterson, J.M. (1985). The double ABCX model of family stress and adaptation: An empirical test by analysis of structural equations with latent variables. *Journal of Marriage and the Family, 47*, 811–825.

Lazarus, R.S. & Launier, R. (1978). Stress-related transactions between persons and environment. In L.A. Pervin & M. Lewis (Eds.), *Perspectives in interactional psychology* (pp. 287–327). New York: Plenum.

Leibowitz, Z.B. & Schlossberg, N.K. (1982). Critical career transitions: A model for designing career services. *Training and Development Journal, 36*(2), 13–18.

Levinson, D.J., Darrow, C.N., Klein, E.B., Levinson, M.H. & McKee, B. (1978). *Seasons of a man's life*. New York: Knopf.

London, M., Crandall, R. & Seals, G. (1977). The contribution of job and leisure satisfaction to quality of life. *Journal of Applied Psychology, 62*, 328–334.

Louis, M. (1980). Surprise and sense making: What newcomers experience in entering unfamiliar organizational settings. *Administrative Science Quarterly, 25*, 226–251.

Marks, S.R. (1977). Multiple roles and role strain: Some notes on human energy, time, and commitment. *American Sociological Review, 42*, 921–936.

Newman, J.E. & Beehr, T.A. (1979). Personal and organizational strategies for handling job stress: A review of research and opinion. *Personnel Psychology, 32*, 1–43.

Newton, T.J. & Keenan, A. (1985). Coping with work-related stress. *Human Relations, 38*, 107–126.

Osipow, S.H., Doty, R.E. & Spokane, A.R. (1985). Occupational stress, strain, and coping across the life span. *Journal of Vocational Behavior, 27*, 98–108.

Parasuraman, S. & Cleek, M.A. (1984). Coping behaviors and managers' affective reactions to role stressors. *Journal of Vocational Behavior, 24*, 179–193.

Parasuraman, S., Zammuto, R.F. & Outcalt, D. (1984). On the role of work/nonwork involvements in influencing job and nonjob attitudes. Paper presented at the *Fourth International Symposium on Forecasting*, London, England.

Pearlin, L.I. & Schooler, C. (1978). The structure of coping. *Journal of Health and Social Behavior, 19*, 2–21.

Pleck, J.H., Staines, G.L. & Lang, L. (1980). Conflicts between work and family life. *Monthly Labor Review, 103*(3), 29–32.

Sarason, I.G. & Johnson, J.H. (1979). Life stress, organizational stress, and job satisfaction. *Psychological Reports, 44*, 75–79.

Schein, E.H. (1978). *Career dynamics: Matching individual and organizational needs*. Reading, MA: Addison-Wesley.

Schlossberg, N.K. & Leibowitz, Z.B. (1980). Organizational support systems as buffers to job loss. *Journal of Vocational Behavior, 17,* 204–217.

Schuler, R.S. (1980). Definition and conceptualization of stress in organizations. *Organizational Behavior and Human Performance, 25,* 184–215.

Sekaran, U. (1985). The paths to mental health: An exploratory study of husbands and wives in dual-career families. *Journal of Occupational Psychology, 58,* 129–137.

Shamir, B. & Salomon, I. (1985). Work-at-home and the quality of working life. *Academy of Management Review, 10,* 455–464.

St. John-Parsons, D. (1978). Continuous dual-career families: A case study. *Psychology of Women Quarterly, 3,* 30–42.

Staines, G.L. & Pleck, J.H. (1986). Work schedule flexibility and family life. *Journal of Occupational Behaviour, 7,* 147–153.

Thoits, P.A. (1983). Dimensions of life events that influence psychological distress: An evaluation and synthesis of the literature. In H.B. Kaplan (Ed.), *Psychosocial stress: Trends in theory and research.* New York: Academic Press.

Vinokur, A. & Selzer, M. (1975). Desirable versus undesirable life events: Their relationship to stress and mental distress. *Journal of Personality and Social Psychology, 66,* 297–333.

PART II: INDIVIDUAL DIFFERENCES

Type A Behavior
and Occupational Stress

Daniel C. Ganster

SUMMARY. Studies of the Type A Behavior pattern in a work context are reviewed in terms of a causal model relating Type A to coronary heart disease. Research supports the hypothesis that Type A's are hyper-responsive to subjective work stressors. However, examination of objective stressors is rare. Furthermore, causal connections between Type A and objective and subjective work environments are consistent with laboratory research, but field studies have yet to provide convincing support for them. Gaps in the empirical literature are delineated and methodological recommendations are made. It is argued that understanding the causal mechanisms by which Type A leads to heart disease has implications for the adoption of treatment strategies, and that the occupational context provides a promising setting for studying these mechanisms.

In the late 1950s Rosenman and Friedman (1959) observed that their coronary heart disease patients shared a characteristic pattern of behaviors and emotional reactions that they labelled Type A behavior. They described this pattern as an "action-emotion complex"

Daniel C. Ganster is affiliated with the Department of Management, University of Nebraska.

This paper was prepared with the support of a grant from the National Institute of Mental Health (1 R01 MH40368).

Grateful acknowledgment is made to Marcelline Fusilier for her helpful comments on a draft of this paper.

that involves hostility, aggressiveness, competitiveness, and a sense of time urgency. This behavior pattern seemed especially prevalent in their younger (under 60 years old) cardiac patients, leading them to hypothesize that it might play a role in the etiology of their disease. These observations mirrored earlier ones of psychiatrists such as Arlow (1945) and Dunbar (1943) who commented on the ambitiousness and goal-directedness of coronary heart disease (CHD) patients. Other cardiologists (Gertler & White, 1954) had made similar descriptions of their young CHD patients.

The first large-scale prospective study to examine the relationship of the Type A pattern with CHD was conducted by Rosenman, Friedman, and their colleagues. Known as the Western Collaborative Group Study, the investigation observed 3500 males for 8.5 years. Those men who were classified as Type A by a structured interview at the beginning of the study were found to have twice the rate of clinical coronary disease, were five times as likely to suffer a second heart attack, and were twice as likely to die from heart attacks as those men classified as Type B (those with an absence of Type A characteristics; Rosenman, Brand, Jenkins, Friedman, Straus & Wurm, 1975). While the exact role of the Type A pattern in the etiology of heart disease is currently under debate, it has been classified as a significant risk factor for CHD that is independent of, and as predictive as, other traditional risk factors (e.g., age, smoking, systolic blood pressure, elevated serum cholesterol; Review Panel on Coronary-Prone Behavior and Coronary Heart Disease, 1981).

Just why individuals who display the Type A behavior pattern should be more susceptible to CHD is not entirely clear. The most likely mechanism appears to involve a heightened physiological reactivity in Type A's when they encounter situations which involve challenge, demands, and a loss of personal control. Chronic exposure to such evoking situations, and its concomitant chronic elevation of physiological responsivity, is believed to cause some initial injury to the lining of coronary arteries, making them susceptible sites for atherosclerotic lesions and deposits. Also, chronic physiological arousal is believed to enhance the development of atherosclerotic lesions by increasing blood clotting and mobilizing circulating lipid substances (Williams, Friedman, Glass, Herd & Schneiderman, 1978). Studies have demonstrated a relationship between Type A and heightened reactivity to certain environmental stimuli (challenge, frustration, demands, threats to control). This reactivity has been shown in cardiovascular variables (such as blood pressure and heart rate) and biochemical variables (such as epinephrine and norepinephrine) (for reviews, see Houston, 1983; Krantz, Glass, Schaeffer & Davia, 1982).

The dominant research paradigm for examining the physiological reactivity of Type A's has been the laboratory experiment in which the experimenter exposes Type A and Type B subjects to various eliciting stimuli in a controlled environment and observes their physiological and behavioral responses. It has been mainly in these, relatively short-term, exposures that the hyper-responsivity of Type A's has been observed. What makes the Type A construct potentially interesting to organizational researchers are the implications of this laboratory research when the findings are generalized to the work environment. Indeed, the primary environmental stimuli that have been implicated in eliciting the Type A response pattern — demands, competition, threats to internal control — are ubiquitous in occupational settings. One might hypothesize, then, that Type A's working in such environments are likely to suffer the consequences of a surfeit of chronic autonomic arousal, including CHD and hypertension. Conversely, to the extent that Type A behaviors might also lead to greater work accomplishments and career advancement, these behaviors may be reinforced by organizations. Work life, then, might not only provide physiologically arousing stimuli to which Type A's are particularly susceptible, but also create the contingencies that shape and reinforce the behavior pattern.

In this paper I will focus on those empirical studies which examined the Type A behavior pattern in the occupational context. The review is organized to address several specific questions regarding potential causal pathways through which Type A behavior might lead to CHD and other health consequences. The model depicting these causal pathways is displayed in Figure 1.

Figure 1 contains a structural model relating Type A behavior to disease outcomes. Embedded within this model is a general model of work stress similar to ones implicitly or explicitly invoked in most stress studies. This general model of work stress involves paths c, d, e, and h. In essence, there are presumed to be certain objective work-related stimuli (e.g., long hours, excessive mental and physical demands) that cause elevations in physiological responses such as serum cholesterol levels, epinephrine, and blood pressure. These stimuli are labelled "objective work stressors." Recognizing that one's cognitive appraisal of an environment might

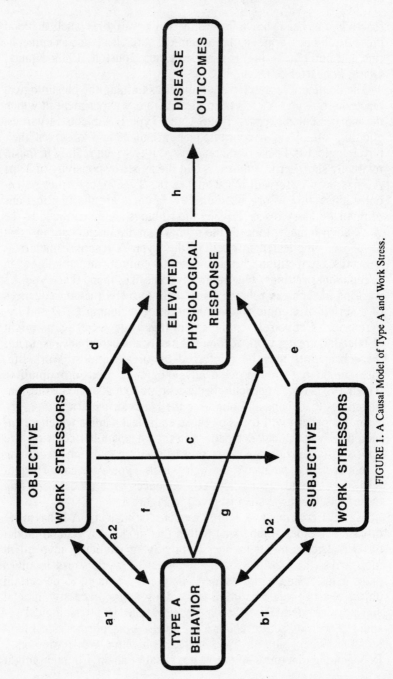

FIGURE 1. A Causal Model of Type A and Work Stress.

cause physiological responses independent of the nature of the objective environment (Lazarus, DeLongis, Folkman & Gruen, 1985), a class of variables labelled "subjective work stressors" is also included in the model. Objective work environments, then, may have an impact on physiological response either directly (path d) or indirectly (via path c) through their effects on the individual's cognitive appraisal of their situation. Path h, depicting a causal relation between elevated physiological response and disease outcomes, is based on a growing corpus of research which attests to its plausibility (e.g., Williams et al., 1978), and thus will not be discussed here. Similarly, the effects of work stressors (paths c, d, and e) are topics of other papers in this issue, so they will not be discussed either.

The remaining paths in the model address three different causal processes, and will guide the discussion of the research in this paper. The first causal process is depicted by paths f and g. These paths denote a moderating effect of Type A on the relationships between work stressors and physiological response. This moderating effect constitutes the hyper-responsivity hypothesis—that is, that Type A's show an exaggerated response (relative to Type B's) to work stressors. A second causal process concerns the eliciting potential of environmental stimuli on the Type A pattern itself. Paths a2 and b2 denote this effect, suggesting that certain stimuli evoke the characteristic behaviors and emotions of the Type A pattern, and that chronic exposure to these environments can actually abet the development of these behaviors into a long-term behavior pattern that generalizes to other work and non-work situations. Finally, paths a1 and b1 reflect the final causal process—that the Type A pattern has a causal effect on the objective and subjective work environments themselves. In the remainder of this paper I will (a) review the empirical studies relevant to each of the three causal phenomena just enumerated, (b) make some methodological suggestions regarding the testing of these causal pathways, and (c) discuss some of the practical implications of understanding the role of the Type A pattern in the context of the work environment.

ARE TYPE A'S HYPER-REACTIVE TO WORK STRESSORS?

Much of the experimental research comparing the reactivity of Type A's and B's suggests that Type A's have stronger physiological responses to certain stimuli (Houston, 1983; Krantz et al., 1982; Matthews, 1982). Generalizing from these studies, the hyper-responsivity of Type A's should be evident in the context of work stressors also. If A's and B's faced equal occupational demands, A's would show more pronounced physiological and emotional reactions. This general hypothesis is denoted by paths f and g in Figure 1, which posit an interaction between stressors (real or imagined) and physiological response.

Investigators examining the moderating effects of Type A on the relationships between job stressors and outcome variables have almost all focused on the effects of subjective work stressors (path g in Figure 1). Studies specifically testing Type A moderating effects are listed in Table 1, which also lists some of the study characteristics.

As noted in Table 1, almost all of the ten studies listed report some significant moderating effect of Type A on the relationships between stressors and some measure of psychological or physiological response. Several characteristics of these studies are worth noting. First, every investigation, except Hurrell (1985), examined work variables that would be classified as "subjective work stressors" in Figure 1; and most of these represent some type of role stress construct such as role conflict, ambiguity, or overload. The general design has been a field survey, and a moderator effect for Type A was inferred if correlations between stressors and outcomes were larger for Type A's than for B's.

While one must be cautious when making inferences from a qualitative review of the literature, it nevertheless is somewhat striking that the only study to fail to find a moderating effect for Type A is that by Hurrell (1985), which is also the only study which examined a work stressor of an objective nature. Hurrell surveyed 5,518 postal workers, 2,803 working on machine-paced letter sorting jobs, and 2,715 working on unpaced jobs. Reasoning that Type A's are particularly responsive to situations in which they lack personal control, in this case over pacing of their work, Hurrell hypothesized a pacing X Type A interaction, expecting Type A's to show more negative reactions to pacing than would Type B's. While pacing was, indeed, found to be stressful, as determined by responses on the Profile of Mood States, Type A's did not respond differently from B's. While physiological or health outcome measures were not used, the anxiety and depression variables were similar to those employed by others (e.g., Caplan & Jones, 1975; Chesney & Ro-

Table 1

Type A Moderator Studies

Study	Sample	Type A Measure	Stressors	Outcomes
Caplan & Jones (1975)	122 Univ. computer users	4 items (Vickers)	Self-report	Psych,HR
Chesney & Rosenman (1980) (1)	145 male mgrs.	SI	Self-report	Psych
(2)	subsample of 76 from above		Self-report (Control)	Psych
Chesney et al. (1981)	384 mgrs.	SI	Self-report	BP
Howard et al. (1986)	217 mgrs.	SI	Self-report	BP,bio-chemical
Hurrell (1985)	5,518 postal workers	20 items (Thurstone)	Mach. pacing (Objective)	Psych
Keenan & McBain (1979)	90 mgrs.	10 items (Vickers)	Self-report	Job Sat.
Ivancevich et al. (1982) (1)	339 mgrs.	8 items	Self-report	Physio, biochemical
(2)	50 nurses	32 items & SI	Self-report	biochemical
Matteson & Ivancevich (1982)	315 med techs.	32 items	Self-report	Psych,health
Orpen (1982)	91 mgrs.	12 items	Self-report	Psych, Physios.
Rhodewalt et al. (1984)	49 Univ. Admins.	JAS	Self-report	symptom checklist

SI=Structured Interview, JAS=Jenkins Activity Scale.

Physios refers to cardiovascular measures such as heart rate (HR) & Blood Pressure (PB).

Psych refers to various psychological outcomes, usually anxiety or depression.

Biochemical refers to serum tests (e.g., cholesterol, triglycerides).

senman, 1980). Moreover, the Type A measure used, the Thurstone Activity Scale, is reliable and has shown some convergence with the Structured Interview method (Mayes, Sime & Ganster, 1984). And, finally, the failure to find an interaction between pacing and Type A in this study cannot be attributed to a lack of statistical power. Perhaps machine pacing is just not the kind of stimulus which evokes the hyper-responsivity of Type A's. However, it would seem to have as many of the eliciting characteristics (demands, low personal control) as do the other more commonly assessed stressors (e.g., role conflict and ambiguity).

A second characteristic shared by most of these studies is that Type A was measured with paper and pencil measures and not the Structured Interview (SI) method, which shows the strongest relationship with CHD. Three studies did use the SI, and they all inferred Type A moderating effects (Chesney & Rosenman, 1980; Chesney et al., 1981; Howard et al., 1986), although the statistical techniques were not always the most appropriate. Chesney and Rosenman (1980) observed the correlations between workload and anxiety and work pressure and anxiety for 145 male managers who were classified as A or B. They found significant correlations for Type A's (A1 on the SI) but not for B's. However, they did not report a test of the difference between the r's of the two samples (nor did they report the r's or the sample sizes of the subgroups). In a further analysis, they gave a random subsample of 76 of these managers a measure of control in the workplace. Using this scale, the sample was divided into high, medium, and low control groups. Chesney and Rosenman reported that A1's in the low control group were more anxious than A1's in the high control group. Type B's, however, reported less anxiety when they were not in control than when they were in control. They apparently did not test for a statistical interaction with an ANOVA, but it seems that they might have found one, given the mean differences. In a later study by Chesney et al. (1981), 384 salaried workers were administered the Work Environment Scale (WES; Insel & Moos, 1974) and were assessed for Type A with the SI. A series of one-way ANOVAs were performed across groups formed on the basis of Type A and trichotomization of the WES subscales. The authors do not explain why two-way ANOVAs were not calculated, since the interactions between Type A and the WES scales were of central interest. Nevertheless, the authors concluded that there were significant interactions between Type A and three of the WES scales (Peer cohesion, physical comfort, and autonomy). Type A's had lower blood pressure (systolic and diastolic) in the high peer cohesion groups than in the low cohesion groups, whereas Type B's showed just the opposite pattern. Similarly, Type A's showed lower blood pressure under conditions of high autonomy, while Type B's showed higher blood pressure under high autonomy. Finally, Type B's had lower systolic blood pressure when they reported high physical comfort than when they did not, while Type A's showed no response to comfort.

A final study which used the SI was reported by Howard et al. (1986). Data were obtained from a panel of 217 managers over a two year period, including measures of role ambiguity at times 1 and 2, physiological measures at times 1 and 2 (blood pressure, cholesterol, triglycerides, uric acid), and job satisfaction and Type A (by the SI) at time 1. Their central thesis concerned the interaction between job satisfaction and changes in ambiguity (predicting changes in the risk factors), consequently, interactions between Type A and ambiguity were not directly tested. However, the regression coefficient relating change in ambiguity to change in systolic blood pressure was higher for A's than for B's. In fact, while more ambiguity was associated with significantly higher blood pressure for A's, it led to significantly lower pressure for B's, suggesting that Type B's are healthier with more role ambiguity.

As a whole these moderators support the notion that Type A's and B's respond differently to certain work factors, especially those involving role stresses and control. However, for several reasons it is difficult to conclude that these findings replicate the kinds of physiological hyper-responsivity results of laboratory research. First, all moderator effects reported in the work environment involve self-reported stressors, while objective manipulations were assessed in the lab. Second, in most studies moderator effects were inferred by examining differences between the correlations of A and B subgroups. Arguments concerning the inappropriateness of this strategy have been made elsewhere (Arnold, 1982), and Type A research would be improved if investigators assessed statistical interactions directly. Finally, there seem to be many disordinal interactions in the field studies, particularly among those using the SI. That is, A's differ from B's not only in responding more vigorously, but often their responses are in the opposite direction. The implication of this disordinal type of interaction is that A's and B's may actually thrive in different kinds of job environments. In fact, other writers such as Ivancevich and Matteson (1984) have proposed a person-environment fit model of Type A in the workplace. The difference between such a P-E fit model and the hyper-responsivity model is the proposition that there may be certain job conditions in which Type B's are hyper-responsive relative to Type A's. A fruitful avenue for future research would involve the delineation of the specific stimulus characteristics (e.g., personal control, competitiveness, time pressure, social support) that best fit Type A and B workers.

TYPE A AND THE WORK ENVIRONMENT:
DOES ONE CAUSE THE OTHER?

In Figure 1 the a and b arrows indicate reciprocal causal relationships between Type A and the objective and subjective work environment. Rosenman and Friedman (1959) originally conceived of Type A persons as having a predisposition to respond in a characteristic way to certain environmental stimuli. That is, when faced with demands they respond with a pattern of hostility, impatience, and aggressiveness. Of course, their response can be to stimuli of either an objective or subjective nature. This model is represented by arrows a2 and b2 in Figure 1. Much of the laboratory research on Type A has explored the specific stimulus conditions which activate the Type A pattern. Generalizing to the work setting, we would expect the Type A pattern to be elicited only in situations which contained such attributes as challenge, deadlines, competition, or loss of control. Indeed, Friedman et al. (1960) noted that researchers studying the biochemical responses of Type A workers should do so during exposure to the milieu in which it is likely to be evoked, since it is not a fixed but a phasic phenomenon. Howard et al. (1977) also proposed a model in which such job conditions as supervisory responsibility, competitiveness, heavy workloads, and conflicting demands would elicit Type A behaviors in individuals so disposed.

In addition to providing the stimulus substrate necessary for evoking the Type A pattern, work (and cultural) environments can also be instrumental in the long-term development of the pattern. Margolis, McLeroy, Runyan, and Kaplan (1983), for example, advocated an ecological approach to Type A, in which interpersonal, institutional, and cultural environments all elicit and strengthen Type A behavior. From this view, we might hypothesize that individuals working in certain occupations, or under certain organizational conditions (such as reward systems that foster competition), will develop the Type A pattern with time.

Conversely, Type A behavior, itself, could be a factor in determining one's exposure to work stressors, as denoted by arrow a1. As Zyzanski and Jenkins (1970) suggested, Type A's may seek out "those vocational settings where intensive involvement in activity and the consequent rewards of high income, responsibility, and prestige are the pattern" (p. 790). Thus, we might hypothesize that Type A's will select themselves into more stressful occupations.

Even within a given occupation, Type A's may redefine their jobs so as to increase stress. Laboratory studies, such as that by Burnam, Pennebaker, and Glass (1975), have demonstrated that Type A's, relative to B's, work at a higher capacity even in the absence of deadlines. Finally, Jenkins (1979) has described the Type A as egocentric, self-centered, abrasive, aggressive, and a poor listener. To the extent that such traits characterize Type A's, they may lead to poor interpersonal relationships with superiors, subordinates, and peers, and a reduction in social support.

Even if exposed to the same objective stressors as Type B's, Type A's may appraise their job demands as being more stressful (path b1). Again, support for this perceptual bias hypothesis is provided by laboratory experiments (e.g., Gastorf, 1981). Thus, Type A and work stressors may be causally related through both behavioral and perceptual processes. The research reviewed in the remainder of this section focuses on this causal linkage between the behavior pattern and the job environment.

A number of organizational studies provide relevant, but ambiguous, data regarding the reciprocal relationship between Type A and work stressors. One type of study has examined differences in the prevalence of Type A across occupations or job types. Haynes, Feinleib, and Kannel (1979) found that working women are more apt to display Type A behavior than are housewives. Lawler, Rixse, and Allen (1983), in comparing a sample of employed women and housewives, found that all the employed women were Type A while less than half of the housewives were. Furthermore, those unemployed women who wanted to work were more likely to be Type A. These studies suggest that Type A women are more apt to be employed, but whether this represents a higher exposure to stressors rests on the assumption that work outside the home is more stressful than housework. Other researchers have made occupational comparisons. Caplan, Cobb, Harrison, French, and Pinneau (1975) compared the Type A scores of workers in 23 occupations, using the 9-item Sales questionnaire. High type A occupations included physicians, administrative professors, and tool and die workers, while low Type A occupations included assemblers on machine-paced lines, continuous flow monitors, programmers, and accountants. From these data it is difficult to conclude either that Type A's select themselves into inherently stressful occupations or that exposure to stressful occupations leads to Type A behavior. It is extremely difficult, conceptually or empirically, to determine which of these occupations is objectively more stressful. On the one hand, administrative professors and physicians report more hours worked and higher quantitative workload than machine-paced assemblers, programmers, and accountants. On the other hand, the level of somatic health complaints is lower for administrative professors and physicians than it is for machine-paced assemblers, programmers, and accountants (Caplan et al., 1975). The report by Haynes et al. (1979) that Type A is more prevalent among white-collar workers than among blue-collar workers is similarly difficult to interpret in terms of the self-selection hypothesis.

Frost and Wilson (1983) evaluated nursing units as "high stress" or "low stress" based on "a subjective assessment of the physical and/or psychological demands placed on the nurse" (p. 404), and found no difference in the levels of Type A. Huang, Hewson, and Singer (1983) compared samples of university students, police officers, police recruits, and the general population on the basis of Type A scores. They found that both officers and recruits had lower Type A scores than did the general population. Similarly, policemen in the Caplan et al. (1975) survey were relatively low on Type A. Hurrell (1985), however, found that male postal workers on machine-paced jobs were more likely to be Type A than non-paced workers. Since the level of Type A was uncorrelated with tenure on the job, Hurrell concluded that Type A's likely selected themselves into the more stressful machine-paced jobs. Hurrell's data directly conflict with those from the Caplan et al. (1975) study, in which machine-paced assemblers were less Type A than non-machine-paced assemblers. In fact, in the Caplan et al. study machine-paced workers had the lowest Type A scores of the 23 occupations studied. Finally, Boyd (1984) examined the Type A scores of small business owners using the Jenkins Activity Survey. Boyd found that 82% of his 368 small business CEO's were classified as Type A's, and that this percentage exceeded those reported for managers in larger firms. Again, however, one must make some assumptions about the inherent stressfulness of being a small business owner if these data are to inform a self-selection hypothesis. In sum, data from occupational comparisons do not convincingly demonstrate that Type A's select themselves into inherently more stressful occupations, nor do they suggest that prolonged exposure to stressful occupations promotes the development of the Type A pattern.

Occupational comparisons of Type A prevalence are difficult to interpret both because of the aforementioned problem of objectively describing the stressfulness of different occupations and because there is likely great individual variability of working conditions within occupations. For these reasons, individual-level studies are apt to be more enlightening regarding the causal relationships between Type A and work stressors. In this vein many investigators have reported relationships between measures of the Type A pattern and various job stressors, although they heavily rely on self-reports. For example, Type A's generally report more workload than do Type B's (Burke & Weir, 1980; Caplan et al., 1975; French & Caplan, 1972; Howard et al., 1977; Ivancevich et al., 1982; Keenan & McBain, 1979; Kelly & Houston, 1985; Sales, 1969), although this is not always the case (Chesney & Rosenman, 1980; Orpen, 1982). In addition to workload, Type A's tend to report higher levels of other stressors as well, including supervisory responsibility (Howard et al., 1977), role conflict (Howard et al., 1977; Ivancevich et al., 1982; Kelly & Houston, 1985; Orpen, 1982), and employer expectations (Mettlin, 1976). Two studies found that Type A's reported more control or influence at work (Burke & Weir, 1980; Chesney & Rosenman, 1980), but one study of over 2,000 men (Kittel et al., 1983) found that Type A white collar workers reported less control over work pacing than did Type B's.

In none of these studies is it possible to determine whether Type A's actually have greater exposure to various stressors (path a1), or whether they tend to cognitively appraise their jobs differently than do B's (path b1). While some laboratory evidence suggests that Type A's will impose more demands on themselves (Burnam et al., 1975), and that they tend to prefer more challenging and demanding tasks (Holmes, McGilley & Houston, 1984), there is no convincing evidence from organizational studies that the objective job demands facing Type A's are really higher than B's. The most nearly objective data, although still supplied by the respondents, indicates that Type A's work longer hours and more overtime hours (Caplan et al., 1975; Howard et al., 1977; Kelly & Houston, 1985), and travel more on the job (Howard et. al., 1977). In concluding this section, one can only state that the reciprocal arrows (a and b) in Figure 1 are supported by research in the lab, but have little corroborating evidence from the field. Thus, there is clearly a need for field research which examines Type A-B differences in exposure to objective job stressors, particularly those most relevant to the construct (e.g., challenges, competition, etc.).

TYPE A AND PERFORMANCE

Before concluding a review of empirical studies, the evidence relating Type A to job performance should be mentioned. This relationship has implications for the prospect of altering the pattern. For one, if Type A's are better performers, organizations might be reluctant to support efforts to change their behavior. Second, to the extent that higher performance is reinforced in organizational contexts, Type A behaviors may be reinforced. As Mettlin (1976) has suggested, the Type A pattern may be so embedded in and reinforced by one's occupational milieu that it would be very resistant to change.

Several studies have reported a positive relationship between Type A and indexes of occupational level or status (Caplan et al., 1975; Kelly & Houston, 1985; Mettlin, 1976; Shekelle et al., 1976; Zyzanski, 1978). These data, while suggestive of a relationship between Type A and job performance, cannot be used to support a relationship between Type A and individual performance within an occupation. Similarly, other researchers have reported that companies with more Type A's have a higher growth rate (Howard et al., 1976) and that small businesses owned by Type A's tend to have a higher return on investment and rate of sales growth (Boyd, 1984). But again, these studies are at best suggestive of a relationship between Type A and individual performance.

Several studies have examined the job performance of Type A's at the individual level, each of them studying employees in one occupation or in one company. Jamal (1985) surveyed 218 white-collar workers of a manufacturing company in Quebec, measuring Type A with the 9-item Sales measure, and obtaining ratings of performance quantity, quality, and effort from their supervisors. Jamal found that Type B's were rated higher on quality, and there were no differences in quantity of performance, although Type A's were rated higher on effort. Similarly, Matteson, Ivancevich, and Smith (1984) examined A-B differences on three objective, quantitative measures of sales performance for 355 life insurance agents. Again, Type A's were no better than B's on any of the performance measures, although, as in Jamal's (1985) study, Type A's reported more health complaints. In contrast, Matthews et al. (1980), studying a group of male, experimental social psychologists, found a positive relationship between Type A and both quality of research publication (as indexed by number of citations) and quantity of research publications. Taylor, Locke, Lee, and Gist (1984) replicated the Matthews et al. (1980) findings on a larger (N = 278) and more diverse sample of research faculty, and used more extensive measures of research quality and productivity. The Taylor et al. (1984) study was particularly interesting because they explored the mechanisms through which Type A might lead to higher performance. Through a path analysis they found that Type A led to higher performance indirectly through the tendency of Type A's to set higher performance goals, to work on multiple projects at once, and to have higher self-efficacy perceptions.

The data regarding the job performance of Type A's, then, is decidedly mixed. While some writers (Friedman & Rosenman, 1974) have speculated that Type A's will perform better only in certain types of jobs (e.g., where a concern for numbers and speed is paramount), there are simply too few studies to make statements about the moderating effect of job type on the relationship between Type A and performance. However, the question is interesting and deserves further attention. The most useful designs would include not only objective as well as subjective measures of performance, but also measures of the intervening behaviors that might determine performance, as in the Taylor et al. (1984) study. Moreover, as discussed below, attention to the assessment of operant behaviors of Type A's on the job would significantly improve any Type A study, not just ones whose primary interest is in job performance.

SUGGESTIONS FOR RESEARCH

The Type A model displayed in Figure 1 is based on a hyperresponsivity model of CHD. Drawing mostly on laboratory research findings regarding the physiological reactivity and behavioral characteristics of Type A's, the model posits several different, though not mutually exclusive, pathways by which Type A may cause CHD in the context of work stress. In reviewing the empirical work done in job settings, few conclusions can be reached about the validity of each of these causal paths. The following conclusions summarize the evidence for each causal process:

1. Support for the hyper-responsivity effect (paths f and g) is fairly general. However, all of the supporting evidence concerns path g (subjective stressors). The only study to test path f (objective stressors) yielded no support.
2. Empirical support for causal relationships between Type A and objective stressors (paths a1 and a2) is very weak. Furthermore, existing field studies yield little insight as to whether Type A's, through their behavior, partially determine their exposure to stressors (path a1) or whether prolonged exposure to such stressors encourages the development of Type A (path a2).
3. The evidence is supportive of a relationship between Type A and subjective stressors (paths b1 and b2), although no research has addressed the magnitude of the causal path from Type A (b1, the perceptual bias hypothesis) relative to the path from subjective stressors (b2).

Assuming that it is worth knowing the validity of the various causal paths in Figure 1 (and I will argue this further below), it seems clear that the major questions tend to concern objective work stressors. However, several methodological issues cut across the various studies of Type A in the work setting, and I think several deserve further attention.

Type A Measurement

The studies reviewed here used a variety of measures of Type A behavior, many of them being questionnaires of uncertain reliability and validity. The original measure of the Type A pattern consists of a structured interview (SI) which, itself, is a social stressor intended to elicit samples of Type A behavior (Chesney, Eagleston & Rosenman, 1980). Responses are typically recorded on audio or video tape and scored by trained observers. Data obtained from the SI differ from those obtained from the questionnaires in several important ways. For one, the interviewer creates stimulus conditions designed to bring out Type A behaviors in respondents so predisposed. Second, the interview is scored for both content of the responses and behavioral stylistics. Typical components of interview content include competition, hostility, speed, and impatience. Typical stylistic components evaluated include hostility, loud and explosive speech, rapid and accelerated speech, and short response latency. These various components are generally combined either into a continuous Type A rating, or into a 4-level classification (A1, A2, X, B) scheme. The component ratings can also be used singly as variables. Scoring of both content and stylistic components is quite reliable when the interviewers and the coders are trained (usually by Rosenman and his colleagues) (Mayes, Sime & Ganster, 1984).

Because the SI is an expensive method of assessing Type A, a variety of questionnaires have been proposed as alternatives. The most common of these is the Jenkins Activity Survey (JAS; Jenkins et al., 1974) which was developed directly from the SI and validated against it. Reviews of these different measures (Chesney & Rosenman, 1980; Matteson & Ivancevich, 1980; Mayes et al., 1984; Sparacino, 1979) suggest several conclusions: (a) the convergence of the various measures, especially the questionnaires with the SI, is not very high, (b) the reliability of many of the questionnaires (including the JAS) is often low, and (c) the SI is the best predictor of CHD and physiological reactivity. Given this evidence, the SI is strongly recommended, despite its higher cost. Researchers using the SI should be trained in administering and scoring it. Furthermore, while most users of the SI employ the 4-level categorization scheme, the National Review Panel on Coronary-Prone Behavior and CHD (1981) recommended using continuous scores. Mayes et al. (1984) also reached this conclusion based on an empirical comparison of the predictability of continuous and categorical scores with physiological reactivity measures.

Measurement of Outcomes

The Type A behavior pattern was originally of interest because it predicted CHD, implying that one should assess CHD in Type A studies. However, this requires an extensive longitudinal design with a large sample. Moreover, organizational researchers are interested not so much in demonstrating a Type A-CHD link as they are in exploring the intervening mechanisms in the workplace. In this regard, short-term outcomes are of interest especially to the extent that they represent CHD risk factors or mental or physical health indicators. In the studies reviewed in this paper some researchers used physiological measures indicative of either cardiovascular or biochemical reactivity. However, many more used questionnaire measures of either physical health symptoms (such as somatic complaints), psychological states (such as anxiety and depression), and even job attitudes (such as job satisfaction).

Physiological measures are preferable on several counts. First, physiological reactivity is the most promising causal mechanism linking Type A behavior to CHD, and thus is the mediating variable of most interest. Second, while non-clinical measures of psychological states (such as anxiety, irritation, and depression) may be of interest in their own right, there is little empirical reason to suspect (a) that they are caused by Type A, (b) that they lead to CHD, or (c) that they are even predictive of clinical mental disorder. Third, there is evidence that when exposed to eliciting stimuli (e.g., challenge) Type A's tend to be physiologically hyper-responsive, but do *not* show similar reactivity in mood states (Dembroski, MacDougall, Shields, Petitto & Lushene, 1978). Even self-reports of physical symptoms are somewhat suspect, given the tendency of Type A's to suppress or deny physical symptoms and fatigue when working on a challenging task (Pittner, Houston & Spiridigliozzi, 1983). Advice regarding the appropriate procedures for reliably and validly assessing physiological reactivity in field settings is proferred in other papers in this issue.

Objective Measurement of Work Stressors

As noted earlier, almost all studies reviewed examined self-reports of job conditions. Some of these (e.g., hours worked, overtime hours) may be relatively objective, but most (e.g., workload, role conflict, competition) are not. In order to determine whether the actions of Type A's serve to increase their exposure to work stressors or whether Type A's just appraise their work environments differently, we simply must devise ways of assessing objective work demands. This has always posed a challenge for work stress research and even for life events stress research. Even the testing of a cognitive appraisal model of stress and health (Lazarus et al., 1985) requires that the objective events and their appraisals be unconfounded (Dohrenwend & Shrout, 1985).

A related issue concerns the measurement of operant behaviors. Though we know something about the beliefs and career aspirations of Type A's (Burke, 1983; 1984), we know little about their actual work behavior. In addition to measuring environmental variables, such as workload, machine-pacing, deadlines, and reward systems, Type A researchers should endeavor to assess the specific work behaviors of Type A's, especially those that alter the environment in such a way as to make it more stressful. A step in this direction was taken by Taylor et al. (1984) who at least asked subjects to report their publication goals and how many projects they worked on at once. More extensive use could be made of diaries of work behavior to assess the extent to which Type A's may volunteer for more projects or delegate fewer tasks. Researchers might also employ direct observation of interpersonal behaviors (related to hostility or aggressiveness) that might affect the amount of social support received from coworkers and supervisors.

CONCLUSIONS

Because the Type A behavior pattern is a predictor of CHD, there is growing interest in methods of changing the behavior of Type A's. However, as Matteson and Ivancevich (1980) noted in their review, relatively little controlled research concerning the alteration of the Type A pattern has been reported. Many of the studies that have been conducted suffer from methodological weaknesses such as small sample size, retrospective designs, lack of experimental controls, and even a failure to measure Type A behavior as an intervention outcome. However, a variety of approaches are currently being tested. Matteson and Ivancevich classified these various techniques as being either attempts to manage the outcomes of Type A or attempts to alter the pattern itself. The various approaches for treating Type A's can also be classified into respondent and operant conditioning categories based on the responses (behavioral, physiological, cognitive) that the technique targets for change. In concluding this brief review, I would like to argue that understanding the causal mechanisms by which Type A's develop CHD, especially in the context of their work life, can inform the selection and development of treatment approaches.

The causal pathways of Figure 1 suggest three different intervention approaches, depending on which of the causal paths is most potent. If Type A's have elevated physiological reactivity primarily because they select themselves into objectively stressful environments, or if they, through their operant behaviors, make their environments more stressful (path a1), then a strategy of modifying these operant behaviors should be pursued. Suinn (1975) has been a leading proponent of this approach. His efforts have concentrated on changing the lifestyles of Type A's, teaching them to replace their rushed and multiphasic behaviors with more healthful ones. Suinn's techniques have been somewhat successful, offering hope that the pattern itself is amenable to change.

As noted in this review, however, the evidence is not clear whether Type A's really are exposed to more objective stressors at work or whether they simply are more apt to appraise their environments as more demanding (path b1). If future research shows the latter causal pathway to be more likely, strategies that focus only on the operant behaviors of Type A's would have limited success. Alternatively, this model would suggest an approach that aimed to intervene directly at the level of these cognitive processes, changing the way that Type A's interpret environmental events. The cognitive behavior modification model of Meichenbaum (1977) is one example of this approach. If, indeed, Type A's are biased in their perceptions and interpretations of work stressors, this perceptual, or cognitive appraisal, process must be addressed. Operant techniques that successfully changed the behaviors of Type A's so that their work environments were the same as Type B's would do little good if Type A's continued to perceive a shortage of time and an excess of employer demands.

Finally, as posited in Figure 1, Type A's may be inherently physiologically hyper-reactive to objective or perceived stressors (paths f and g), even if they are exposed to the same objective and subjective work environments as Type B's. If this is the primary mechanism linking Type A to elevated physiological responsiveness, the two operant intervention approaches mentioned so far would both have limited utility. In this model techniques whose aim is to alter this physiological reactivity directly would be recommended. These techniques might include various forms of progressive relaxation training or biofeedback training of autonomic responses. These techniques might even be combined with a focus on specific work environment stimuli to which the client is especially responsive, as in classical desensitization therapy. The difference in this approach is its targeting of the physiological responses themselves rather than their behavioral or cognitive precursors.

Further research that clarified the causal mechanisms of the Type A behavior pattern should yield important implications regarding different therapeutic approaches. Moreover, organizational researchers have perhaps become disaffected with individual differences variables, given our experience with such constructs as "growth need strength." The Type A pattern, however, is a complex constellation of cognitive, behavioral, and physiological responses that has tangible health implications. Research has ranged from large-scale prospective studies to experiments in the laboratory. As such, Type A offers clear opportunities for combining lab and field methods to achieve a better understanding of how the pattern may determine, be determined by, or interact with events in the occupational experience.

REFERENCES

Arlow, J.A. (1945). Identification of mechanisms in coronary occlusion. *Psychosomatic Medicine, 7*, 195–209.

Arnold, H.J. (1982). Moderator variables: A clarification of conceptual, analytic, and psychometric issues. *Organizational Behavior and Human Performance, 29*, 143–174.

Boyd, D.P. (1984). Type A behaviour, financial performance, and organizational growth in small business firms. *Journal of Occupational Psychology, 57*, 137–140.

Burnam, M.A., Pennebaker, J.W. & Glass, D.C. (1975). Time consciousness, achievement striving, and the Type A coronary-prone behavior pattern. *Journal of Abnormal Psychology, 84*, 76–79.

Burke, R.J. (1983). Career orientations of Type A individuals. *Psychological Reports, 53*, 979–989.

Burke, R.J. (1984). Beliefs and fears underlying Type A behavior: What makes Sammy run — so fast and aggressively? *Journal of Human Stress*, Winter, 174–182.

Burke, R.J. & Weir, T. (1980). The Type A experience: Occupational and life demands, satisfaction and well-being. *Journal of Human Stress*, December, 28–38.

Caplan, R.D., Cobb, S., French, J.R.P., Jr., Van Harrison, R. & Pinneau, S.R., Jr. (1975). *Job demands and worker health.* HEW Publication No. (NIOSH) 75–160.

Caplan, R.D. & Jones, K.W. (1975). Effects of workload, role ambiguity, and Type A personality on anxiety, depression, and heart rate. *Journal of Applied Psychology, 60*, 713–719.

Chesney, M.A., Eagleston, J.R. & Rosenman, R. (1980). The Type A Structured Interview: A behavioral assessment in the rough. *Journal of Behavioral Assessment, 2*, 255–272.

Chesney, M.A. & Rosenman, R.H. (1980). Type A behaviour in the work setting. In C.L. Cooper and R. Payne (Eds.), *Current concerns in occupational stress.* New York, Wiley, 187–212.

Chesney, M.A., Sevelius, G., Black, G., Ward, M., Swan, G. & Rosenman, R. (1981). Work environment, Type A Behavior, and coronary heart disease risks. *Journal of Occupational Medicine, 23*, 551–555.

Dembroski, T.M., MacDougall, J.M., Shields, J.L., Pettito, J. & Lushene, R. (1978). Components of the Type A coronary-prone behavior pattern and cardiovascular responses to psychomotor challenge. *Journal of Behavioral Medicine, 1*, 159–176.

Dohrenwend, B.P. & Shrout, P.E. (1985). "Hassles" in the conceptualization and measurement of life stress variables. *American Psychologist, 40*, 780–785.

Dunbar, H.F. (1943). *Psychosomatic Diagnosis.* New York: Paul H. Hoeber.

French, J.R.P., Jr. & Caplan, R.D. (1972). Organizational stress and individual strain. In A.J. Marrow (Ed.), *The failure of success.* New York: AMACOM.

Friedman, M., St. George, S., Byers, S.O. & Rosenman, R.H. (1960). Excretion of catecho-lamines, 17-ketosteroids, 17-hydroxycorticoids and 5-hydroxyindole in men exhibiting a particular behavior pattern (A) associated with high incidence of clinical coronary artery disease. *Journal of Clinical Investigations, 39,* 758–764.

Friedman, M. & Rosenman, R.H. (1974). *Type A behavior and your heart.* New York: Alfred Knopf.

Frost, T.F. & Wilson, H.G. (1983). Effects of locus of control and A-B personality type on job satisfaction within the health care field. *Psychological Reports, 53,* 399–405.

Gastorf, J.W. (1981). Physiologic reaction of Type As to objective and subjective challenge. *Journal of Human Stress, 7,* 16–20.

Gertler, M.M. & White, P.B. (1954). *Coronary heart disease in young adults.* Cambridge, MA: Harvard University.

Haynes, S.G., Feinlieb, M. & Kannel, W.B. (1979). The relationship of psychosocial factors to coronary heart disease in the Framingham study: III. Eight year incidence of coronary heart disease. Unpublished manuscript. Bethesda: National Heart, Lung, and Blood Institute.

Holmes, D., McGilley, B. & Houston, B.K. (1984). Task-related arousal of Type A and Type B persons: Level of challenge and response specificity. *Journal of Personality and Social Psychology, 46,* 1322–1327.

Houston, B.K. (1983). Psychophysiological responsivity and the Type A behavior pattern. *Journal of Research in Personality, 17,* 22–39.

Howard, J.H., Cunningham, D.A. & Rechnitzer, P.A. (1977). Work patterns associated with Type A behavior: A managerial population. *Human Relations, 30,* 825–836.

Howard, J.H., Cunningham, D.A. & Rechnitzer, P.A. (1986). Role ambiguity, Type A behavior, and job satisfaction: Moderating effects on cardiovascular and biochemical responses associated with coronary risk. *Journal of Applied Psychology, 71,* 95–101.

Huang, M.S., Hewson, V.A. & Singer, A.E. (1983). Type A behavior in the police and general population. *The Journal of Psychology, 115,* 171–175.

Hurrell, J.J., Jr. (1985). Machine-paced work and the Type A behaviour pattern. *Journal of Occupational Psychology, 58,* 15–25.

Ivancevich, J.M. & Matteson, M.T. (1984). A Type A-B person-work environment interaction model for examining occupational stress and consequences. *Human Relations, 37,* 491–513.

Ivancevich, J.M., Matteson, M.T. & Preston, C. (1982). Occupational stress, Type A behavior, and physical well being. *Academy of Management Journal, 25,* 373–391.

Jamal, M. (1985). Type A behavior and job performance: Some suggestive findings. *Journal of Human Stress, 11,* Summer, 60–68.

Jenkins, C.D. (1979). The coronary-prone personality. In W.D. Gentry & R.B. Williams (Eds.), *Psychological aspects of myocardial infarction and coronary care.* St. Louis: Mosby.

Jenkins, C.D., Rosenman, R.H. & Zyzanski, S.J. (1974). Prediction of clinical coronary heart disease by a test of the coronary-prone behavior pattern. *New England Journal of Medicine, 290,* 1171–1275.

Keenan, A. & McBain, G.D.M. (1979). Effects of Type A behaviour, intolerance of ambiguity, and locus of control on the relationship between role stress and work-related outcomes. *Journal of Occupational Psychology, 52,* 277–285.

Kelly, K.E. & Houston, B.K. (1985). Type A behavior in employed women: Relation to work, marital, and leisure variables, social support, stress, tension, and health. *Journal of Personality and Social Psychology, 48,* 1067–1079.

Kittel, F., Kornitzer, M., DeBacker, G., Dramaix, M., Sobolski, J., Degré, S., Denolin, H. (1983). Type A in relation to job stress, social and bioclinical variables: The Belgian physical fitness study. *Journal of Human Stress,* December, 37–45.

Krantz, D.S., Glass, D.C., Schaeffer, M.A. & Davia, J.E. (1982). Behavior patterns and coronary disease: A critical evaluation. In J.T. Cacioppo & R.E. Petty (Eds.), *Perspectives in cardiovascular psychophysiology,* pp. 315–346. New York: Guilford Press.

Lawler, K.A., Rixse, A. & Allen, M.T. (1983). Type A behavior and psychophysiological responses in adult women. *Psychophysiology, 20,* 343–350.

Lazarus, R.S., DeLongis, A., Folkman, S. & Gruen, R. (1985). Stress and adaptational outcomes: The problem of confounded measures. *American Psychologist, 40,* 780–785.

Margolis, L.H., McLeroy, K.R., Runyan, C.W. & Kaplan, B.H. (1983). Type A behavior: An ecological approach. *Journal of Behavioral Medicine, 6,* 245–258.

Matteson, M.T. & Ivancevich, J.M. (1980). The coronary-prone behavior pattern: A review and appraisal. *Social Science and Medicine, 14A,* 337–351.

Matteson, M.T. & Ivancevich, J.M. (1982). Type A and B behavior patterns and self-reported health symptoms and stress: Examining individual and organizational fit. *Journal of Occupational Medicine, 24,* 585–589.

Matteson, M.T., Ivancevich, J.M. & Smith, S.V. (1984). Relation of Type A behavior to performance and satisfaction among sales personnel. *Journal of Vocational Behavior, 25,* 203–214.

Matthews, K.A. (1982). Psychological perspectives on the Type A behavior pattern. *Psychological Bulletin, 91,* 293–323.

Matthews, K.A., Helmrich, R.L., Beane, W.E. & Lucker, G.W. (1980). Pattern A, achievement striving, and scientific merit: Does Pattern A help or hinder? *Journal of Personality and Social Psychology, 39,* 962–967.

Mayes, B.T., Sime, W.E. & Ganster, D.C. (1984). Convergent validity of Type A behavior pattern scales and their ability to predict physiological responsiveness in a sample of female public employees. *Journal of Behavioral Medicine, 7,* 83–108.

Meichenbaum, D. (1977). *Cognitive Behavior Modification: An Integrative Approach.* New York: Plenum.

Mettlin, C. (1976). Occupational careers and the prevention of coronary-prone behavior. *Social Science and Medicine, 10,* 367–372.

Orpen, C. (1982). Type A personality as a moderator of the effects of role conflict, role ambiguity, and role overload on individual strain. *Journal of Human Stress,* June, 8–14.

Pittner, M.S., Houston, B.K. & Spridigliozzi, G. (1983). Control over stress, Type A behavior pattern, and response to stress. *Journal of Personality and Social Psychology, 44,* 627–637.

Review Panel on Coronary-Prone Behavior and Coronary Heart Disease (1981). A critical review. *Circulation, 63,* 1199–1215.

Rhodewalt, F., Hays, R.B., Chemers, M.M. & Wysocki, J. (1984). Type A behavior, perceived stress, and illness: A person-situation analysis. *Personality and Social Psychology Bulletin, 10,* 149–159.

Rosenman, R.H., Brand, R.J., Jenkins, D., Friedman, M., Straus, R. & Wurm, M. (1975). Coronary heart disease in the Western Collaborative Group Study: Final follow-up experience of 8.5 years. *Journal of the American Medical Association, 233,* 872–877.

Rosenman, R.H. & Friedman, M. (1959). The possible relationship of the emotions to clinical coronary heart disease. In G. Pincus (Ed.), *Hormones and Atherosclerosis.* New York: Academic Press.

Sales, S.M. (1969). Differences among individuals in affective, behavioral, biochemical, and physiological responses to variations in work load (Doctoral Dissertation, University of Michigan). *Dissertation Abstracts International, 30,* 2407–B. (University Microfilms No. 69–18098).

Shekelle, R.B., Schoenberger, J.A. & Stamler, J. (1976). Correlates of the JAS Type A behavior pattern score. *Journal of Chronic Diseases, 29,* 381–394.

Sparacino, J. (1979). The Type A behavior pattern: A critical assessment. *Journal of Human Stress, 5,* 37–51.

Suinn, R. (1975). Behavior therapy for Type A patients. *The American Journal of Cardiology, 36,* 269–270.

Taylor, M.S., Locke, E.A., Lee, C. & Gist, M.E. (1984). Type A behavior and faculty research productivity: What are the mechanisms? *Organizational Behavior and Human Performance, 34,* 402–418.

Williams, R.B., Friedman, M., Glass, D.C., Herd, J.A. & Schneiderman, N. (1978). Section summary: Mechanisms linking behavioral and pathophysiological processes. In T.M. Dembroski, S.M. Weiss, J.L. Shields, S.J. Haynes, and M. Feinlieb (Eds.), *Coronary-prone behavior,* pp. 119–128. New York: Springer-Verlag.

Zyzanski, S.J. (1978). Associations of the coronary-prone behavior pattern. In T.M. Dembroski, S.M. Weiss, J.L. Shields, et al. (Eds.), *Coronary-prone behavior.* New York: Springer-Verlag.

Zyzanski, S.J. & Jenkins, C.D. (1970). Basic dimensions within the coronary-prone behavior pattern. *Journal of Chronic Diseases, 22,* 781–795.

Perspectives on Social
Support and Research
on Stress Moderating Processes

Susan Gore

SUMMARY. This article provides a guide to current approaches in research on social support processes in stress moderation. It describes three major models of social support processes and emphasizes the importance of making explicit the particular model of stress buffering that is being investigated. The article underscores the importance of designing a study that leads to statements about the effects of specific supports in specific types of situations. This can be achieved through study of single stress situations as they occur or through study of more ongoing stress in particular life roles. The relationship between social support and personality moderators is discussed as well as the debate on objectivity and subjectivity in measurement.

In much of our past work on the role of social support in moderating the effects of stress we spoke of "testing the stress buffering hypothesis." Researchers now speak of examining the stress process. This change in terminology reflects a new orientation to research on social support and stress, one that aims to build theory rather than test it.

In this paper I would like to consider some of the critical features of this new approach. For a fuller appreciation of the breadth of the field and complexity of the issues, I refer the reader to several recent volumes.[1] I can best review the issues by dividing the material into three major domains or problem areas, each of which is multi-faceted. After a brief consideration of definition, I will turn my attention to the following matters:

Susan Gore is affiliated with the University of Massachusetts-Boston.

1. Models of stress-buffering
2. Process study of stress
3. Objectivity, subjectivity and confounding in measurement

DEFINITIONS AND MEASUREMENT
OF SOCIAL SUPPORT

Since in most research on stress and support, the data are obtained through the self reports of the individuals studied, all measures of social support are subjective in this regard. However, questions about social support differ according to whether they request information about the existence of relationships, and their availability for different purposes, versus about the feeling of satisfaction with these provisions, that is, the perceived adequacy of social support. In addition, there has been some attention to documenting the helpful and nonhelpful behaviors of others in response to stress.

Questions about the availability of support are seen to measure the resource aspect of support and are, as Kessler and McLeod (1985) note, one of the major means through which support has been measured. Most measures of support functions are derived from direct questions about the availability of a type of support. For example, from Cohen and associates' (Cohen, Mermelstein, Kamarch & Hoberman, 1985) Interpersonal Support Evaluation List, an indicator of the *belonging* dimension of support is: "No one I know would throw a birthday party for me." A true/false response is called for. Other measures of resource availability include measures of social integration, which tap typical amounts of social interaction and extent of group memberships (cf. Berkman & Syme, 1979). Defining support in terms of such social embeddedness has its theoretical roots in the rich tradition of epidemiological study of social isolation. (For a discussion of this tradition see Thoits, 1982.) Measures of social integration or participation, which, for example, include marital status as an indicator of support, are a step removed from other means of assessing resource support since having social ties are a necessary but not sufficient condition for fostering supportive interactions.

The rationale for a focus on measures of the perceived adequacy of social support is evidenced in the significant and growing body of research on support attempts that fail (cf. Dunkel-Schetter & Wortman, 1982, and Wortman & Lehman, 1985). This research also points to the limitation of relying on the investigator's a priori ideas about the behaviors that constitute support, and lends support to the recommendation of House and Kahn (1985) that researchers should attempt to measure a variety of aspects of social relationships in any particular study.

In sum, a definition of support may emphasize the availability of help, which is a resource perspective on support, the occurrence of interactions or behaviors that have the purpose of meeting varying needs, and the "result" or long and short term impact of receiving/ not receiving support, the sense of being supported by others.

MODELS OF STRESS REDUCTION AND STRESS BUFFERING

Most research on the relationship between the social environment and disease has identified a set of stressors, or risk factors; indicators of health or illness status, the outcomes; and other variables that alter exposure or responses to the stressors. Of the many ways of conceptualizing the ordering and relationships among these variables perhaps most popular has been the idea of a stress-buffering function of social supports (and other coping resources.)

Wheaton (1985:356) has described two such models of stress-buffering and differentiated these from another three models in which social support plays a prominent role in the stress process but cannot be said to buffer the effects of stress.[2] In the first stress-buffering model, social support is seen as a moderator variable interacting with stress such that the effects of stress are attenuated at high levels of social support. This is the more familiar idea of stress buffering which requires an interaction between stress and support such that high levels of support will attenuate the effects of stress.

Wheaton's second stress-buffering model is more complex and of interest to researchers who study the mobilization of resources (Eckenrode, 1983), in that it emphasizes a sequence of activity that begins with the occurrence of the stressor. This is seen to lead to subsequent increases in the support variable, which is evidenced by a positive (and counterintuitive) relationship between stress and the support variable, and which in turn leads to a reduction of symptoms. In both these cases of stress-buffering Wheaton argues that the support variable must be understood as intervening and therefore having something to do with stress.

Investigations of the help that is actually received in particular stress situations are also best guided by the second model of stress buffering. This measurement strategy is part of an overall objective to develop an understanding of the significant dimensions of stressors and the coping behaviors that would be most relevant to their mastery. Such work would eventually advance the field by addressing what is perhaps the central question in all stress-buffering work, namely, what types of supports or coping work in what types of situations. This is often referred to as the "matching" strategy (Wheaton, 1983), and although the goal is at this time somewhat elusive, the planning of supportive interventions depends upon some middle-level understanding of this kind. I call this a middle-level understanding since with respect to the wide range of life events and situations that could be regarded as stressful, the strategy is to learn something about clusters of situations, which is more general than our understandings of particular situations, but less general than the idea of an all-purpose stress-buffering variable.

In contrast with this emphasis on social support behaviors that occur at the time of a life crisis, and in specific response to it, Brown and associates (Brown & Bifulco, 1985:353; Brown & Harris, 1978) have been more inclined to think that the protective function of social support arises from an ongoing sense of "continuing emotional concern well prior to any such provoking crisis." Moreover, Brown has documented stress processes that are chronic or ongoing, which contradicts the dominant image of a stress buffering process as temporally moving through neatly demarcated stages, from stressor, to response, to health impact. Specifically, in his model the episode of depression is set in motion by chronic stressors, called long term life difficulties, such as a husband's infidelity. This situation may go on for some time until a "provoking crisis" serves to confirm the loss (of a faithful partner, a viable marriage, etc.). In most instances, the onset of depression quickly follows.

What can be said about the importance of supportive interventions? According to Brown and Bifulco (1985:362): ". . . In hardly any of the provoking events was it possible to conceive of practical intervention that would lead to some kind of quick resolution of the situation resulting from the crisis—a point already implicit in our argument concerning the way the event often confirms some ongoing sense of failure or disappointment. It follows that effective intervention would in many instances need to concern itself with combatting the woman's developing judgement of hopelessness."

Brown's work suggests that ideas about stress buffering and especially the measurement of social support will have to be modified to suit designs in which chronic or relatively stable conditions rather than singular acute crises are studied. Furthermore, House (1981:139) has argued that in cross sectional studies in general and when studying the effects of chronic stressors in particular, stress-buffering processes may not be evidenced in statistical interactions. Moreover, both House and associates (House, Strecher, Metzner & Robbins, 1986:70) and Kasl and Wells (1985) note that in large scale epidemiologic studies global measures that capture rather stable or chronic conditions are likely to be the best predictors of outcomes since more "state" or situational measures of person or environment at one point in time are less likely to predict much of importance many years hence. House maintains that this dynamic would explain why in their analyses of the mortality data from the Tecumseh community health study, they did not find "any significant (p < .05) prospective associations of the job characteristics or perceived stresses . . . over the approximately 10-year follow-up period."

Stress researchers have been hesitant to study chronically stressful life conditions since the time of onset of such conditions cannot be reliably documented, making difficult inferences about these stressors causing changes in health status. Nevertheless, the pervasiveness of long term stressors in social life makes this an important area of study. It is for this reason that Pearlin and Schooler's (1978:377) strategy for assessing chronic life problems has been so well received. Basically, Pearlin (1982) defines chronic or repeated stressful experiences as deriving from the institutional level of society and "built into the fabric of daily life" through our participation in major social roles. Thus, for study of adults, he has focussed on the ongoing problems associated with marital, parental and occupational statuses and relationships. His analyses have aimed to identify the extent to which different types of role strains contribute to psychological distress and how the occurrence of distress may be offset or reduced through regular use of different coping strategies. While it is true that such research fails to track what goes on in specific stress situations and therefore misses the intraindividual and intrasituational variation that characterizes study of single acute stressors, the approach has been popular precisely because it yields a matching of stressor and effective coping resource, which I noted about provides the middle level understandings we seek.

A final matter that must be considered is the outcome of the stress process. Much epidemiological work concerns itself with the incidence, prevalence and mortality from major diseases. In a review of this research from the viewpoint of the effects of social networks and social supports, Berkman (1984:419) has emphasized that although in mortality studies various aspects of networks have predicted to mortality with a relative risk of at least two, findings on morbidity, such as those on coronary heart disease, have been equivocal with respect to the social support measures utilized. Thus, we see that we know very little about the incidence and course of particular diseases even regarding more straightforward additive models of risk. Berkman points to the inconsistencies among measures of social supports, which is certainly an important issue.

In stress-buffering research we have most often studied mental health outcomes, although in studies of occupational stress we do see more of a focus on diseases such as CHD and their physiological precursors. However, for the most part we have used scales of psychological distress, measures that Dohrenwend and colleagues (Dohrenwend, Shrout, Egri & Mendelsohn, 1980) see as measuring a broad construct of demoralization. We typically examine stress-buffering by differentiating the highly symptomatic from the less highly symptomatic, often using cross-sectional designs. Depue and Monroe (1985) have pointed to our relative inattention to the fact that most of the high scoring respondents on such scales are chronically disturbed, (that prior disorder is always the single best predictor of subsequent disorder), and that at least for this significant subsample many of the other assumptions and expectations derived from our dominant causal model can't hold. For example, they point out that low correlations between events and disorder are in part due to the fact that the chronically ill are already at the inventory's ceiling. They recommend a refocus in stress research away from such aggregated conceptions and measures of human disorder to consider problems, like the maintenance of chronic disorder by life stress, which would require differentiating initiation, relapse and maintenance processes. Such work requires longitudinal data sets and is beginning to be reported (Lin & Ensel, 1984; Aneshensel, 1985).

PROCESS STUDY OF STRESS

Early research on life stress was concerned with the fundamental question of whether life stress affects health status, in much the same way that current research tends to address the question of whether social support moderates the health effects of life stress. Initially, at least, process study meant turning our attention to questions of the second type since study of stress moderation entails finding an explanation for the fact that individuals are not equally affected by exposure to identical stress situations.

Kessler (1979) and Brown and Harris (1978) among many others have referred to these variables that operate in the presence of stress as "vulnerability factors." Vulnerability differentials between groups, Kessler argues, can be caused by: biological influences, that make some groups more fragile than others; and environmental influences, including the influence of subjective meaning in interpreting the threat of events, the provision of social support or other resources, socialization experiences that provide self-esteem and other coping resources.[3] Social support, then, is one of a class of environmental factors that may define vulnerability as opposed to resilience in the face of stress. Consistent with the term social support, we tend to emphasize the stress-reducing effects of positive social interactions. However, some researchers have focussed on vulnerability due to support deficits. For example, Brown and Harris (1978) demonstrated vulnerability effects of a lack of intimacy and to loss of a parent in early life.

Thus, in its narrowest sense process study of social support has concerned itself with whether individuals having different levels of support resources are more or less resilient in the face of similar stressors. In addressing this question, research on social support and stress buffering processes has emphasized obtaining greater detail about the social and psychological variables that shape the experience of stress and responses to it. Basically, there have been two means for obtaining this detail. First, there has been a turning away from conceptions of stressors as aggregated life crises or in fact, any aggregated approach to stress measurement. In a parallel manner, measures of social support are now geared to assessing specific features of social interaction rather than more global features of the social environment. As I mentioned earlier in discussing middle level understandings, and have noted elsewhere (Gore, 1985), a basic strategy in stress research today is to identify which of a limited set of variables have an impact on specific classes of stressors. For example, an early finding of this nature by House and associates (La Rocco, House & French, 1980; and studies summarized in House, 1981) was that social support of the spouse was relatively ineffectual in reducing the effects of a variety of stresses deriving from job conditions, in contrast to the moderating effects observed for coworker and supervisor support.

Most researchers in the 1980s have worked to achieve this linking of the stressor and moderating variables by focussing on the following types of disaggregated stress:

— singular stressful events, such as divorce, job loss, bereavement and childbirth, among many other life events;
— clusters of stressors associated with various role domains, such as work or family; and
— stressors and stress responses on a daily basis.

We might say that in each case there is an attempt to get a better handle on the types of problems that people confront and how they deal with them, and that this focus on the particular has allowed stress-buffering research to be better guided by existing theory. Thus, some issues that have received considerable attention include: individual differences in needs for support, the help seeking process and satisfaction with social contacts, types and sources of helping and differential stress-buffering effects, the relationship between social support and social conflict in network relationships, the role of intimacy versus having more diffuse social ties, sex differences in exposure and vulnerability to the effect of stress, and many others.

A second means through which researchers have gained the detail essential to process study has been through retaining more large scale designs, while expanding consideration of the mediating variables that may constitute the critical features of the stress response. In other words, the stress process is to be reconstructed in analysis, rather than observed as it unfolds. Among recent reports this is well illustrated in the work of Pearlin and associates (Pearlin, Lieberman, Menaghan & Mullan, 1981) on involuntary job disruption and stressful outcomes. Pearlin (1985:56–57) summarizes their results as follows:

> Briefly, the loss of the job can be seen as initiating a process that eventually results in psychological depression. The linkages between job loss and depression are as follows: The job loss leads to a decrease in earnings and the decreased earnings result in an increase in the level of economic strain that is experienced; the economic strain, in turn, diminishes positive self concepts, self-esteem and mastery; the diminution of the self, finally, results in the depression. . . . We actually found that social supports appear to have little or no direct efficacy in reducing depression. However, they do have a rather special and important indirect effect. Specifically, within the context of the problems under scrutiny in this example, supports function primarily to buttress self-esteem and mastery in the face of hardship; the effects of social supports in protecting against psychological depression are very important but entirely indirect.

Pearlin and Lazarus and their colleagues (cf. Pearlin & Schooler, 1978; Lazarus & Folkman, 1985) are strongly identified with the study of coping styles and behaviors, "the things people do to avoid being harmed by life strains" (Pearlin & Schooler, 1978:2). Something brief should be said here about the relationship between the social support and coping constructs since most studies of stress-moderating processes now seek detail in both these areas. The idea of coping emphasizes what people do toward stress resolution so it is necessarily individualistic in its techniques of assessment. As I mentioned earlier, one thing people do is talk to others and seek guidance, support and information. Thus, in one sense social support is a subset of a broader domain of coping. Alternatively, it may be important to recognize the independent status of social networks as containing resources that exist apart from the person, but on which he or she can draw.

By expanding the range of variables for study — which I noted is a defining feature of a process orientation to stress-buffering, we are able to trace complex pathways of influence, as we have seen above in the work of Pearlin and associates. At the present time I think many studies include so many coping and social support variables that analyses are inevitably contaminated, and the absence of any guiding theory is often sorely evident.[4]

However, on the constructive side, there are, as I see it, at least five important questions to be asked about the relationship between social support and other individual (personality or behavioral) variables:

1. What are the personal characteristics of individuals that make for individual differences in needs for social support or social affiliation? An important instance of this issue is evidenced in an increasing attention to sex differences in support and distress (Kessler, McLeod & Wethington, 1985).

2. What are the personal characteristics that make it likely or unlikely that social supports will be utilized, that is, that the social network will be mobilized? This question has been addressed in a few investigations (Sandler & Lakey, 1982; Eckenrode, 1983) concerned with how personality characteristics, such as having an internal locus of control, predispose individuals to certain types of coping behaviors. It is important to know, for example, whether individuals with low self-esteem do not attempt to solicit the help of others in problem solving due to fear of social rejection.

3. Can social support offset the negative effects of other personal characteristics, such as low self-esteem and Type A personality, and vice versa? Here we have to understand that these personality traits are stressors in their own right and that they are activated under certain conditions.

4. Is social support irrelevant if other personal strengths are evident and vice versa? For example, Pearlin and associates (1981) found that social support operated indirectly in reducing psychological distress through bolstering self-esteem, and Brown and Bifulco (1985) report that either high esteem or high support operate to reduce the risk of depression. (See an excellent review by Lefcourt, 1985, on many of these issues with reference to the locus of control construct.)

5. Is satisfaction with social ties and their provisions something other than a function of the individual's psychological status? This question is becoming a central one in support research because it addresses the concern whether stress-buffering ef-

fects are due to the actual interventions of others or whether to long term sustaining affiliation and the sense of social support (Wethington & Kessler, 1986).

In sum, process study calls for an increasing attention to the details of responses to stressors. This is evident in research on specific stressful situations, including life crises or transitions, and also in study of the chronic or ongoing stresses associated with major domains of role functioning. However, it must be emphasized that the emphasis on gaining a fuller appreciation of a particular slice of the picture — the psychosocial responses to stressors — should not displace concern with other essential elements of design. Kasl and Wells (1985:191) emphasize that if the ultimate objective of research on social support is to link the support process to health outcomes, "then investigators need to try to reconstruct as much of the causal network of other influences on the health outcome of interest as they can: prior health status, biological risk factors, health-related behaviors, and medical care data."

OBJECTIVITY, SUBJECTIVITY AND CONFOUNDING IN MEASUREMENT

In a recent review of research on stress in the workplace, Baker (1985:377–378) contrasted the two dominant etiologic models of stress, the Michigan Person-Environment Fit (P-E fit) model (Caplan, Cobb, French, Harrison & Pinneau, 1975) and the Job-Demands-Control (JD-C) model (cf. Karasek, 1979). According to Baker, both models share the view that stress arises from an imbalance between the individual and environment, and both also have identified the same classes of occupations as exposed to the greatest stress. He is critical, however, of the P-E fit model for its focus on individual perceptions as the determinants of occupational stress and the use of modifier variables (e.g., defense and coping predispositions, genetic and social background characteristics, and unmet needs) that are also largely characteristics of the individual. In contrasting this distinctively American approach to the study of stress with the Scandinavian based JD-C, Baker argues:

This emphasis on individual perceptions is more consistent with a clinical psychological paradigm than with a public health approach to the prevention of workplace hazards. . . . Specifically, the individual level focus has tended to convert the social problem of the work environment into a private problem of the individual. Thus, stress research is able to avoid the basic conflict that exists between the perspectives of health and safety and the imperatives of the production system. . . .

Even within this more individual-centered emphasis of stress research, which does characterize much of the research on social support as a stress moderator, there has been considerable discussion of the problem of relying on individual reports of all important constructs: sources of stress, mediating reactions, and illness outcomes (Gore, 1981, 1985; Dohrenwend, Dohrenwend, Dodson & Shrout, 1984). Furthermore, many of these questionnaire measures are regarded as subjective or perceptual because individuals are asked to evaluate their experiences of stress, support and distress. For example, the problem of subjectivity has most often been discussed in regard to obtaining reports of stress and disorder. In measuring disorder we are definitely interested in the person's experience of worry, upset, sadness, etc. The critical question from an etiologic perspective is whether some life conditions or events brought on these states. Thus, researchers who view stress as harmful stimuli emerging from outside the individual, view stress as what has happened or is happening.

The goal of measurement from this perspective is to gain access to these happenings in as simple and direct a manner as possible and to establish their meaning from contextual data but not from the respondents' own judgments about these episodes. The problem with such judgments is that they are highly likely to be a function of existing and preexisting psychological disorder. Thus, while the objective of most studies is to show that stress is producing disorder, the data in fact may only be documenting that one measure of disorder, i.e., judgments about overwhelming stress, is correlated with another highly related measure of disorder, i.e., feelings of distress. This is why despite numerous critiques of the Holmes and Rahe techniques for assessing exposure to stress, researchers primarily interested in the stress-disease linkage usually come back to some measurement vehicle of this nature. And, while it is recognized that many of the items on such inventories of acute stress are also likely to be the consequence of disorder, it has been possible to develop probes that make for more sensitive measurement of this kind (Dohrenwend, Link, Kern, Shrout & Markowitz, 1985).

Moderating variables such as social support and coping predispositions may also overlap with both stressor and illness constructs. For example, most measurement strategies that assess support in terms of help received or not received with problems yield indirect measures of the existence of life problems, which is a variable of stress. Other measures of feeling socially supported by others are usually moderately to highly correlated with outcome measures such as depression. In much of the research on stress-buffering, the sole focus of investigation is the extent of depressive symptoms. In such instances the use of brief, global measures of feeling supported or having support available is not an optimal measurement strategy.

I emphasize the problem of brevity in measurement to point to the fundamental problem with many of these self report measures. Brown and associates (Brown, Andrews, Bifulco, Adler & Bridge, unpublished; Brown & Bifulco, 1985) have argued that a considerable degree of probing is required to even obtain valid measures of objective conditions, and that such probing can also reveal whether more subjective attitudes and feelings about support have a little or lot to do with what is actually received from relationships in an objective sense. Thus, they maintain that the distinction between measuring objective versus subjective conditions is often falsely drawn, and call for a focus on measurement adequacy rather than debating the inherent superiority of more personally distant "objective" measures of supports versus the more immediate and "subjective" perceptions of adequacy.

CONCLUSION

In concluding, I'd like to return to Baker's critique of the American brand of stress research. This might suggest to managers some of the importances of social support and research in this area. First we see that from the viewpoint of prevention it is indeed important to identify the environmental conditions that promote significant risk. If this is accomplished, the structural interventions that Baker would like to see are not necessarily incompatible with attention to some subjectively measured stressors and more personal intervening processes. For example, in their analyses of findings from the Framingham Heart Study, Haynes and Feinleib (1980) found female clerical workers to be at greater risk for developing CHD than housewives and other female workers. Specifically those with children and married to blue collar workers had five times the incidence rate of the housewives. Interestingly, among these workers, having a non-supportive boss (a subjective variable) predicted incidence independently of other standard risk factors including other subjective variables such as suppressed anger. Although in this instance the stresses of female clerical work are not directly measured, theoretically guided study of objectively existing stress situations such as this gender-related configuration of conditions could provide the clues to the non-clinical interventions that might be sought.

Second, while it is important to target particular groups at risk for experiencing distress and disorder, managers should not presume to know the stresses experienced or supports needed. Existing scales may be seriously flawed. Moreover, strategies for measuring occupational stress and support will inevitably be affected by particularities of the setting, and the personal and occupational characteristics of the workers. Thus, intervention studies in organizational settings can always benefit from pilot data collections in which data that reflect employees perceptions' are first collected. Otherwise, planned supportive interventions may be irrelevant or harmful.

Finally, serious efforts to promote worker health will have to recognize that work is only one of the significant domains of individual functioning. The permeability of the boundaries between work and family life is reflected in the idea of "spillover." We will probably see fewer and fewer studies of occupational stress that deal only with work experience variables like job stress and support on the job, to the extent they also concern themselves with outcome variables (e.g., mental health, substance abuse, absenteeism, CHD) that are also influenced by a broader range of life roles and circumstances.

NOTES

1. Recent volumes on social support include: *Social support and health*, edited by Cohen and Syme, and *Social support: Theory, research and application*, edited by Sarason and Sarason.

2. Wheaton's other models present three more possibilities: In a third model the occurrence of stress is found to lead to a reduction in support. Thus, while stress affects support, the relationship is in the wrong direction, suggesting that stress depletes social support. In a fourth model, support is understood to precede and deter the occurrence of stress. Thus, support protects by virtue of reducing exposure. Finally, in his last model, that which is usually characterized as an additive or main effects model, support is seen to independently promote good health, but bears no relationship to the operation of the stress variable.

3. Furthermore, Kessler notes two methodological problems that might lead the researcher to find a vulnerability differential when subgroups in fact are no different in their stress reactivity.

4. For example, Cohen and Edwards (forthcoming) have provided a comprehensive and workmanlike review of coping-related personality characteristics which may function as stress-moderators. It necessarily covered so many variables that it might have been simpler to review variables not related to the coping construct. Nevertheless, they seem to concur with other researchers that Type A personality, self-esteem and locus of control remain central stress-moderating concepts.

BIBLIOGRAPHY

Aneshensel, C. (1985). The natural history of depressive symptoms: Implications for psychiatric epidemiology. In J. Greenley (Ed.), *Research in Community and Mental Health*, Volume 5. Greenwich, CT: JAI Press.

Baker, D. (1985). The study of stress at work. *Annual Review of Public Health*, 6, 367–381.

Berkman, L. (1984). Assessing the physical health effects of social networks and social support. *Annual Review of Public Health*, 5, 413–432.

Berkman, L. & Syme, S. (1979). Social networks, host resistance and mortality: A nine year follow-up of Alameda County residents. *American Journal of Epidemiology*, 189, 186–204.

Brown, G. & Bifulco, A. (1985). Social support, life events and depression. In I. Sarason & B. Sarason (Eds.), *Social support: Theory, research and applications*. The Hague, Netherlands: Martinus Nijhoff.

Brown, G. W. & Harris, T. (1978). *The social origins of depression*. New York: The Free Press.

Caplan, R., Cobb, S., French, J., Harrison, R. & Pinneau, R. (1975). Job demands and worker health. Washington, DC: HEW Publ. No. (NIOSH) 76–160.

Cohen S. & Edwards, J. (forthcoming). Personality characteristics as moderators of the relationship between stress and disorder. In R. Neufeld (Ed.), *Advances in the investigation of psychological stress*. New York: John Wiley & Sons.

Cohen, S., Mermelstein, R., Kamarck, T. & Hoberman, H. (1985). Measuring the functional components of social support. In I. Sarason & B. Sarason (Eds.), *Social support: Theory, research and applications*. The Hague, Netherlands: Martinus Nijhoff.

Depue, R. & Monroe, S. (1985). Life stress and human disorder: Conceptualization and measurement of the disordered group. In I. Sarason & B. Sarason (Eds.), *Social support: Theory, research and applications*. The Hague, Netherlands: Martinus Nijhoff.

Dohrenwend, B. S., Dohrenwend, B., Dodson, M. & Shrout, P. (1984). Symptoms, hassles, social supports and life events: Problem of confounded measures. *Journal of Abnormal Psychology*, 93, 222–230.

Dohrenwend, B., Link, B., Kern, R., Shrout, P. & Markowitz, J. (unpublished). Measuring life events: The problem of variability within event categories. New York City: Columbia University and New York State Psychiatric Institute.

Dohrenwend, B., Shrout, P., Egri, G. & Mendelsohn, F. (1980). Nonspecific psychological distress and other dimensions of psychopathology. *Archives of General Psychiatry, 37,* 1229–1236.

Dunkel-Schetter, C. & Wortman, C. (1982). The interpersonal dynamics of cancer: Problems in social relationships and their impact on the patient. In H. S. Friedman & M. R. DiMatteo (eds.), *Interpersonal issues in health care.* New York: Academic Press.

Eckenrode, J. (1983). The mobilization of social support: Some individual constraints. *American Journal of Community Psychology, 11,* 509–528.

Gore, S. (1985). Social support and styles of coping with stress. In S. Cohen & S. Syme (Eds.), *Social support and health.* New York: Academic Press.

Haynes, S. & Feinleib, M. (1980). Women, work and coronary heart disease: Prospective findings from the Framingham heart study. *American Journal of Public Health, 70,* 133–141.

Holmes, T. H. & Rahe, R. H. (1967). The social readjustment rating scale. *Journal of Psychosomatic Research, 11,* 213–218.

Henderson, S., Duncan-Jones, P. & Byrne, D. G. (1981). *Neurosis and the social environment.* New York: Academic Press.

House, J. (1981). Work stress and social support. Reading, MA: Addison-Wesley.

House, J. & Kahn, R. (1985). Measures and concepts of social support. In S. Cohen & S. Syme (Eds.), *Social support and health.* Orlando, FL: Academic Press.

House, J. S., Strecher, V., Metzner, H. & Robbins, C. A. (1986). Occupational stress and health among men and women in the Tecumseh community health study. *Journal of Health and Social Behavior, 27,* 62–77.

Karasek, R. (1979). Job demands, decision latitude and mental strain: Implications for job redesign. *Administrative Science Quarterly, 24,* 285–308.

Kasl, S. & Wells, J. (1985). Social support and health in the middle years. In S. Cohen & S. Syme (Eds.), *Social support and health.* Orlando, FL: Academic Press.

Kessler, R. (1979). A strategy for studying differential vulnerability to the psychological consequences of stress. *Journal of Health & Social Behavior, 20,* 100–107.

Kessler, R. & McLeod, J. (1985). Social support and mental health in community samples. In S. Cohen & S. Syme (Eds.), *Social support and health.* Orlando, FL: Academic Press.

Kessler, R., McLeod, J. & Wethington, E. (1985). The costs of caring: A perspective on the relationship between sex and psychological distress.

LaRocco, J., House, J. & French, J. (1980). Social support, occupational stress and health. *Journal of Health & Social Behavior, 21,* 202–218.

Lazarus, R. & Folkman, S. (1984). *Stress, appraisal and coping.* New York: Springer.

Lefcourt, H. (1985). Intimacy, social support and locus of control as moderators of stress. In I. Sarason & B. Sarason (Eds.), *Social support: Theory, research and applications.* The Hague, Netherlands: Martinus Nijhoff.

Lin, N. & Ensel, W. (1984). Depression-mobility and its social etiology: The role of life events and social support. *Journal of Health & Social Behavior, 25,* 176–188.

Pearlin, L. (1985). Social structure and processes of social support. In S. Cohen & S. Syme (Eds.), *Social support and health.* Orlando, FL: Academic Press.

Pearlin, L. I., Lieberman, M. A., Menaghan, E. G. & Mullan, J. T. (1981). The stress process. *Journal of Health and Social Behavior, 22,* 337–356.

Pearlin, L. & Schooler, C. (1978). The structure of coping. *Journal of Health & Social Behavior, 19,* 2–21.

Sandler, I. & Lakey, B. (1982). Locus of control as a stress moderator: The role of control perceptions and social support. *American Journal of Community Psychology, 10,* 65–80.

Thoits, P. (1982). Conceptual, methodological and theoretical problems in studying social support as a buffer against life stress. *Journal of Health & Social Behavior, 23,* 145–159.

Wethington, E. & Kessler, R. (1986). Perceived support, received support, and adjustment to stressful life events. *Journal of Health and Social Behavior, 27,* 78–89.

Wortman, C. & Lehman, D. (1985). Reactions to victims of life crises: Support attempts that fail. In I. Sarason & B. Sarason (Eds.), *Social support: Theory, research and applications*. The Hague, Netherlands: Martinus Nijhoff.

Wheaton, B. (1985). Models for the stress-buffering functions of coping resources. *Journal of Health & Social Behavior, 26*, 252–364.

Wheaton, B. (1983). Stress, personal coping resources and psychiatric symptoms: An investigation of interactive models. *Journal of Health & Social Behavior, 24*, 208–229.

Assessment of Physiological Indices Related to Cardiovascular Disease as Influenced by Job Stress

Lisa R. Balick

J. Alan Herd

SUMMARY. Accurate assessment of physiological indices of job stress is necessary in order to help us identify individuals most susceptible to stress-related ailments such as cardiovascular disease. The physiological indicators examined, blood pressure and heart rate, catecholamines, cortisol and lipids have all evidenced a relationship to physical and psychological stressors. Assessment of these indicators must address the difficulties involved in doing such studies. Individual differences in responding, the specifics of each physiological process, and the constraints of doing such research in the natural setting must be considered. Only if strict attention is paid to the myriad of processes influencing the variables under study is accurate assessment possible.

Lisa R. Balick, PhD, Associate Professor, Departments of Medicine and Psychiatry, Baylor College of Medicine.

J. Alan Herd, MD, Professor, Department of Medicine, Baylor College of Medicine and Medical Director, Institute for Preventive Medicine, The Methodist Hospital, Houston, Texas.

INTRODUCTION

The realization that behavior influences cardiovascular and metabolic functions has drawn many observers to suppose that psychological factors contribute to cardiovascular disease. In addition, epidemiological studies have demonstrated relationships between cardiovascular disease and various social, psychological, and behavioral factors. From these clinical and epidemiological observations, the concept of stress has arisen. By common usage, the concept of stress implies a psychological effect of some influence that is usually considered undesirable or even harmful in some way. In addition, notions of perception, meaning, and previous experience influence personal uses of the concept.

The concept of job stress arises naturally from the realization that behavior is influenced by occupational conditions, and many individuals can identify influences in the workplace they consider undesirable and possibly harmful. The difference between job stress and other occupational hazards is the contribution from social and psychological factors as distinct from purely physical factors. Because psychological factors are more difficult to measure than physical factors, they have assumed a somewhat mysterious quality. The attempt to identify physiological indices of job stress arises from the proposition that physical effects of social and psychological factors may allow us to quantitate job stress more readily and help to identify individuals most susceptible to any adverse physical effects.

This search for physiological indicators of job stress is necessary because individual perceptions of stress and stressful situations are not well defined and are not consistent between individuals. If there were no observable physiological consequences and no apparent relations between job stress and cardiovascular disease — for example, measurement of stress could be so simple as questions concerning subjective effects. We must do better than this, by as accurately as possible assessing the effects of job stress on physiological processes.

The physiological indicators of greatest interest are those related to cardiovascular and metabolic functions most likely to contribute to cardiovascular disease. Other medical conditions have been associated with social and psychological factors, but the prevalence and severity of cardiovascular diseases draw our attention. The realization that cardiovascular diseases progress for many years before clinical manifestations appear brings us to make great efforts to prevent these diseases at an early stage.

Studies have been conducted indicating occupational influences on cardiovascular disease. Karasek, Baker, Marxer, Ahlbom and Theorell (1981) demonstrated that individuals experiencing demanding work with few opportunities to control the job situation had increased prevalence of coronary heart disease and increased incidence of mortality. Similarly, Alfredsson, Karasek and Theorell (1982) conducted a case-controlled study of incident myocardial infarction cases and reported that individuals in occupations characterized by hectic work and low control over work tempo and skill variety had an increased risk of myocardial infarction. Thus it is evident that perceived work demand, which may be interpreted as job stress, has a predictive relation to cardiovascular risk factors and potential development of coronary heart disease. In order to best assess the physiological effects of job stress which may lead to coronary heart disease, we need to conduct research in both experimental and natural work settings which will accurately monitor physiological indicators predictive of heart disease.

The physiological indicators which will be addressed that are important predictors of heart disease are blood pressure and blood lipids. Heart rate and blood levels of catecholamines and cortisol also are linked to blood pressure and lipid metabolism. Blood pressure (and heart rate which is often linked with blood pressure) and lipid metabolism are both known risk factors of heart disease. Catecholamines are linked to heart disease through their relationship to blood pressure and lipid metabolism. Cortisol levels also are linked to heart disease through effects on lipid metabolism. Thus, blood pressure and lipid metabolism are viewed as direct risk factors while catecholamines and cortisol levels serve as intermediate measures.

Recommendations for conducting research which assesses the effects of stress on blood pressure and heart rate, catecholamines, cortisol, and lipids arise from the relations of physiological indices to cardiovascular risk factors. Also described are some of the studies which have been executed in these areas, revealing some of the types of stressors frequently introduced and results obtained.

HEART RATE AND BLOOD PRESSURE

High blood pressure is one of the most important risk factors for coronary heart disease. Measurements of blood pressure and heart rate have been used by many investigators to assess cardiovascular responses to physical and psychological factors. These measures, as physiological indices of job stress, provide a rapid and sensitive measure of response to physical and psychological stressors.

The first detailed studies of cardiovascular and renal function during psychological testing were performed by Brod and his colleagues (1959). They used mental arithmetic as a psychological stimulus administered in both normotensive and hypertensive subjects. During the stimulus of mental arithmetic, the systolic, diastolic, and mean blood pressures rose in association with an increase in cardiac output and a reduction in total peripheral vascular resistance.

Obrist and his colleagues (1974 & 1978) and Light and Obrist (1980) assessed the influence of psychological stimuli on heart rate and contractility, finding that, in a reaction-time task, heart rate and blood pressure rose during the preparatory phase, then returned toward baseline until the time of responding occurred. Additionally, it was noted that intensity of efforts to cope with behavioral challenges, which is influenced by the role of perceived controllability, affected cardiovascular responses. Greater changes in heart rate and blood pressure occurred in subjects with control over aversive stimuli when they continued their efforts to control them than in subjects without control.

In addition to laboratory studies assessing the effects of stress or heart rate and blood pressure, a prospective study reporting the relationship between responses to the cold pressor test and coronary heart disease was conducted by Keys, Taylor, Blackburn, Brozek, Anderson and Somonson (1971). They found that the magnitude of subjects' diastolic blood pressure responses to cold immersion was associated significantly with the development of coronary heart disease during a 23-year follow-up.

Certainly, the aforementioned studies and several others inform us that physiological and psychological stressors in both laboratory and natural conditions can influence heart rate and blood pressure. However, several considerations must be taken into account when conducting such studies. The fact that some subjects are responders and some are nonresponders to physical and psychological stressors provides a source of difficulty in assessing effects for subjects who simply do not respond in a test situation. In addition, blood pressure and heart rate are influenced by posture, physical activity, intake of caffeine, absorption of nicotine, and dietary intake of sodium. Levels of blood pressure and responses of blood pressure and heart rate also are influenced by heredity and body composition. Although levels of blood pressure and heart rate and their responses to test situations are fairly reproducible within individuals, many of these factors may influence results differently under different conditions.

Ideal conditions for measuring the influence of physical and psychological stress on blood pressure and heart rate may be difficult to attain but are worthy of pursuit. Ideal conditions include measurements under baseline conditions with subjects resting comfortably in a bland environment. The most restful conditions would be obtained while subjects were on relief from usual daily activity such as during vacation. In addition, measurements should be made repeatedly to obtain reliable resting values. Once reliable baseline measures are obtained, the potential for response in each subject should be tested using physical and psychological stressors. Physical stressors may include the cold pressor test, isometric hand grip, and dynamic work under an exercise tolerance test. Response to psychological stressors also should be measured using standard procedures such as mental arithmetic with measures of competence and performance included. These procedures would indicate the potential each subject has for response in test situations.

The response to test situations such as job conditions should be made during 24-hour periods. The periodic measurement of both blood pressure and heart rate should be recorded automatically and correlated with features of the test situation objectively measured, perceptions of impact on a subject by self-report, and behavior of the subject observed and measured objectively by others. In addition, the relation of heart rate to blood pressure should be tracked and analyzed.

Using this approach, it becomes possible to use responders as probes of test situations. Even those subjects who do not respond vigorously to physical and psychological stressors can be observed for their response to job situations, but the intensity of response may be less. Ultimately, the long-term rise in average level of blood pressure is more important than short-term responses. Consequently, the average level of blood pressure in a test situation during periods of several hours on different days will be the most important measure of response to a job situation.

Although the ideal study of blood pressure and heart rate can be specified, there are many constraints imposed under normal conditions. Baseline values are difficult to obtain during rest and repeated measures frequently are difficult to obtain. The measurement of blood pressure and heart rate during 24-hour periods is expensive, and analysis of data is time-consuming. Furthermore, all subjects must be used as their own controls, since each will respond more or less vigorously than others in similar situations. In fact, some subjects simply do not respond to physical and psychological stressors, and assessing the impact of test situations becomes difficult if blood pressure and heart rate are the only measures available.

CATECHOLAMINES

Measurement of catecholamine levels in blood and urine has contributed a great deal of information concerning physical and psychological stressors in test situations. Januszewicz, Szajderman, Wocial, Feltynowski, and Klenowicz (1979) found that in both normotensive and hypertensive subjects, measurements of plasma demonstrated significant increases in epinephrine, norepinephrine, and plasma renin activity in response to a mental arithmetic test. A study by LeBlanc, Cote, Jobin and Labrie (1979) evidenced differential responses of epinephrine and norepinephrine in test situations. Results indicated that psychological factors (mental arithmetic test) have a greater effect on epinephrine responses than on norepinephrine responses, whereas physical factors (cold water hand immersion) have a greater effect on norepinephrine responses. Timio and Gentili (1976) and Timio, Gentili and Pede (1979) have studied the neuroendocrine responses of industrial workers under different natural working conditions. Results showed that mean daily urinary excretion of epinephrine, norepinephrine, and 11-hydroxycorticosteroids increased under such working conditions as a payment by results schedule or while working on an assembly line, as compared to a fixed salary schedule or working outside of the assembly line. Additionally, Timio et al. (1979) found that the enhanced neuroendocrine responses persisted, perhaps indicating that chronic exposure to psychological factors may have enduring effects on neuroendocrine processes.

Thus, investigations have shown that catecholamine levels are influenced by physical and psychological stressors. Although the presence of sensitive and accurate measurements of catecholamines exist, many difficulties which intrude on interpretation of results must be addressed. Many factors influence rates of secretion and levels of concentrations in blood and urine. The amount of sodium in the diet, posture of subjects, their physical activity, their intake of caffeine, and their absorption of nicotine influence rates of secretion and levels of concentration in blood. In addition, the amount of norepinephrine in urine is influenced not only by filtration from blood into the urine, but also by secretion of norepinephrine from adrenergic nerve terminals in the kidney itself. Furthermore, collection of urine frequently is difficult because of poor understanding and poor cooperation by subjects in providing specimens.

In the ideal situation, very useful information can be obtained. The baseline values must be obtained under resting conditions, and values should be obtained on several different days to ensure that baseline values are reliable and as low as possible. After baseline values have been obtained, the potential for response should be evaluated under standardized laboratory situations using both physical and psychological stressors. Physical stressors such as isometric muscle contraction, dynamic exercise under exercise tolerance testing, and postural stress on a tilt table are useful to assess the potential for response to physical stressors. In addition, turnover rates of epinephrine and norepinephrine can be measured using labelled substances injected intravenously by continuous infusion during several hours and then the rate of their disappearance measured as the infused substances are degraded or absorbed into adrenergic nerve terminals. Effects of psychological stressors also can be tested using mental arithmetic for cognitive challenges and psychological stress interviews to elicit emotional responses.

In natural settings, continuous measurements of levels in blood can be obtained using a constant withdrawal pump and periodic sampling of blood obtained. Urine can be sampled frequently and measurements made on samples obtained at precise times during a period of 24 hours. These measurements of levels in blood and urine can be related to situations which are evaluated objectively, to perceptions reported by subjects concerning their effect, their cognitive effort, and their sense of competence, and behavior can be measured by other observers. In each of the samples of blood and urine, the proportion of epinephrine to norepinephrine should be determined, both in the free hormone levels and their metabolic products.

Although the ideal situation might provide substantial information, many constraints are found in natural settings. The 24-hour urine collections are difficult to obtain, and the use of a continuous withdrawal pump is costly and difficult to operate. All subjects must be used as their own controls, and responses to test situations must be repeated several times to overcome effects of novelty or fear in an experimental situation. Although the ideal conditions of the laboratory seldom can be obtained in natural settings, by using precautions and observing test conditions carefully, it should be possible to obtain good information concerning effects on catecholamine levels of physical and psychological stressors in job situations.

CORTISOL

In addition to heart rate and blood pressure and catecholamine levels, the effect of physical and psychological stressors on the secretion of cortisol has been examined (Brandenberg, Follenius, Wittersheim, Salame, 1980; Davis, Gass, Bassett, 1981; Rose, Hurst, Livingston & Hall, 1982; Ursin, Baade & Levine, 1978). For example, Davis et al. (1981) tested normal young men under a graded exercise tolerance test, with one group of subjects having experience in exercise testing and the others having no experience. The authors found that post-exercise increase in serum cortisol was greater in nonexperienced subjects, concluding that novelty was the major determinant of this increase. Additionally, Ursin et al. found that, for young men receiving parachute training on three successive days, reported fear reduced from day-to-day as did plasma levels of cortisol. The authors interpreted these results as demonstrating that improved performances and reduction of fear reduced the magnitude of the physiological responses. Importantly, studies in natural settings conducted over long periods of time have demonstrated enduring effects of psychological factors on cortisol secretion. Rose et al. (1982) measured levels of cortisol and growth hormone in blood on at least three different occasions in 201 air traffic controllers while at work. Comparing controllers with themselves and across three repeated endocrine studies, results showed a consistent but modest relationship between increases in workload and increases in cortisol.

Importantly, it is evident that stressors such as novelty, fear, and workload can influence cortisol levels. However, there are many difficulties in studies involving measurements of cortisol which must be considered. The change in diurnal pattern secretion rates of cortisol preclude the measurement of a steady baseline state during minutes or hours under resting conditions. Repeated measures on several different days can provide some confidence that baseline values have been obtained. However, any changes observed must be interpreted against a background of constant change in relation to the diurnal pattern. Other effects of eating meals, physical activity, changes in posture, and change in ambient temperature must be noted and considered in analyzing results. Finally, difficulties of collecting urine and obtaining complete samples are ever-present hazards in conducting studies of cortisol secretion.

In the ideal experimental situation, cortisol levels in blood and urine would be obtained under restful conditions over periods of several days. In addition, a sufficient number of samples must be obtained to fully document the diurnal pattern and to capture the maximal and minimal values for concentration of cortisol in blood at the appropriate times of day. After determining the diurnal pattern and its reliability, the potential for response should be obtained using both physical and psychological stressors. As in studies of catecholamines, the physical stressors commonly used are cold pressor test, isometric muscle contraction, and dynamic exercise under exercise tolerance testing. The psychological stressors that have been tested include mental arithmetic, and some assessment of competence, effort, motivation, and adaptation should be obtained.

In natural settings, measurements should be made during 24-hour collections. A constant withdrawal pump provides frequent samples of blood so that small changes in concentration can be detected. In addition, frequent samples of urine provide estimates of amounts filtered into urine. Along with measurements of cortisol and its metabolites, measurements of potassium in blood and urine and measurements of sodium in urine provide information concerning the effects of cortisol on electrolyte metabolism.

As with studies of cardiovascular function and catecholamines, there are many constraints in the natural situation. The use of a constant withdrawal pump is artificial and intrudes on normal daily activities. Its operation is cumbersome and costly. All subjects must be used as their own controls, and studies must be repeated on as many days as possible to overcome effects of novelty and to determine the adaptation which might occur in test situations. The result is that the ideal test situation seldom can be obtained. Again, however, with the best possible use of the aforementioned techniques, substantial information concerning effects of physical and psychological stressors on cortisol secretion can be obtained in the natural job setting.

LIPIDS

Results of many epidemiological and clinical investigations have demonstrated the relation of lipid metabolism to risk for cardiovascular disease. Measurements of lipid substances in blood provide rapid and sensitive indices of physiological and psychological stressors. Dimsdale and Herd (1982) reviewed results of 60 studies in which plasma lipid levels were observed to respond to psychological factors. The majority of studies involved effects of psychological factors over short periods of time (few minutes or few hours), while only a few studies involved effects over days, weeks, or months. In all studies, the effects of unpleasant, novel or arousing situations were observed in relation to levels of free fatty acids, triglycerides, and cholesterol in blood. In these studies, levels of free fatty acids were almost invariably elevated. Levels of triglycerides also increased but did so more slowly. Often, they were not elevated during the test experience but increased several hours after the task. Most studies also found that levels of cholesterol increased, with the effects being particularly evident in subjects exposed to natural situations for several weeks or months.

Certainly, lipid responses provide important information regarding the effect of physical and psychological stressors. The major difficulty encountered in studying lipid responses is the influence of a variety of factors on the levels. Such factors include heredity, gender, body composition, dietary intake of fat, physical activity, and cigarette smoking.

Under the ideal conditions, the baseline measures would be obtained from individuals under resting conditions on several different days under constant conditions of nutrition, physical activity, and other factors. In addition to responses that would be elicited by typical physical and psychological stressors, the metabolic responses to glucose and triglycerides would be observed. In this way, assessment of clearance, as well as secretion, would be obtained. The obvious importance of cholesterol level in its low-density lipoprotein and high-density lipoprotein components makes the measurement of these substances most important for assessing risk induced by test situations.

In the natural setting, design of experiments would be appropriate which examine the gradual changes occurring over several weeks with as much control exerted as possible over physical activity, nutrition, and other factors known to influence lipid metabolism. The individuals most likely to be responsive will be those with high levels of cholesterol in low-density lipoproteins and high levels of triglycerides in blood. In these individuals, changes in neuroendocrine function will have an effect on insulin sensitivity and on degradation of triglycerides into high-density and low-density lipoproteins. Any individuals with low levels of cholesterol and triglycerides in blood will likely be unresponsive to most physical and psychological stressors.

CONCLUSION

It is evident that many factors must be considered in order to most accurately assess the effects of stress on physiological processes. The most compelling feature in all studies of individual responses to physical and psychological stressors is the enormous range of individual variability. Although each subject may have similar responses under similar situations on different days, the differences between subjects frequently are large. Consequently, ipsative analyses must be performed in which all subjects serve as their own controls. A corollary of this is the necessity of comparing all subjects under different conditions with well-established baseline measurements followed by thorough studies under test conditions. Also, it is important to consider that some individuals can be termed responders in one system or another, but little information is available to determine whether individuals respond with similar intensity in all physiological systems. Additionally, an appreciation of the physiological processes under study is imperative for interpretation of results. Levels of substances in blood and amounts appearing in urine often have little relation to rates of secretion or metabolic activity. An appreciation for turnover rates, metabolic pathways, and physiological consequences must be obtained for each system under study.

It is noted that three measures might prove useful for screening subjects during normal daily activities in natural situations. The first of these is the ratio of epinephrine to norepinephrine in urine or blood. It is expected that psychological factors would stimulate epinephrine secretion more than norepinephrine secretion, and the ratio of the catecholamines and their metabolic products should change under the varying influences of psychological and physical factors. The second of these measures is the ratio of potassium to sodium in urine. It is expected that the diurnal pattern of this ratio would be flattened when cortisol secretion is high and stays high without the usual diurnal pattern for its secretion when psychological factors have a strong influence over physiological function. The third of these measures involves lipoproteins, both total cholesterol and triglyceride levels in blood. It is expected that triglyceride levels would be high, and HDL-cholesterol levels would be low when cortisol and catecholamine secretions are elevated under the influence of strong psychological factors. These measures are worthy of exploration to determine whether subjects are responding to situations with intense cognitive effort, strong emotional effects, or psychological distress.

In the corporate setting, it would be difficult for a corporate health director to conduct a thorough program for monitoring and assessing. A practical screening program to monitor and assess the effects of job stress on physiological indicators of employees would look as follows: Pre-employment measurement of blood pressure, serum cholesterol, blood glucose for diabetes, and amount of cigarette smoking would be obtained. Additionally, an electrocardiogram would be recorded. Those found with cardiovascular risk factors would be given information regarding control of risk factors. Additionally, they would be monitored on a regular basis to determine if the risk factors were increasing. If continuous measurement revealed that the levels of risk factors were increasing and/or that there was any indication that risk factors were higher when in work settings than in nonwork settings (when on vacation for example), indicating that the job made control hard to achieve, then it would be advisable to counsel employees at high risk to change their jobs.

The prevalence of heart disease and other stress-related ailments underscores the importance of examining factors which contribute to the development of such diseases. The progress that has been made in physiology, psychology, and behavioral technology makes it possible to study the physiological indices of job stress. However, strict attention must be paid to the myriad of processes influencing the variables under study.

REFERENCES

Alfredsson, L., Karasek, R. & Theorell, T. (1982). Myocardial infarction risk and psychosocial work environment: An analysis of the male Swedish working force. *Soc Sci Med, 16*, 463–467.

Brandenberger, G., Follenius, M., Wittersheim, G. & Salame, P. (1980). Plasma catecholamines and pituitary adrenal hormones related to mental task demand under quiet and noise conditions. *Biological Psychology, 10*, 239–252.

Brod, J., Fencl, V., Hejl, Z. & Zirka, J. (1959). Circulatory changes underlying blood pressure elevation during acute emotional stress (mental arithmetic) in normotensive and hypertensive subjects. *Clinical Science, 18*, 269–279.

Davis, H., Gass, G. & Bassett, J. (1981). Serum cortisol response to incremental work in experienced and naive subjects. *Psychosomatic Medicine, 43*, 127–132.

Dimsdale, J. & Herd, J.A. (1982). Variability of plasma lipids in response to emotional arousal. *Psychosomatic Medicine, 44*, 413–430.

Januszewicz, W., Sznajderman, M., Wocial, B., Feltynowski, T. & Klonowicz, T. (1979). The effect of mental stress on catecholamines, their metabolites and plasma renin activity in patients with essential hypertension and in healthy subjects. *Clinical Science, 57*, 229s–231s.

Karasek, R., Baker, D., Marxer, F., Ahlbom, A. & Theorell, T. (1981). Job decision latitude, job demands and cardiovascular disease: A prospective study of Swedish men. *American Journal of Public Health, 71*, 694–705.

Keys, A., Taylor, H.L., Blackburn, H., Brozek, J., Anderson, J.T. & Somonson, E. (1971). Mortality and coronary heart disease among men studied for 23 years. *Arch. Int. Med., 128*, 201–214.

LeBlanc, J., Cote, J., Jobin, M. & Labrie, A. (1979). Plasma catecholamines and cardiovascular responses to cold and mental activity. *Journal of Applied Physiology: Respiratory Environment Exercise Physiology, 42*, 1207–1211.

Light, K.C. & Obrist, P.A. (1980). Cardiovascular response to stress: Effects of opportunity to avoid shock, shock experience, and performance feedback. *Psychophysiology, 17*, 243–252.

Obrist, P.A., Gaebelein, C.J., Teller, E.S., Langer, A.W., Gringnolo, A. (1978). The relationship among heart rate, carotid dP/dt, and blood pressure in humans as a function in the type of stress. *Psychophysiology, 15*, 102–115.

Obrist, P.A., Lawler, J.E., Howard, J.L., Smithson, K.W., Martin, P.L. & Manning, J. (1974). Sympathetic influences in carotid rate and contractility during acute stress in humans. *Psychophysiology, 11*, 405–427.

Rose, R.M., Jenkins, C.D., Hurst, M., Livingston, L. & Hall, R.P. (1982). Endocrine activity in air traffic controllers at work. I. Characterization of cortisol and growth hormone levels during the day. *Psychoneuroendocrinology, 7*, 101–111.

Timio, M. & Gentili, S. (1976). Adrenosympathetic overactivity under conditions of work stress. *British Journal of Preventive and Social Medicine, 30*, 262–265.

Timio, G., Gentili, S. & Pede, S. (1979). Free adrenaline and noradrenaline excretion related to occupational stress. *British Heart Journal, 42*, 471–474.

Ursin, H., Baade, E. & Levine, S. (Eds.). (1978). *Psychobiology of Stress. A Study of Coping Men.* New York: Academic Press.

Stress:
Psychobiological Assessment

India Fleming
Andrew Baum

SUMMARY. A multidimensional approach to stress measurement which includes assessment of self-report, behavioral, physiological, and biochemical components of the stress response is described. The strengths and weaknesses of each measurement domain are considered. The use and interpretation of physiological and biochemical measures less familiar to behavioral scientists are discussed in detail. Arguments in favor of the inclusion of physiological and biochemical measures in studies examining the stress-illness relationship are presented.

One reason the study of stress has generated so much interest is that stress is involved in the etiology of both physiological and psychological illness. Stress appears to contribute to the development of physical disorders such as peptic ulcers, hypertension, and suppression of the immune system (Amkraut & Solomon, 1977; Rose & Glomset, 1976; Selye, 1956; Weiner, 1977), and to the development of psychological disorders including anxiety and depression. Some researchers have suggested that stress is a useful concept in explaining the link between environmental and psychological events and the physical and emotional disturbances that sometimes follow. The stress response is complex; it involves both psychological and

India Fleming and Andrew Baum are affiliated with the Uniformed Services University of the Health Sciences.

This work was partially supported by research grants from the Uniformed Services University of the Health Sciences (C07205) and the National Science Foundation (BNS 8317997). The opinions or assertions contained herein are the private ones of the authors and are not to be construed as official or reflecting the views of the Department of Defense or the Uniformed Services University of the Health Sciences.

biological changes. The physiological and biochemical changes that are part of the stress response are probably important mediators between the experience of stress and subsequent physical illness. Study of the way that stress affects these systems is necessary if we are ever to understand the association between stress and illness. In spite of the importance of these biological changes they are seldom measured in studies of stress and stress consequences.

The study of stress is of particular importance to researchers interested in job settings. Several studies have found that perceived job stress is related to employee health, work satisfaction, and job performance (e.g., Beehr & Newman, 1978). For example, French & Caplan and their colleagues (e.g., Caplan, Cobb, French, Harrison, Pinneau, 1975; French & Caplan, 1972) noted that workload and role conflict predicted somatic symptoms such as headaches, and psychological symptoms including depression and anxiety. Similarly, the incidence of hypertension appears to be greater in "high stress" occupations than in other jobs (Cobb & Rose, 1973). Many sources of occupational stress are chronic rather than acute. Although most stress research has focused on acute stressors, such as laboratory stimuli and the taking of final exams, there is evidence that chronic stressors may be more related to physical and psychological health problems (Baum, Singer & Baum, 1981; Selye, 1976). Job related stressors are probably among the most common chronic or recurrent stressors experienced in our society and therefore, study of the relationships between occupational stress and health is an important field of investigation.

This paper describes a multidimensional approach to the measurement of stress. Because of the multifaceted nature of the stress response concurrent measurement of psychological and biological aspects of the stress response have been suggested (Baum, Grunberg & Singer, 1982). In our research we collect simultaneous measures of psychological, behavioral, physiological and biochemical states (e.g., Baum, Fleming & Singer, 1985). Because behavioral scientists are generally familiar with psychological and behavioral assessment this discussion will focus primarily on the physiological and biochemical measures. Several factors, including limited resources, time, money, and techniques make the infrequent use of biological assessment of stress by behavioral scientists understandable. However, recent advances in instrumentation to measure physiological changes and the development of relatively inexpensive biochemical assays for stress related hormones should make inclusion of these measures in studies of stress more practical.

PSYCHOBIOLOGICAL BASIS OF STRESS

Early stress research focused on primarily biological aspects of the stress response. Cannon (1929; 1936) described the emergency "fight/flight" response and identified epinephrine, a hormone produced and secreted by the adrenal glands, as a key mediator of that response. Cannon suggested that the arousal of the sympathetic nervous system (SNS) and the physiological changes occurring in response to a threat prepared the organism to cope with the danger. When confronted by threatening or upsetting situations, SNS arousal and the release of epinephrine allow an individual to react more strongly or quickly — to fight harder or to flee faster. This is accomplished by increased blood flow to muscles, increased heart rate and respiration, and decreased blood flow to areas not needed for such confrontations, including the skin and viscera. Protective aspects of the emergency response were also noted, such as reduced blood flow to the skin, reducing bleeding if the individual is cut.

Mason (1975) later characterized stress as a catabolic process, adding several dimensions to the model described by Cannon. During stress, stores of energy are broken down for use and the primary activity of the body is to draw energy out of storage and into action. Anabolic processes are reduced; sugar is not transported into cells for storage as readily as at rest, and substances needed in the breakdown and use of energy increase in the system. Thus, hormones and enzymes that produce ready energy increase in concentration during stress, while those involved in building the body and storing energy are reduced.

In between the work of Cannon and Mason were the highly influential theories advanced by Selye (1956; 1976). He focused on a different biological system than did Cannon, and referred to an almost immune-like stress response. First noting that a range of stressors caused the same three physiological pathologies (enlargement of the adrenals, shrinkage of the thymus gland, and ulceration of the gastro-intestinal tract), Selye went on to describe the "general adaptation syndrome" — a three part response that he believed was common to all dangers or threats. The first part, the alarm phase, represented mobilization and initial response as well as recurring response if the stressor was persistent. Resistance, the second phase, was a period of rebuilding bodily stores to do further combat and, when replenishment was no longer possible, the third stage — exhaustion — occurred.

Selye's (1956; 1976) work focused on a different set of hormones — corticosteroids — produced by a different part of the adrenals. When the body senses the presence of a stressor (Selye called them noxious agents) it reacts much as does the immune system when it detects the presence of an antigen. Instead of immunoglobins, however, the body responds to stressors with massive release of corticosteroids in an attempt to overcome the incursion. It is important to keep in mind that most of the stressors that Selye studied were biological insults such as introduction of pathogens, exposure to X-rays, cold, heat, and so on. Psychological stressors were not eliminated from the system but were not explicitly discussed.

Mason's (1975) work as well as that of other investigators has shown that the corticosteroids are involved in stress as Selye (1956; 1976) suggested, but that catecholamines (epinephrine and norepinephrine) and other hormones are as well. More recent investigative studies have confirmed the notion of multiple response during stress, including psychological responses and important mediation of stress by cognitive processes. Modern stress research indicates that stress is a whole body response, involving all major biological and psychological systems in response to threats, dangers, irritants, and the like.

As behavioral scientists began to study stress, new models of the stress process developed. Stress can be viewed as a process linking an individual's or organisms perception of a threat, harm, or challenge to its well-being with the responses of the organism (Baum et al., 1981; Lazarus, 1966; Lazarus & Launier, 1978). Responses to a potential stressor depend upon the appraisal of an event as a threat and on the appraisal of one's resources for coping with it. Research has shown that many events and situations can be stressful including crowding (D'Atri, 1975), noise (Cohen, Evans, Krantz & Stokols, 1980), job loss (Kasl & Cobb, 1970), and commuting (Singer, Lundberg & Frankenhaeuser, 1978). Many factors affect the interpretation and response to potential stressors. The individual's ability to cope with the particular threat, the duration of the threat, its predictability, and the number of people affected all influence the stress response.

The stress response is a whole body response. It involves physiological, cognitive, emotional, and behavioral changes. These changes may help prepare the organism to cope with the stressor by enabling it to avoid the threat, minimizing its impact, or they may reflect the costs of coping. Psychological response to stress may include emotional changes such as negative affective tone, anxiety and depression; cognitive changes such as a narrowing of attention, and changes in motivation and skill levels. Physiological response to stress primarily involves increased physiological arousal. Somatic distress may also accompany or follow the stress response; increases of symptoms such as headaches and gastrointestinal discomfort are frequently reported.

MEASUREMENT OF STRESS

There are four basic dimensions along which the stress response can be measured: self-report, behavioral, physiological, and biochemical. Self-report measures assess appraisal of a stressor, affective and somatic states, and coping styles. These measures generally involve directly asking subjects about their attitudes, beliefs, feelings and behaviors. Behavioral measures are used to examine coping, the effects of stress on skilled performance, and aftereffects of stress. These measures generally involve direct observation of behavior, or performance measures on tasks likely to reflect stress related deficits in motivation or performance. Physiological measures assess stress through its impact on specific physiological systems or organs. For example, changes in heart rate and blood pressure reflect the impact of stress on the cardiovascular system, and changes in skin conductivity (the galvanic skin response) reflects stress related increases in perspiration. Finally, biochemical measures assess stress related changes in the endocrine system or in enzyme changes in many systems. Although stress appears to affect many hormones, epinephrine, norepinephrine and the corticosteroids appear to be the primary stress hormones — generating response to stress and mediating many aspects of physiologic responses to stress. Thus, these hormones are the most frequently measured in studies of stress. Moderate correlations between measures in these different domains are often found; however, they are not necessarily correlated as they assess overlapping but separate processes. Each measurement domain has its own particular strengths and weaknesses; each is influenced by factors other than stress; many of these measures have large variances, and they may follow different time courses. Because each measurement domain is subject to variance caused by factors other than stress, multimodal stress measurement strategies promise to provide more reliable assessment of stress.

Self-Report Measures

The easiest and most direct way of finding out if people are stressed is to ask them. Interviews and questionnaires are easy and inexpensive to administer, and often have a high degree of face validity. Generally self-report measures assess the affective, cognitive and somatic experience of stress. Questions designed to assess response to a specific stressor are often used. Some scales have been designed to measure general levels of stress, though most assess particular aspects of the stress response or the stressful situation. For example, the Perceived Stress Scale (Cohen, Kamarck & Mermelstein, 1983) assesses respondents' recent feeling of being stressed, but focuses most heavily on notions of overload, control, and depressed affect. Other scales originally designed for other uses have been useful in studying stress. The Symptom Checklist-90 (Derogatis, 1977) a multidimensional symptom inventory with several subscales measuring such stress related affect as somatization, depression and anxiety, has been used by several researchers examining stress, and related mental health changes (e.g., Baum, Gatchel & Schaeffer, 1983; Bromet, 1981). Still other scales have been designed to quantify the frequency of stressful or potentially stressful events including life events and daily hassles (e.g., Holmes and Rahe, 1967; Kanner, Coyne, Shaefer & Lazarus, 1982). Finally, inventories measuring how people deal with stressors have been used; the Ways of Coping Inventory (Folkman & Lazarus, 1980; Vitaliano, Russo & Carr, 1985), assessing appraisal of the stressor and several possible coping styles, has been frequently used in stress research.

Self-report measures are subject both to deliberate and to unconscious sources of error. For example, self-report measures of affective and somatic states may be influenced by changes in symptom awareness due to increased concern about the effects of a stressor, attitudes toward or against something if the stressor is controversial, and by coping styles which may involve repressing or denying that there is a problem. Furthermore, symptoms that ordinarily would have been ignored or gone unnoticed before a major stressful event may not only be noticed and reported after the event because they now may have meaning, but may also become a subject for additional worry and upset. At Three Mile Island, for example, increased reporting of symptoms could reflect worry about what the symptoms might mean — is this sore throat a symptom of radiation exposure? cancer? On the job, exposure to toxins could cause the same pattern.

Behavioral Measures

Behavioral measures of stress generally examine the ways people cope with stress or assess performance on tasks which may be affected by stress. Where possible, observation of actual behavior can be used, and several laboratory tasks have been used as well. For example, a behavioral measure of crowding stress might involve counts of the frequency and duration of interpersonal interactions. Measures similar to this have been used in studies of residential crowding (Baum, Davis & Aiello, 1981), and could be adapted for use in work environments. Persistance and performance on tasks requiring motivation and concentration are based on the notion that arousal or distress can reduce motivation, concentration, and attention to detail. For example, Glass and Singer (1972) found that stressed subjects performed more poorly on a proofreading task that required concentration than did less stressed subjects. These measures will be subject to their own sources of variance. For example, the proofreading task is likely to be affected by skill, educational level, practice, and interest. Further complicating matters, practice and interest are often independently affected by stress. Thus, interpreting task performance as a measure of stress can be difficult.

Physiological Measures

Physiological stress measures often assess arousal of the sympathetic nervous system through its effects on specific organ or system function. The cardiovascular system, the respiratory system, muscle tension, and electrodermal response all reflect stress related physiological arousal. Sympathetic arousal during stress should heighten levels of heart rate, blood pressure, muscle tension, breathing, and so on; increased sweating during stress should reduce skin resistance. Each of these has been used as an index of stress in previous research. Because of large individual differences and continuous fluctuation in these systems it is important to collect baseline readings whenever possible. Unfortunately, the equipment required for many of these measures is expensive and some techniques require intrusive and novel procedures, such as the placement of electrodes, which may in themselves be stressors or which may make movement, and therefore realistic response, less likely. In addition many of these are not suitable for field use, since the equipment is difficult to move and subject to decalibration. However, advances in telemetry and ambulatory monitoring may enable more use of these measures in the future.

Heart rate and blood pressure are among the more frequently reported physiological measures of stress. Because the necessary equipment is lightweight, relatively easy to transport, and easy to learn to use, they are practical for studies of stress in field settings which allows them to be used in studies of naturally occurring stress in real world settings. They are also important links between stress and illness and are used frequently for this as well. Changes in heart rate and blood pressure reflect changes in the cardiovascular system resulting from increased activity of the sympathetic nervous system. These cardiovascular changes direct blood flow to organs potentially needed to enable the organism to respond quickly and decreases blood flow to less critical organs. Specifically, blood flow to the heart and skeletal muscle is increased while blood flow to the skin, digestive tract and the kidneys is decreased. Generally, heart rate and systolic and diastolic blood pressure increase in response to stress. These changes are somewhat independent of one another, and they may be differentially affected by specific aspects of a stressor. As with other physiological measures baseline values are important, and, because heart rate and blood pressure are influenced by activity and posture, it is critical that these are held constant across subjects and conditions. Subjects should be seated quietly at least 15–20 minutes before heart rate and blood pressure readings are taken. Ambulatory heart rate and blood pressure monitors have been developed which allow frequent readings of heart rate and blood pressure to be taken as a person goes about daily activities. Generally subjects on ambulatory monitors are asked to record the activities they were engaged in at the onset of each measurement. Although this technique may facilitate study of physiological response to activity and stress in daily life, it does have limitations. The equipment is cumbersome and the knowledge that one is being monitored may limit normal physical and social activities. Also, these machines are expensive and can be used on only one subject at a time.

Biochemical Measures

The catecholamines, epinephrine and norepinephrine, are hormones secreted by the adrenal medulla that reflect activation of the sympathetic nervous system.[1] They are a crucial element in sympathetic nervous system arousal. The adrenal medulla is innervated by the sympathetic nervous system, and arousal of the SNS, stimulated by the hypothalamus, controls the secretion of both epinephrine and norepinephrine. Epinephrine and norepinephrine stimulate increases in the blood pressure and heart rate, and selectively constrict blood vessels to channel blood to appropriate organs. They also prolong the effects of neural activation of the SNS. The catecholamines contribute to many of the more general physiological changes associated with stress.

Research clearly shows that increased secretion of epinephrine and norepinephrine is associated with stress. Increases of epinephrine and norepinephrine have been found with exposure to a variety of stressors including commuting stress (Singer et al., 1978) and job stress (Frankenhaeuser, 1978). In addition, psychosocial stimuli such as failure, threat, loss of control, and uncertainty may increase secretion of the catecholamines (Mason, 1975). For example, Johansson, Aronsson, and Lindstrom (1978) found evidence of control related differences in catecholamines in a Swedish sawmill industry. Catecholamine levels in a group of sawmill workers whose work pace was largely machine-controlled was compared with levels in a group of workers whose work pace was self-determined. During working hours the machine-controlled group had higher catecholamine levels than did the self-determined group suggesting that control associated with self-paced tasks reduced stress on the job or prevented stress due to loss of control.

Catecholamines also vary as a function of factors other than stress. Exercise, posture, diet, and pharmacological substances all influence catecholamine levels. Epinephrine and norepinephrine also show circadian rhythms, though there is some debate over whether all people show these patterns. The exact time of peak levels is also unclear, though as a general rule it is safe to conclude that they peak at noon or in the early afternoon and drop to their lowest levels overnight. This cycle is likely to be different for individuals who work different hours or who are on rotating shifts. Hence increases in catecholamines are not necessarily indicative of stress. It is crucial to control for these factors in studies in which epinephrine and norepinephrine are used as indicators of stress. Questionnaires asking about physical activity, food consumption, and use of pharmacologic agents provide an easy way of getting the necessary information to statistically control for these sources of variation. The impact of circadian rhythms can be minimized by collecting specimens at the same time of day for each subject, by collecting discrete measures for each subject across the daily cycle, or at least by counterbalancing specimen collection time across groups or conditions.

Accurate estimates of stress related catecholamines can be obtained from both blood plasma and urine. The choice of using blood or urine specimens depends upon the goals of the study and the research setting. Blood samples are appropriate if one is interested in immediate catecholamine response to specific acute stressors. For example, Glass and his colleagues (Glass et al., 1980) have used repeated blood samples taken over short periods of time to compare acute catecholamine changes of Type A and B subjects in response to challenging tasks. Urine samples, on the other hand, are particularly useful for studies of prolonged or recurrent stress, and for studies of stress in real world settings. For example, Rissler (1977) examined catecholamine changes associated with increased work load (up to 15 hours of overtime work per week) in employees of an insurance company in Sweden. Catecholamines were measured before during and after this period. Epinephrine excretion increased during the period of overtime work and returned to normal after the employees returned to their normal schedules.

Collection of blood samples for catecholamine assay is tricky because of the potentially reactive nature of the procedures and because of the short duration of the response. Plasma catecholamines fluctuate rapidly (the half-life of catecholamine levels in the blood is less than two minutes), they reflect very brief periods of arousal, and must be assessed repeatedly. In addition, there is evidence that catecholamine levels are sensitive to the stress of venipuncture (Davis et al., 1962). Venipuncture is invasive and a potentially reactive procedure; as a result it is difficult to obtain appropriate samples. Dimsdale (in press) described a procedure to minimize the problem of measurement reactivity in blood samples by using an indwelling catheter inserted in a peripheral vein. This allows one to draw repeated samples and to minimize the impact of venipuncture on the catecholamine levels. After insertion of the catheter it is important to let the subject rest for at least 20 minutes prior to taking baseline samples or exposing the subject to the stressful stimulus; otherwise the catecholamine levels may reflect changes due to the venipuncture itself. Because catecholamine response occurs rapidly and dissipates quickly in the blood frequent sampling during or after exposure to a stressor is vital; otherwise one may miss the response entirely. To increase the probability of catching the catecholamine surge and to reduce the variability associated with abrupt changes in epinephrine and norepinephrine, Dimsdale advocates the use of multiple integrated three minute samples taken at different points during a stressful experience. This technique requires the use of a continuous withdrawal pump which can slowly draw a sample over a few minute period. Once one sample is completed the collection tube can be replaced and another sample drawn when appropriate (e.g., Dimsdale & Moss, 1980). One difficulty inherent in any multidraw procedure is the necessity of an anticoagulant to prevent the blood in the catheter from clotting. Anticoagulating agents, such as heparin, can be infused into a catheter, but such agents may affect physiological function and they require frequent attention and adjustment. Some catheters, available for use with continuous withdrawal pumps, have been treated with a substance which binds heparin and prevents coagulation in the catheter without entering the subject's system. Use of blood samples to estimate circulating catecholamine levels generally requires a laboratory setting and physician supervision.

Catecholamines in the blood are very unstable and blood samples must be handled properly to assure valid measurement. The blood must be placed on ice immediately after collection and centrifuged to separate the plasma from the red blood cells within two hours. Otherwise, an enzyme in the red blood cells (catechol o-methyl transferase) will degrade the catecholamines. Anti-oxidizing agents may also be added to the samples to delay degradation. Once separated, the plasma should be frozen as quickly as possible. If the assays will be performed within one week the samples may be frozen at $-20°$ C, if they must be kept longer they should be stored at $-70°$ C.

In contrast with the collection of blood samples, the collection of urine specimens is relatively easy. Urine collection is noninvasive, not painful, is easily incorporated into field studies, and does not require physician supervision. In addition, collection of urine samples requires only minor changes in subject's normal activities and, therefore, is particularly useful for studies of naturally occurring stress. Also, urinary catecholamine levels change more slowly than do plasma levels and reflect all catecholamine production over the previous few hours. Thus there is more leeway in the timing of sample collection and one is unlikely to miss the catecholamine response entirely; however, if the response is particularly brief it may not show up in the urine whereas it might show up in an appropriate plasma sample (e.g., Williams et al., 1982).

We have used two basic strategies to collect urine samples: a double void procedure and a collection of all urine voided over several hours. The double void procedure is useful in studying the effects of specific short term events and is often used in laboratory studies. Two single void samples are collected, one prior to exposure to the stressor and one an hour or an hour and a half subsequent to the stressor. The first sample serves as a baseline measure or as a covariate to control for individual differences. It is best if the baseline specimen is from the first morning void as samples taken immediately prior to the study will be more variable. If the morning void is used as a baseline the subject should void just prior to participating in the study to minimize the impact of other events on catecholamine levels in the urine collected after the session. To minimize the impact of circadian rhythms on urine samples it is important to run subjects at the same time of day or to counterbalance conditions by time of day. Collection of all urine voided over several hours, long term samples, are useful if one is interested in catecholamine response to ongoing or prolonged stressors. In these studies all urine voided for a set period of time, usually 15–24 hours, is collected. A 24 hour collection is preferable as variation due to individual differences in circadian rhythms and idiosyncratic events will be minimized. For example, if a subject is late for an appointment and runs to save time there would probably be an elevation in catecholamines in the next void, but this type of elevation would be diluted in a 24 hour sample. However, subjects may be reluctant to carry collection containers and urine specimens around with them during the day; therefore we often collect all urine voided for 15 hours, between 6 pm and 9 am — when most subjects are home. A 15 hour collection has many of the advantages of the 24 hour collection, including reduction of variation associated with idiosyncratic events. In addition, we feel that this collection period increases the likelihood that the subjects will provide a complete sample. For some studies it may be desirable to collect all urine voided over a specific period, but to keep each void separate. For example, if one were interested in stress associated with changes in work schedules it might be best to collect urine over a 24 hour period, but to separate urine voided at work and urine voided during non-working hours.

Regardless of the procedure, care of the urine samples is critical if the estimates of epinephrine and norepinephrine are to be reliable. A preservative (hydrochloric acid or sodium metabisulfate) must be added to the urine at the time of collection to prevent oxidation of the catecholamines. Following collection of the specimen, the volume should be measured, the sample stirred, and a small amount frozen at $-29°$ C or $-70°$ C depending on the duration of storage and the assays to be done.

Not all circulating catecholamines show up in the urine; rather a constant fraction of circulating catecholamines are excreted in the urine as free epinephrine and norepinephrine (Frankenhaeuser, 1975). Because urinary catecholamines represent only a fraction of circulating epinephrine and norepinephrine the absolute levels of these substances in the urine are not as meaningful as are relative levels and changes within individuals over time. Epinephrine levels in urine provide a reliable estimate of adrenal medullary activity because the adrenal medulla is the only source of epinephrine. Norepinephrine, on the other hand, is secreted by the SNS fibers as well as the adrenal medulla, and a substantial portion of circulating norepinephrine is reabsorbed by nerve endings and is not reflected in the urine. In spite of this, estimates of epinephrine and norepinephrine from urine provide a useful index of SNS arousal.

Several types of assays have been developed to assess catecholamine levels in blood and urine. These include spectrophotofluorometric, radioenzymatic, and high performance (power) liquid chromotography procedures (Axelrod, 1962; Axelrod & Tomchick, 1958; Euler & Lishajko, 1961). Radioenzymatic assays are particularly cost effective as a hundred or more samples can be processed in a week by one or two trained technicians. In the radioenzymatic procedure a radiolabeled enzyme (catechol o-methyl transferase) added to the samples produces a reaction in which the catecholamines are converted to radioisotope labeled amine metabolites. Organic solvent extraction separates the catecholamine metabolites from excess radioisotope. These metabolites are separated from one another using thin layer chromotographic procedures. The remaining radioactivity is measured and the resulting values converted to indicate epinephrine and norepinephrine concentration in the sample. In long term samples the concentration of catecholamines should be adjusted by the sample volume to create an estimate of the average rate of catecholamine excretion over the urine collection period.

Corticosteroids are the most extensively studied aspect of the endocrine response to stress. They are secreted by the adrenal cortex in response to a wide range of physical and psychosocial stressors. The pathway leading to secretion of corticosteroids appears to begin in the hypothalamus which stimulates the pituitary adrenal cortical axis. The pituitary evokes corticosteroid release from the adrenal glands by releasing adrenocorticotropic hormone (ACTH) which can also be measured and is correlated with corticosteroid levels.

Research has found elevated levels of corticosteroids in response to stress in both animals and humans. For example, researchers have reported increased adrenal cortical activity in response to shock, noise, crowding, and restraint in animals (e.g., Christian, 1963; Elmadjian & Pincus, 1945; Harrington & Nelbach, 1942; Selye, 1956). Furthermore, Selye demonstrated that the differences in circulating corticosteroids found between stressed and unstressed animals could be prevented by removing the adrenal glands. In humans increased corticosteroid levels have been found to be associated with stressors such as anticipating surgery, taking final exams, athletic competition, airplane flights, and emergency duty in hospitals (Frost, Pyer & Kohlstaedt, 1951; Pincus & Hoagland, 1943; Thorn, Jenkins & Laidlaw, 1953; Schwartz & Shields, 1954). Mason (1975) reported a series of studies linking increased adrenal cortical activity with situations involving loss of control, uncertainty, and pain.

The pituitary-adrenocortical axis appears to be highly sensitive to psychosocial stress (Mason, 1968). Elevations in corticosteroids do not appear to reflect specific emotional states; but rather they seem to reflect undifferentiated arousal or preparation for coping, as Selye (1956; 1976) suggested. However, interpretation of changes or differences in corticosteroid levels is more complex than is interpretation of changes in catecholamines because corticosteroids show a bipolar response to stress. Psychological factors can cause both increases and decreases in corticosteroid secretion depending on the type of threat, the quality of the emotional reaction, the style and effectiveness of coping and defensive reactions, and whether the threat is acute or chronic. For example, in one study of medic units in Vietnam, some subjects showed decreases rather than increases in corticosteroid levels during and after exposure to stress (Bourne, Rose & Mason, 1967). Due to the bipolar response of corticosteroids the adrenal medullary hormones (epinephrine, norepinephrine) may provide clearer indications of stress.

Like the catecholamines, the corticosteroids are influenced by factors other than stress. Cortisol levels also show diurnal variation; cortisol levels are generally highest between 5 am and 10 am and lowest between 8 pm and 4 am. Several pharmacologic agents, including oral contraceptives, may also affect cortisol levels, so it is important to collect information from subjects about their use of these substances.

Corticosteroids serve many important physiological functions including the regulation of water and electrolytes, the metabolism of carbohydrates, fats and proteins, and the inflammation of body tissue. The corticosteroids are believed to be responsible for many of the effects Selye (1956; 1976) noted as consequences of stress. The primary corticosteroid in humans is cortisol.

Accurate estimates of cortisol in both blood and urine can be obtained using existing assay procedures. Kits are available for a competitive binding radioimmunoassay (Yalow & Berson, 1971) that are relatively easy for an experienced laboratory technician to use. These allow several hundred samples to be processed in a single day. The radioimmunoassay relies on competitive binding principles. Special tubes, coated with an antibody which binds with cortisol, are used. The samples of plasma or urine are added to these tubes along with a known amount of cortisol tracer — radiolabeled cortisol. The samples are then incubated. The cortisol from the sample and the radiolabeled cortisol tracer bind with the antibodies coating the tube in proportions reflecting their relative amounts. The contents of the tube are decanted; the remaining radioactivity is measured, and the resulting values are converted to indicate cortisol levels in the sample. Because sample cortisol competed with radiolabeled cortisol for binding sites, measured radioactivity is inversely associated with cortisol levels in the sample.

USE OF MULTIDIMENSIONAL STRESS MEASURES

Evaluation of reliability of these measures of stress is difficult. Stress is not a static state and the normal fluctuations of levels of various stress indicators poses problems for those wishing to show some stability of response. Test-retest approaches, therefore, are unlikely to reveal much, and moderate to low correspondence across time in one or another measure does not necessarily mean that the assessment is flawed. Internal consistency of self-report measures or standardized scales can be assessed, but this is more difficult when considering estimates of bodily response. In our lab, urine samples frozen and assayed several times over a period of two years yield correlations of .8 or better, including the effects of slow deterioration of the samples over time. This suggests that the catecholamine assays used in our work are reliable and that a sample can be read several times with similar results. However, correlations between sample values for a given individual over time are lower. The cortisol assay is also reliable; samples assayed several times vary by about 5%. The fact that stress levels change is another reason for use of multiple levels of assessment of stress responding.

The choice of particular measures, and the method of administration obviously depend on the nature and goals of the specific study. As we have noted, some of the physiological measurement techniques are more appropriate for studies of response to acute stressors and others are more useful in studies of chronic stress. If one is interested in chronic stress then it is necessary to collect repeated measures of stress over time. The timing and frequency of the assessment should depend upon factors such as whether the stressor is continuous, episodic, or cyclic, the occurrence of other predictable sources of stress such as holiday seasons, and whether one wishes to assess changes in stress response associated with changes in environmental sources of stress. For example, in a study of changes in stress associated with a change in work schedule it would be important to assess stress response both before and after the change. Furthermore, measurements taken immediately pre- or post-change may reflect disruption due to the change itself rather than stress responses associated with the two different schedules. Measures taken two or more weeks before and after the change may more accurately reflect differences due to schedule. If one is interested in chronic stress in a relatively static environment several measures taken over a year or more are probably adequate. In our ongoing studies of chronic stress we measure stress two to four times a year.

Comparison groups are essential in the interpretation of any of these measures of stress. Although normative data are available for many of the self-report and physiological measures this seldom provides a useful comparison because the "normal" range is often large, and sample idiosyncracies may bias the results. In addition, stress related elevations in somatic and emotional distress, blood pressure, heart rate, the catecholamines, and corticosteroids, and decrements in behavioral performance are generally still within normal ranges. Therefore, it is important to have a comparable comparison group.

We have argued that no single measure of stress should be used alone. Rather, measurement of multiple domains is necessary to evaluate the complexities of the stress response. Stress is not a simple stimulus-response reaction, but instead is a process in which a physical or psychological stressor impinges on an individual, appraisals by the individual, and psychological, behavioral and physiological responses of the individual. Understandably, most behavioral researchers have relied primarily on paper and pencil self-report measures assessing only a few of these domains. However, as interest in the health consequences of stress has increased more researchers have incorporated behavioral and physiological measures into their studies. Assessment of these domains of stress response is important if we are to understand the processes linking stress with health consequences. We have discussed the strengths and weaknesses of the four domains of stress measurement, focusing particularly on the biochemical measures likely to be less familiar to behavioral scientists.

STRESS RELATED HEALTH CONSEQUENCES

Most of the measures described above assess aspects of the stress response itself. Many other biological and health consequences of stress can also be measured. Two responses which may reflect physiological changes resulting from the stress response, and which may more directly mediate specific health consequences are cardiovascular reactivity and immune system function. These are both being measured with increasing frequency in studies of stress consequences.

Heightened cardiovascular reactivity may be a marker of risk for the development of cardiovascular disorders including essential hypertension and coronary heart disease (Eliot, Buel & Dembroski, 1982; Krantz & Manuck, 1984). Cardiovascular reactivity involves changes in generalized arousal including increases in heart rate and blood pressure which occur in response to acute stressors or challenges. Although cardiovascular reactivity involves the physiological responses described earlier, assessment of reactivity is conceptually distinct. Many people will show some elevation in heart rate and blood pressure in response to acute stressors; however there are individual differences in the magnitude and duration of these responses. For example, there is evidence that Type A individuals are more reactive than are Type B individuals (e.g., Contrada et al., 1982; Glass, Lake, Contrada, Kehoe & Erlanger, 1982). Further, the experience of chronic stress appears to increase cardiovascular reactivity to acute stressors even when baseline measures of heart rate and blood pressure fail to distinguish stressed from unstressed groups (Fleming, Baum, Davidson, Rectanus & McArdle, 1986). Chronic stress may potentiate acute stress response and cardiovascular reactivity may be a factor linking chronic stress with health outcomes. In addition, assessment of reactivity may prove to be an additional marker of chronic stress.

The immune system is an important mediator of environmental effects on health, and recent evidence of psychological and central nervous system influences on immunity suggests that it may be an important intervening variable during stress. Traditionally, the immune system has been viewed as a primary factor in host resistance — how well an organism can fend off pathogens and disease-causing agents. Antibodies and a variety of T cell variants were seen as engaging in seek and destroy missions against foreign particles, agents, substances, and so on. If this immunity shield was weakened, resistance declined and illness was more likely. Our current view of the immune system is far more complex, though its effects are clearly the same — the protection of the body from pathogens. Stress appears to reduce measures of immunocompetence — how well immune cells function or how many cells there are — and stress reduction improves immune status (e.g., Kiecolt-Glaser et al., 1985; Stein, in press).

It is probably premature to make any strong conclusion about stress and immunity. Whether the changes observed during stress have any clinical significance is not clearly known; however, with recent advances in technology and immunology, new types of cells and cell-functions are being continually discovered and new measures developed, advances in the understanding of stress and immune function are likely. Choice of measures, ultimately dependent on questions being asked, are also heavily influenced by available equipment and supplies. Regardless, further study of stress-related changes in immunity promises to provide important information about psychobiological mechanisms of the stress-illness relationship.

UNEMPLOYMENT STRESS – AN EXAMPLE

The usefulness of this multidimensional stress measurement strategy can be demonstrated by considering research on unemployment stress. Interest in the consequences of unemployment began in the 1930s during the Great Depression. Since that time research on unemployment stress has investigated a variety of effects including the impact on feelings of self-worth (e.g., Goodchilds & Smith, 1977), negative emotional response (e.g., Warr, 1984), increased somatic complaints (e.g., O'Brian, 1978), and hormonal changes (Cobb, 1974). However, little attention has been given to how these responses are related. In addition, some studies have found results contradicting those of other studies. For example, Little's (1976) finding that self-evaluations were more positive following job loss is discrepant from most research examining feelings of self-worth following job loss (e.g., Goodchilds & Smith). Likewise, studies of physiological changes associated with unemployment have found differences in catecholamine levels between employed and unemployed groups at some times (anticipatory and post unemployment) but not at others. There are several possible explanations for this type of discrepancy, and interpretation of such contradictory findings would be easier if they were presented in the context of other changes accompanying unemployment.

Baum, Fleming, and Reddy (in press) examined catecholamine levels and behavioral and catecholamine responses to frustrating tasks in three groups of subjects that varied in their employment or unemployment status. Subjects were either employed, had been unemployed less than three weeks, or had been unemployed for more than three weeks. The procedures involved a double void urine collection — the first sample collected when the subjects arrived to participate in the study and the second collected at the end of the session, approximately an hour after the subjects worked on the task. Because these investigators were particularly interested in the role of loss of control and learned helplessness in unemployment stress the behavioral task was drawn from a learned helplessness paradigm. Subjects were presented with a version of the Levine task (Levine, 1975). For half the subjects in each employment/unemployment group, feedback on the problems was contingent on performance; the remaining subjects received noncontingent feedback.

The baseline urine samples collected prior to the task revealed group differences in urinary catecholamines. Unemployed subjects had higher levels of catecholamines in their urine than did employed subjects; further, baseline catecholamine levels increased with length of unemployment. The correspondence between catecholamine and behavioral responses to the task is even more interesting. Under conditions of contingent feedback, catecholamine levels decreased in all groups. However, under noncontingent conditions the groups showed varied catecholamine responses. Employed and recently unemployed subjects showed increases in catecholamines in response to noncontingent feedback, whereas subjects unemployed longer than three weeks showed decreases in catecholamines in response to the same task. These catecholamine changes paralleled behavioral performance. Subjects unemployed for a longer time showed decreases in task persistence under conditions of noncontingent feedback. The fact that the biochemical and behavioral responses correspond increases one's confidence that these changes indicate a stress response.

CONCLUSIONS

Inclusion of biological assessment strategies in studies of psychosocial stressors can contribute greatly to the understanding of the stress response to specific types of stressful situations. Many of the measures described in this paper could be incorporated into existing research protocols with minimal impact on the study procedures and at minimal additional expense. Further, the use of multidimensional stress measurement can add greatly to the understanding of how the complex changes associated with stress are related to one another.

Stress is a broad concept which is used in different ways by different researchers. Some have argued that it is useless. We believe that it is an important concept because it is useful in understanding the relationships between psychological and environmental stimuli and the range of psychological, behavioral, and biological changes that often follow. However, there is a danger in the use of stress as an explanation for an association between psychological events and subsequent increases in illness reports when the studies have not assessed the physiological and biochemical changes likely to mediate that relationship. The processes intervening between psychological and environmental stressors and health consequences are complex. Examining only the two endpoints of this process — the stressors and subsequent physical or psychological health status — precludes real understanding of this relationship.

NOTE

1. Norepinephrine is found in relatively small quantities in the adrenals, and most systematic norepinephrine is secreted by sympathetic neurons in vascular beds or throughout the body. Thus, increases in norepinephrine, independent of epinephrine, may reflect activity, muscle tension, and general nervousness as well as stress.

REFERENCES

Amkraut, A. & Solomon, G.F. (1977). From the symbolic stimulus to the pathophysiologic response: Immune mechanisms. In Z.J. Lipowski, D.R. Lipsitt & P.C. Whybrow (Eds.), *Psychosomatic medicine: Current trends and clinical applications*. New York: Oxford Press.

Axelrod, J. (1962). Catechol-O-methyltransferase from rat liver. In S.P. Colowick & N.O. Kaplan (Eds.), *Methods in enzymology: Vol. 5*. New York: Academic Press.

Axelrod, J. & Tomchick, R. (1958). Enzymatic O-methylation of catecholamines. *Journal of Biological Chemistry, 233*, 702.

Baum, A., Davis, G. & Aiello, J.R. (1978). Crowding and neighborhood mediation of urban density. *Journal of Population, 1*, 266–279.

Baum, A., Fleming, R. & Reddy, D.M. (in press). Unemployment stress: Loss of control, reactance and learned helplessness. *Social Science in Medicine*.

Baum, A., Fleming, R. & Singer, J.E. (1985). Understanding environmental stress: strategies for conceptual and methodological integration. In A. Baum & J.E. Singer (Eds.), *Advances in environmental psychology: Vol. 5* (pp. 185–205). Hillsdale, NJ: Lawrence Erlbaum Associates.

Baum, A., Gatchel, R.J. & Schaeffer, M.A. (1983). Emotional, behavioral and physiological effects of chronic stress at Three Mile Island. *Journal of Consulting and Clinical Psychology, 51*, 565–572.

Baum, A., Grunberg, N.E. & Singer, J.E. (1982). The use of psychological and neuroendocrinological measurements in the study of stress. *Health Psychology, 1*, 217–236.

Baum, A., Singer, J.E. & Baum, C.S. (1981). Stress and the environment. *Journal of Social Issues, 37*(1), 4–34.

Beehr, T.A., Newman, J.E. (1978). Job stress, employee health and organizational effectiveness. A facet analyses, model, and literature review. *Personnel Psychology, 31*, 665–669.

Bourne, P.G., Rose, R.M. & Mason, J.W. (1967). Urinary 17-OHCS levels: Data on seven helicopter ambulance medics in combat. *Archives of General Psychiatry, 17*, 104.

Bromet, E. (1980). Three Mile Island: Mental health findings. Pittsburgh, PA: Western Psychiatric Institute and Clinic and the University of Pittsburgh.

Cannon, W.B. (1929). *Bodily changes in pain, hunger, fear, and rage.* Boston: Branford.

Cannon, W.B. (1936). *Bodily changes in pain, hunger, fear, and rage* (2nd ed.). New York: Appleton-Century-Crofts.

Caplan, R.D., Cobb, S., French, J.R.P. Jr., Harrison, R.V., Pinneau, S.R. Jr. (1975). *Job demands and worker health* (HEW Publication No. NIOSH 75-160). Washington, DC: U.S. Government Printing Office.

Christian, J.J. (1963). The pathology of overpopulation. *Military Medicine, 128*, 571–603.

Cobb, S. (1974). Physiological changes in men whose jobs were abolished. *Journal of Psychosomatic Research, 18*, 245–258.

Cobb, S. & Rose, R.M. (1973). Hypertension, peptic ulcer, and diabetes in air traffic controllers. *Journal of the American Medical Association, 224*, 489–492.

Cohen, S., Evans, G.W., Krantz, D.S. & Stokols, D. (1980). Physiological, motivational, and cognitive effects of aircraft noise on children: Moving from the laboratory to the field. *American Psychologist, 35*, 231–243.

Cohen, S., Kamarck, T. & Mermelstein, R. (1983). A global measure of perceived stress. *Journal of Health and Social Behavior, 24*, 385–396.

Contrada, R.J., Glass, D.C., Krakoff, L.R., Krantz, D.S., Kehoe, K., Isecke, W., Collins, C. & Elting, E. (1982). Effects of control over aversive stimulation and Type A behavior on cardiovascular and plasma catecholamine responses. *Psychophysiology, 19*, 408–419.

D'Atri, D. (1975). Psychophysiological responses to crowding. *Environment and Behavior, 1*, 237–252.

Davis, J., Morrill, R., Fawcett, J., Upton, V., Bondy, P.K. & Spiro, H.M. (1962). Apprehension and elevated serum cortisol levels. *Journal of Psychosomatic Research, 6*, 83.

Derogatis, L.R. (1977). *SCL-90-R: Administration Scoring and Procedures Manual 1.* Baltimore, Maryland: Clinical Psychometrics Research.

Dimsdale, J.E. (in press). Measuring human sympathoadrenomedullary responses to stressors. In A. Baum & J.E. Singer (Eds.), *Handbook of psychology and health: Vol. 5.* Hillsdale, NJ: Lawrence Erlbaum Associates.

Dimsdale, J.E., Moss, J. (1980). Short-term catecholamine response to psychological stress. *Psychosomatic Medicine, 42*, 493–497.

Eliot, R.S., Buell, J.C. & Dembroski, T.M. (1982). Bio-behavioral perspectives on coronary heart disease, hypertension, and sudden cardiac death. *Acta Medica Scandinavia, 660* (Suppl.), 203–213.

Elmadjian, F. & Pincus, G. (1945). The adrenal cortex and the lymphoctopenia of stress. *Endocrinology, 37*, 47.

Euler, U.S. von & Lishajko, F. (1961). Improved technique of the fluorimetric estimation of catecholamines. *Acta Physiologica Scandinavica, 51*, 348–355.

Fleming, I., Baum, A., Davidson, L.M., Rectanus, E. & McArdle, S. (1986). *Chronic stress as a factor in physiological reactivity to challenge.* Manuscript submitted for publication.

Folkman, S. & Lazarus, R.S. (1980). An analysis of coping in a middle-aged community sample. *Journal of Health and Social Behavior, 21*, 219–239.

Frankenhaeuser, M. (1975). Experimental approaches to the study of catecholamines and emotions. In L. Levi (Ed.), *Emotions: Their parameters and measurement* (pp 209–234). New York: Raven Press.

Frankenhaeuser, M. (1978). Coping with job stress: A psychobiological approach. Reports from the Department of Psychology, University of Stockholm, (532).

French, U.R.P. Jr. & Caplan, R.D. (1972). Organizational stress and individual strain. In A.J. Morrow (Ed.), *The failure of success* (pp. 30–66). New York: Amacon.

Frost, J.W., Dryer, R.L. & Kohlstaedt, K.G. (1951). Stress studies on auto race drivers. *Journal of Laboratory and Clinical Medicine, 38*, 523.

Glass, D.C., Lake, R.C., Contrada, R.J., Kehoe, K.K. & Erlanger, L.R. (1983). Stability of individual differences in physiological responses to stress. *Health Psychology, 2*, 317–341.

Glass, D.C., Krakoff, L.R., Contrada, R.J., Hilton, W.F., Kehoe, K., Mannucci, E.G., Collins, C., Snow, B. & Elting, E. (1980). Effect of harassment and competition upon cardiovascular and plasma catecholamine responses in Type A and Type B individuals. *Psychophysiology, 17*, 453–463.

Glass, D.C. & Singer, J.E. (1972). *Urban Stress*. New York: Academic Press.

Goodchilds, J.D. & Smith, E.E. (1977). The effects of unemployment as mediated by social status. *Sociometry, 26*, 287–295.

Herrington, L.P. & Nelbach, J.H. (1942). Relation of gland weights to growth and aging processes in rats exposed to certain environmental conditions. *Endocrinology, 30*, 375.

Holmes, T.H. & Rahe, R.H. (1967). The social readjustment rating scale. *Journal of Psychosomatic Research, 11*, 213–218.

Johansson, G., Aronsson, G. & Lindstrom, B.O. (1978). Social psychological and neuroendocrine stress reactions in highly mechanized work. *Ergonomics, 21*, 583–599.

Kanner, A.D., Coyne, J.C., Schaefer, C. & Lazarus, R.S. (1981). Comparison of two modes of stress management: Daily hassles and uplifts versus major life events. *Journal of Behavioral Medicine, 4*, 1–39.

Kasl, S.V. & Cobb, S. (1970). Blood pressure changes in men undergoing job loss: A preliminary report. *Psychosomatic Medicine, 32*, 19–38.

Kiecolt-Glaser, J.K., Glaser, R., Willinger, D., Stout, J., Messick, G., Sheppard, S., Ricker, D., Romisher, S., Briner, W., Bronell, G. & Donnerberg, R. (1985). Psychosocial enhancement of immunocompetence in a geriatric population. *Health Psychology, 4*, 25–41.

Krantz, D. & Manuck, S. (1984). Acute psychophysiologic reactivity and risk of cardiovascular disease: A review and methodologic critique. *Psychological Bulletin, 96*, 435–464.

Lazarus, R.S. (1966). *Psychological stress and the coping process*. New York: McGraw-Hill.

Lazarus, R.S. & Launier, R. (1978). Stress-related transactions between person and environment. In L.A. Pervin & M. Lewis (Eds.), *Perspectives in interactional psychology* (pp. 287–327). New York: Plenum.

Levine, M. (1975). *A Cognitive Theory of Learning*. Hillsdale, NJ: Lawrence Erlbaum Associates.

Little, C.B. (1976). Technical-professional unemployment: middle-class adaptability to personal crisis. *Social Quarterly, 17*, 262–274.

Mason, J.W. (1968). A review of psychoendocrine research on the sympathetic adrenal medullary system. *Psychosomatic Medicine, ˙30*, 631.

Mason, J.W. (1975). Emotion as reflected in patterns of endocrine integration. In L. Levi (Ed.), *Emotions: Their parameters and measurement* (pp. 143–181). New York: Raven Press.

O'Brien, G.E. (1978). Adjustment of the unemployed. *Working Paper Series*, No. 29.

Pincus, G. & Heagland, H. (1943). Steroid excretions and the stress of flying. *Journal of Aviation Medicine, 14*, 173.

Rissler, A. (1977). Stress reactions at work and after work during a period of quantitative overload. *Ergonomics, 20*, 13–16.

Ross, R. & Glomset, J.A. (1976). The pathogenesis of atherosclerosis. *New England Journal of Medicine, 295*, 369–377, 420–425.

Schwartz, J.B. & Shields, D.R. (1954). Emotional tension and excretion of corticoids and creatinine. *American Journal of Medicine, 16*, 608.

Selye, H. (1956). *The stress of life*. New York: McGraw-Hill.

Selye, H. (1976). *The stress of life*. New York: McGraw-Hill.

Singer, J.E., Lundberg, U. & Frankenhaeuser, M. (1978). Stress on the train: A study of urban commuting. In A. Baum, J.E. Singer & S. Valins (Eds.), *Advances in environmental psychology*, (Vol. 1). Hillsdale, NJ: Lawrence Erlbaum Associates.

Stein, M. (in press). Psychosocial perspectives on aging and the immune response. In R. Wiley, J.D. Matarazzo & A. Baum (Eds.), *The Aging Dimension*. Hillsdale, NJ: Lawrence Erlbaum Associates.

Thorn, G.W., Jenkins, D. & Laidlaw, J.C. (1953). The adrenal response to stress in man. *Recent progress in hormone research, 8*, 171.

Weiner, H. (1977). *Psychobiology and human disease*. New York: Elseucer.

Williams, R.B., Lane, J., Kuhn, C., Melosh, W., White, A. & Schanberg, S. (1982). Type A behavior and elevated physiological and neurendocrine responses to cognitive tasks. *Science, 218*, 483–485.

Vitaliano, P.P., Russo, J., Carr, J.E., Maiuro, R.D. & Becker, J. (1985). The Ways of Coping Checklist: Revision and Psychometric Properties. *Multivariate Behavioral Research, 20*, 3–26.

Yalow, R.S. & Berson, S.A. (1971). In W.D. Odell & W.H. Daughaday (Eds.), *Principles of competitive protein binding assays*. Philadelphia: J.B. Lippincott.

Beyond Negative Affectivity: Measuring Stress and Satisfaction in the Workplace

David Watson
James W. Pennebaker
Robert Folger

SUMMARY. Stress researchers frequently use self-report measures to assess stress, health, psychological adjustment, and subjective dissatisfaction. We present evidence demonstrating that all of these variables are highly intercorrelated and reflect a common underlying factor of Negative Affectivity (NA). NA is a stable and pervasive personality dimension — high NA individuals report more stress, distress and physical complaints, even in the absence of any objective stressor or health problem. Thus, NA may operate as a substantial nuisance factor in many areas of research. To circumvent its influence, investigators can use non-subjective measures of stress and health. Finally, we present a two-factor model of stress and satisfaction that includes, in addition to NA, the independent factor of Positive Affectivity (PA), a trait reflecting positive feelings about oneself and one's life.

Researchers measure job stress because of its importance to employers and employees alike. But when a self-report assessment is used, what really gets measured? Does the self-report instrument tap the construct (stress) that is considered so important? We will address such questions by examining the affective, perceptual, and

---

David Watson and James W. Pennebaker are affiliated with Southern Methodist University.

Robert Folger is affiliated with the A. B. Freeman School of Business, Tulane University.

Correspondence should be addressed to David Watson or James W. Pennebaker, Department of Psychology, Southern Methodist University. This research has been funded by NIH grant HL32547.

dispositional correlates of self-reported stress, physical symptoms, and health.

Two themes receive emphasis. First, we argue that Negative Affectivity (NA; Watson & Clark, 1984) is a stable and general disposition with broad implications for stress, health, and job satisfaction. A major implication is that the interrelationships among various measures of self-reported stress, symptoms, mood, and personality all reflect the same underlying construct of NA (cf. Depue & Monroe, 1986). Among the respondent "selves" who provide self-report data, some people are more highly disposed than others to respond negatively to almost any kind of questionnaire item.

Second, we consider the need to go beyond stress, distress, and symptoms—to measure, in addition, positive feelings about work and the workplace. There is evidence that variations in positive feelings occur independently of variations in Negative Affectivity, suggesting that the separable construct of Positive Affectivity (PA) also deserves measurement attention. Along these lines, we present a two-factor model derived from extensive investigations of self-rated mood (described in Watson & Tellegen, 1985).

STRESS, SYMPTOMS AND NA

The Nature and Definition of Stress

Because stress is a fuzzy concept whose definition is problematic (cf. Horowitz, 1976; Mason, 1975; Selye, 1976), the following component elements or aspects should be differentiated: (a) Some objective or perceived stimulus, the *stressor*, presumably precedes and evokes a stress response. One early approach adopted by researchers (e.g., Holmes & Rahe, 1967) focused on major life changes (e.g., divorce, job change, death of spouse) as acute stressors. Because this life-change inventory approach to measuring stressors is methodologically suspect (see B. P. Dohrenwend, 1974, 1979; Rabkin & Struening, 1976; Schroeder & Costa, 1984) and because scores on such inventories are only weakly related to long-term health and adjustment (see Delongis, Coyne, Dakof, Folkman & Lazarus, 1982; Goldberg & Comstock, 1976; Rahe, 1974), researchers have increasingly studied such alternatives as chronic stressors or "role strains" (e.g., recurrent financial problems, an unsatisfactory job or marriage; see Eckenrode, 1984; Pearlin, 1983;

Pearlin, Lieberman, Menaghan & Mullan, 1981) and minor daily stressors or "hassles" (e.g., DeLongis et al., 1982; Kanner, Coyne, Schaefer & Lazarus, 1981; Monroe, 1983). (b) *Cognitive and perceptual factors* influence how a person evaluates and responds to stressors (e.g., the stress response can be mediated by the perceived significance of the stressor for one's well-being; see Lazarus, DeLongis, Folkman & Gruen, 1985). (c) *Individual differences* can influence how — and how well — a person copes with a stressor (Depue & Monroe, 1986), perhaps because different people use different strategies for coping with stress (e.g., Folkman, Lazarus, Gruen & DeLongis, 1986). (d) Notions such as Selye's (1976) General Adaptation Syndrome imply that stress has an important *physiological substrate*. (e) Finally, the response to a stressor may include *overt changes in behavior*.

Despite the importance of each component, we will focus primarily on ways people perceive and report their feelings of stress (linking the cognitive/perceptual and individual differences components) and discuss the other aspects only as they relate to these self-reported feelings. For an extended discussion of the various components of stress and their interactions, see B. P. Dohrenwend & Shrout (1985) or Lazarus et al. (1985).

Components and Correlates of Perceived Stress

Several years ago the second author asked a sample of over 400 undergraduates to rate the degree to which they felt each of the following during "the average day": under stress, sad, guilty, angry, frustrated, headache, upset stomach, dizzy, racing heart, tense muscles. As might be expected, self-reports of stress correlated + .40 to + .70 with each of the other items. This and later surveys continued to suggest that perceptions of stress are highly related to the experience of both negative emotions and to physical symptoms (see Pennebaker, 1982 for a review). Indeed, the magnitudes of the relationships were sufficiently high to suggest that the items all represented the same underlying construct.

Watson (1986) obtained similar results in an extensive longitudinal investigation of 80 individuals. Subjects filled out a daily questionnaire over a 6-7 week period. On each day the subjects reported: (a) the level of stress they had experienced, (b) the extent to which they had felt each of 28 emotional states, and (c) the degree to which they had experienced 18 physical symptoms and complaints.

Mean levels of symptoms, moods, and stress responses were calculated for each person and subjected to a factor analysis. Stress, physical complaints, and negative moods all loaded on the same factor, again suggesting that they reflect a common construct.

What is this common factor? In a comprehensive review of a large number of commonly-used personality tests, the first author (with Lee Anna Clark) demonstrated that a variety of trait measures were all highly intercorrelated and thus reflected the same underlying factor, namely, Negative Affectivity or NA (Watson & Clark, 1984). This conclusion was reached from a review of dozens of studies that had included such measures as the IPAT Anxiety Scale (Krug, Scheier & Cattell, 1976), the Eysenck Personality Inventory Neuroticism Scale (Eysenck & Eysenck, 1968), the Taylor Manifest Anxiety Scale (Taylor, 1953), and the State-Trait Anxiety Inventory (Spielberger, Gorsuch & Lushene, 1970), as well as various measures of repression/sensitization, depression, defensiveness, ego strength, social desirability, and general maladjustment. Any of these scales is an acceptable measure of NA (see Watson & Clark, 1984, for a discussion of commonly-used NA measures). In our own research we most frequently use the 14-item Negative Emotionality Scale from Tellegen's Multidimensional Personality Questionnaire, a general inventory of normal personality (Tellegen, 1982; MPQ. The MPQ was formerly called the Differential Personality Questionnaire). Watson and Clark (1984) demonstrate that high NA individuals are more likely to experience discomfort at all times and across situations. Further, high NA subjects tend to be more introspective and dwell on the negative side of themselves and the world (see also Watson & Tellegen, 1985).

The identification of this pervasive affective disposition suggested to us that NA might be the factor accounting for the relatedness of stress perceptions, negative moods and physical symptoms. To test our hypothesis, we had a sample of approximately 150 healthy adults complete a battery of tests including scales of NA and stress reactions (from the MPQ; Tellegen, 1982), reports of physical symptoms (the PILL, as described in Pennebaker, 1982), and a measure of current emotional states (using the mood descriptors presented in Zevon & Tellegen, 1982). Again, we find that self-reports of physical symptoms, stress reactivity, and negative moods are highly intercorrelated (approximate mean intercorrelation among measures = .50). In other words, the domains of stress, symptoms, and negative moods overlap considerably. The overlap is sufficiently high to suggest that perceptions of stress, symptoms and negative moods represent the same basic construct. We are currently testing the generality of these relationships by looking at a wider range of measures in both normal adult and college student samples. To date, we have examined over 300 subjects on measures of NA, physical status (the PILL, physical symptom checklists, etc.), stress (e.g., the Hassles Scale of Kanner et al., 1981), psychological adjustment (e.g., the Beck Depression Inventory; Beck, Ward, Mendelson, Mock & Erbaugh, 1961; and the Hopkins Symptom Checklist; Derogatis, Lipman, Rickels, Uhlenhuth & Covi, 1974). We continue to find that all of these measures reflect the common influence of NA.

Implications of NA for the Measurement of Stress

The Dispositional Nature of Stress and Distress

That self-reports of stress, physical symptoms, and negative moods reflect a common psychological factor is both reassuring and disquieting. On the one hand, it is comforting to know that the researcher has access to a diverse array of inter-related stress measures. And, by the same token, the stress researcher can draw on an immense body of relevant data—from the areas of personality, mood research, health, and so on—when analyzing and interpreting specific phenomena.

On the other hand, the existence of this very broad NA factor causes several conceptual and methodological problems. Some of these stem from the fact that NA is a *dispositional* construct. First, there are large individual differences in NA. These individual differences have a substantial heritable component (Fuller & Thompson, 1978; Lykken, 1982; Scarr, Webber, Weinberg & Wittig, 1981), and are stable over time and consistent across contexts. For example, trait NA measures show significant stability over periods of up to 30 years (Leon, Gillum, Gillum & Gouze, 1979; see also Watson & Clark, 1984); similarly, NA tests can predict transient levels of negative mood states measured as long as 10 years later (Costa & McCrae, 1980). Taken together, such studies show that high NA individuals are likely to report more stress, distress and physical discomfort over time and regardless of the situation, *even in the absence of any overt or objective stressor.* Thus, presumed measures of job stress or dissatisfaction can be expected to correlate strongly with NA tests. Any simple between-subjects surveys that compare different employee groups will have to use sample sizes large enough to overcome potential NA group differences. Moreover, high NAs may be selectively drawn to different types of jobs than low NAs, thus artifactually building in group differences in distress and perceived stress. As a general rule, it is advisable to measure the NA levels of respondents wherever feasible; if this is impossible, the researcher must rely on random group assignment or pre/post designs.

At a more basic level, the strong influence of NA on stress and symptom measures indicates that researchers must consider the person—the individual employee—as well as environmental factors such as office environments, job responsibilities, noise levels, and so on. Stress research has traditionally focused on the environment, attempting to identify acute events (e.g., traffic and pollution levels, financial problems) that generate stress responses. Underlying such studies is the implicit idea that once relevant stressors are identified they can be reduced or eliminated, thereby attenuating these stress reactions.

Identifying external sources of stress is no doubt important, but our research demonstrates that dispositional sources are crucial as well. High NA individuals are capable of experiencing a great deal of stress and discomfort even in relatively benign contexts. Their high levels of distress will likely persist in the face of dramatically altered working conditions. As Hackman (1969) notes, "For some men dissatisfaction is a way of life. These men will find something to be irritated by, no matter what the situation" (p. 127).

The recent work on job attitudes by Staw and his colleagues (Staw, Bell & Clausen, 1985; Staw & Ross, 1985) demonstrates the importance of dispositional factors such as NA in organizational research. Staw and Ross (1985) report a longitudinal analysis of the job attitudes of 5,000 middle-aged men. They found that a single-item index of job satisfaction measured in 1966 accounted for more job-attitude variance in 1971 than could objective changes in job context (including changes in employer, occupation, job status, and pay). Similarly, Staw et al. (1985) developed a multi-item index of general emotional temperament (which they found to be stable over a 40-year period) that predicted job satisfaction across time and contexts, even as subjects changed jobs and occupations. Staw et al. conclude:

The stability of job attitudes identified by Staw and Ross and the present finding that job attitudes are influenced by affective disposition both imply that it may be extremely difficult to improve job attitudes via external interventions. Job redesign efforts may, for example, be prone to failure since they must contend with strong forces for stability—forces that either make individuals resistant to change or prompt individuals to return over time to their baseline states. (p. 23)

Clearly these comments have implications not only for researchers who study stress, but also for management practitioners who design job-related interventions.

Stress and Health

In light of the NA construct, and of the interrelatedness of stress, symptoms, and negative moods, we must re-examine the question of how stress affects long-term health status. As we have seen, people who report a great deal of stress also have a large number of physical complaints and problems. DeLongis et al. (1982) report similar findings with the Hassles Scale—people who cite many hassles in their lives also report more physical problems. But beyond reporting more aches and pains and other discomforts, do highly stressed people really suffer from poorer health—that is, are they more susceptible to major diseases, chronic disability, and premature death, as Selye (1976) proposed?

The answer is not entirely clear, but research to date suggests that NA itself is not highly predictive of long-term health status. Research in our laboratory indicates that NA measures are uncorrelated with various indices of cardiovascular status (e.g., blood pressure and heart rate levels, chronic hypertension; see Pennebaker & Watson, 1986). We have also found NA to be a poor predictor of objective measures of health-relevant behavior, such as number of doctor visits during the past year, or number of work days missed due to illness.

Costa and McCrae (1980) report similar results. They note, for example, that while NA (they call it "Neuroticism") correlates significantly with reports of chest pain, it is unrelated to objective indicators of coronary artery disease. After reviewing a number of such studies, they conclude that NA "influences perceptions of health, but not health itself" (p. 24).

Thus, in health research NA may represent a substantial nuisance factor — a major source of variance in measures of stress and symptoms that is ultimately unrelated to long-term objective health status. This problem may be especially severe owing to the potential for substantial common method variance in self-report data (cf. Kasl, 1978). One obvious way around this problem is to go beyond simple self-report symptom scales and use more objective indicators of health status and health-related behaviors. These might include: (a) physicians' ratings of health, (b) physiological measures (e.g., blood pressure), (c) number of days of work missed due to illness or injury, (d) number of days hospitalized during the past year, and (e) number of medical visits due to illness or injury (see Folger & Belew, 1985, for a discussion regarding the use of various behaviorally based, unobtrusive or nonreactive measures of stress reactions).

NA as a Nuisance Factor

This leads us to the more general issue of NA's influence on work performance. Watson and Clark (1984) document the consequences of NA for the individual: A high NA person is extremely distressed and self-dissatisfied, suffers from poor self-esteem, and is likely to seek relief in the form of therapy or another type of psychological intervention. But is NA a concern for the employer as well — that is, because high NA workers are likely to report more dissatisfaction with their jobs (along with everything else in their lives), are they thereby poorer workers? We know of no relevant data, but we would caution researchers and management practitioners against making such an inference. High NA workers are likely to report stress and dissatisfaction, but this may not translate into meaningful behavioral deficits in areas such as productivity and absenteeism. As in the area of health, we caution researchers and practitioners against making a simple correspondence between subjective factors (i.e., symptoms, dissatisfaction) and objective, behavioral effects (long-term health, work performance). Once again, NA may operate largely as a nuisance factor.

The Causality Problem

Another disquieting implication of the NA construct concerns the general problem of causality. As an example of the problem, consider the following common sense causal model: Some aspect of a job is extremely frustrating and so causes undue stress. Over time, according to this simple causal model, the stress will cause health problems that are measured by symptom reports. The NA findings demonstrate that such a model is not tenable without *very* careful testing. That is, perceptions of frustration, stress, and physical symptoms all represent the same construct. To say that one of the three components—frustration, stress, or symptoms—causes the other (without measurement of all three at three different points in time) simply has no meaning.

A particularly relevant example of this problem is evident in the current popularization of the Hassles Scale (Kanner et al., 1981). According to the authors of the scale, the degree to which we perceive minor irritants in our daily lives (e.g., waiting in line, being in traffic) is related to chronic low levels of stress. Over time, these hassles are causally related to health problems. In testing this, Delongis et al. (1982) and, more recently, Lazarus et al. (1985) note that the measurement of hassles is related to reports of psychological distress and physical symptoms. Based on our discussion, it is clear why this claim cannot be validated. *The process related to the perception of hassles is the same process related to the perception of symptoms.* In short, a person who feels bad will perceive hassles and symptoms. To some extent, each undoubtedly causes the other and both reciprocally influence one another; surely, causality in this instance can not be simply or easily discerned.

One way around this problem, similar to that proposed for health measures, is to assess stressors as objectively as possible, independent of subjective reactions to these stimuli. This is the general approach advocated by Dohrenwend and Shrout (1985; but see Lazarus et al., 1985, for an opposing point of view). Measures that assess subjective reactions to events (e.g., by asking employees to identify sources of discomfort and stress in their work environment, or by asking them to evaluate the aversiveness of various aspects of their jobs) will likely contain a very sizable NA component. To minimize NA's influence, one must bypass this subjective element. For example, rather than merely asking people how pleasant or aversive they find the noise level in their office, researchers might directly measure the noise level in the environment. Similarly, rather than simply asking people how well they like their co-workers, researchers might assess objective patterns of social activity (e.g., frequency of contact).

Of course, ideally researchers should measure *both* subjective and objective components of stress. The point we are making here is that researchers need to go beyond simple subjective measures, and that they should try to assess subjective and objective factors as independently as possible. Only in this manner can their separate effects be evaluated. An overreliance on self-report as the exclusive method of measurement, by contrast, neglects opportunities for objective assessment at several levels: not only at the level of the stressor's objective features as discussed above (e.g., decibel levels, frequency of contact), but also with regard to the physiological substrate (e.g., changes in blood pressure) and overt behavior (e.g., absenteeism). Folger and Belew (1985) have discussed some of the advantages, as well as the challenges, in adopting a multi-measure approach that combines subjective and objective indicators.

BEYOND STRESS AND DISTRESS: THE TWO DIMENSIONS OF FEELING

Thus far we have discussed various issues relating to the definition and measurement of stress. We have seen that stress perceptions are part of the larger, more general NA construct, which subsumes stress, physical symptoms, and negative emotional states. Although NA is clearly an important and pervasive psychological factor, by itself it provides an incomplete picture of the individual's overall level of coping and well-being. A comprehensive account requires considering an additional, independent dimension of positive feeling — Positive Affectivity.

The Two-factor Structure of Mood

Two dominant, independent dimensions consistently emerge in factor analyses of self-rated mood (Watson, Clark & Tellegen, 1984; Watson & Tellegen, 1985). The first, negative affect, has already been discussed. The second, positive affect, is quite different in its nature and in its implications. Positive affect reflects a state of pleasurable arousal, activation or engagement — it represents the degree to which one feels excited and enthusiastic, full of life and energy. Mood descriptors such as *excited, enthusiastic, delighted, active, energetic, alert* and *determined* best capture the distinctive flavor of this mood factor.

Positive affect and negative affect have quite different correlates. For example, positive affect is related to diverse measures of social activity, including frequency of contact and satisfaction with friends and relations; making new acquaintances; involvement in social organizations; and general patterns of social activity, such as interacting with people versus being alone or not interacting (e.g., Beiser, 1974; Bradburn, 1969; Clark & Watson, 1986; Moriwaki, 1974). Positive affect is also correlated with a variety of environmental factors, and biological or socially determined rhythms, including weather variables (e.g., rainfall, hours of sunshine), the circadian cycle, the day of the week, and the season of the year (Clark & Watson, 1986; Rossi & Rossi, 1977; Sanders & Brizzolara, 1982; Smith, 1979; Stone, Hedges, Neale & Satin, 1985; Thayer, 1978). Like negative affect, positive affect also has a strong dispositional component (Positive Affectivity, or PA). PA is strongly associated with trait measures of extraversion and well-being (Costa & McCrae, 1980; Tellegen, 1982; Watson & Clark, 1984). In our research we most commonly use the 11-item Positive Emotionality Scale from Tellegen's MPQ (Tellegen, 1982) as our PA measure.

In contrast to NA, PA is completely unrelated to stress perceptions and physical complaints. A person can feel energetic and enthusiastic about life, for example, even in the face of substantial stress and discomfort (or conversely, one can feel listless, apathetic and bored in the absence of stress). It is easy to generate examples illustrating this pattern. In the job context, for example, it is entirely possible that a promotion provokes transient (or perhaps even long-term) increases in both positive and negative affect. That is, a promotion may increase both the employee's distress (because of heightened responsibilities, pressures, and time demands) and enthusiasm (because of increased power and status, better perquisites, etc.).

The Type A coronary-prone personality provides an especially interesting illustration of this point. In our studies of normal adults we have found that the Type A pattern (as measured by the Jenkins Activity Survey; Jenkins, Rosenman & Friedman, 1967) is associated with high levels of both PA and NA. It is easy to see why. A hard-driving, ambitious and time-pressured person will undoubtedly experience much stress and strain (high NA); but at the same time, he or she may lead an interesting and stimulating life (high PA).

The important point is that positive and negative affect (and their corresponding dispositions, PA and NA) are independent, unrelated dimensions. Researchers seeking a comprehensive assessment of well-being and satisfaction in the work environment are thus advised to measure both factors (see Watson & Clark, 1984; Watson & Tellegen, 1985).

Other Two-Factor Models

Somewhat similar two-factor models have at times captured the attention of organizational scientists. Noteworthy among these are Maslow's Need Hierarchy (Maslow, 1954, 1968) and Herzberg's Motivation-Hygiene Theory (Herzberg, 1966, 1976; Herzberg, Mausner & Snyderman, 1959). Although our PA/NA framework may superficially resemble these models in certain aspects, there are also important differences, which we will briefly note.

Maslow's Need Hierarchy

In Maslow's view, higher-level human needs emerge only as stronger, more basic needs are satisfied. He distinguishes between two fundamental types of motives: The lower, or deficiency (D) needs (for physical comfort and security, self-esteem, love and belongingness), and the higher growth or self-actualization (SA) needs. One can largely identify the D-needs with NA, and the SA-needs with PA. The D-needs operate on a tension-reduction model: An unfulfilled deficiency need causes subjective distress (high NA), while its satisfaction produces feelings of relief (low NA). The D-need is itself aversive, and represents an unpleasant state of arousal; only its satisfaction is pleasurable. Prolonged frustration of the D-needs can lead to illness and maladjustment.

The SA-needs, on the other hand, generate pleasurable states of arousal or activation that the individual is motivated to maintain or even enhance. Failure to satisfy these needs produces feelings of apathy and boredom (low PA); their fulfillment generates feelings of excitement and delight (high PA) and produces a positive state of health.

Maslow's model can thus be easily translated into PA and NA terms. One obvious difference is that in his hierarchical view NA is prepotent; that is, the SA-needs (generating PA) will emerge only after the D-needs (generating NA) are basically satisfied. And, according to Maslow, most people remain stuck at this D-need/NA level. Our studies, on the other hand, indicate that PA and NA are parallel dimensions that exist simultaneously. PA is, therefore, a factor relevant to all individuals, not simply those who have reached a certain stage of development (see also Herzberg, 1976, p. 48).

Herzberg's Motivation-Hygiene Theory

Herzberg's model stipulates that the factors producing job satisfaction and dissatisfaction are distinct and independent. Specifically, he argues that intrinsic factors (e.g., achievement, responsibility, the nature of the work itself), which he calls "motivators," produce satisfaction; while extrinsic factors, or "hygienes" (e.g., benefits, working conditions, interpersonal relations) generate dissatisfaction.

It is easy to identify satisfaction with PA and dissatisfaction with NA, and in this respect our view resembles Herzberg's. Like Herzberg, we believe that these two affects are distinct and independent dimensions that have very different causes and correlates. However, unlike Herzberg, we do not feel that the factors related to PA and NA can be distinguished according to a simple dichotomy of intrinsic versus extrinsic. We have already noted various factors differentially related to the two dimensions of affectivity; for example, stress and physical complaints correlate with NA, while social parameters are strongly associated with PA. But the matter of which factors affect NA, and which influence PA, is an empirical question; rather than proposing a general scheme along these lines, we instead suggest that researchers study both positive and negative feelings concerning the job and job environment, and determine empirically the distinctive correlates of these two important affective dimensions.

Herzberg's work has been controversial, and we certainly do not endorse either his intrinsic/extrinsic dichotomy (as he has described it in relation to satisfaction/dissatisfaction) or his list of presumed correlates of satisfaction and dissatisfaction. Moreover, NA and PA emerge as independent factors in a wide variety of mood and personality measures; as such, the identification of these affective dimensions is not subject to the methodological criticisms that have dogged Herzberg's analysis of "critical incidents" reported in semi-structured interviews. The point is that one can be critical of Herzberg's motivation-hygiene theory and yet at the same time endorse a two-factor structure of affect. As we have suggested, this two-factor approach offers promising leads for especially fruitful new research directions on the topic of stress.

CONCLUSIONS

Our concluding recommendations can be highlighted by first noting some topics we have had to slight in this review. Space limitations have precluded, for example, a discussion of factors that influence how people perceive and report physical symptoms and sensations (see Pennebaker, 1982). Likewise, it has been impossible to devote adequate attention to the problems and prospects of objective (e.g., behavioral, nonreactive) measures—along with the fascinating issues that arise when speculation turns to the possible varieties of relationships among subjective and objective indicators (see Folger & Belew, 1985). As noted, however, these issues have been addressed elsewhere.

Instead, our focus has centered on what we consider to be some exciting new research and measurement strategies. Our chief recommendation is that stress researchers take note of the dual nature characterizing affective responses. The dichotomy of NA and PA is now well established at the level of self-report, and there are intriguing possibilities that the independence of these factors may reflect a fundamental dichotomy at the physiological level as well.

We have also emphasized the dispositional nature of both NA and PA, and the existence of stable individual differences on these dimensions has implications for management practitioners. As was mentioned in connection with the work on job attitudes by Staw and his colleagues (Staw et al., 1985; Staw & Ross, 1985), the stability of affective reactions is a phenomenon with which practitioners will have to contend when implementing organizational change. Objectively positive changes (e.g., improvements in working conditions) may not be reflected in attitude changes by employees, or at least not by some employees. High-NA employees, for example, are particularly likely to remain expressively dissatisfied on self-report measures despite workplace improvements. The consequence is that assessments of both the need for change as well as the effects of change will be prone to misinterpretation unless the possible influence of these temperamental dispositions is taken into account (e.g., in the most problematic case, where a surveyed workforce contained a large number of high-NA individuals, the need for change would be overestimated and the positive impact of change would be underestimated).

Thus, in addition to broader implications of the two-factor structure underlying affective responses, our discussion has highlighted that NA may operate as a nuisance factor in self-report data. To the extent various self-report measures all tap the same underlying NA construct, presumed "independent variables" and "dependent variables" in many stress studies may represent little more than different measures of the same thing — and that *thing* is not necessarily the construct of stress, but perhaps merely the predisposition to respond negatively.

REFERENCES

Beck, A. T., Ward, C. H., Mendelson, M., Mock, J. & Erbaugh, J. (1961). An inventory for measuring depression. *Archives of General Psychiatry, 4*, 561–571.

Beiser, M. (1974). Components and correlates of mental well-being. *Journal of Health and Social Behavior, 15*, 320–327.

Bradburn, N. M. (1969). *The structure of psychological well-being.* Chicago: Aldine.

Clark, L. A. & Watson, D. (1986). *Mood and the mundane: Relations among daily life events and self-reported mood.* Manuscript submitted for publication.

Costa, P. T. & McCrae, R. R. (1980). Influence of extraversion and neuroticism on subjective well-being: Happy and unhappy people. *Journal of Personality and Social Psychology, 38*, 668–678.

DeLongis, A., Coyne, J. C., Dakof, G., Folkman, S. & Lazarus, R. S. (1982). Relationship of daily hassles, uplifts, and major life events to health status. *Health Psychology, 1,* 119–136.

Depue, R. A. & Monroe, S. M. (1986). Conceptualization and measurement of human disorder in life stress research: The problem of chronic disturbance. *Psychological Bulletin, 99,* 36–51.

Derogatis, L. R., Lipman, R. S., Rickels, K., Uhlenhuth, E. H. & Covi, L. (1974). The Hopkins Symptom Checklist (HSCL): A self-report symptom inventory. *Behavioral Science, 19,* 1–15.

Dohrenwend, B. P. (1974). Problems in defining and sampling the relevant population of stressful life events. In B. S. Dohrenwend & B. P. Dohrenwend (Eds.), *Stressful life events: Their nature and effects* (pp. 275–310). New York: Wiley.

Dohrenwend, B. P. (1979). Stressful life events and psychopathology: Some issues of theory and method. In J. E. Barrett & R. M. Rose (Eds.), *Stress and mental disorder* (pp. 1–15). New York: Raven Press.

Dohrenwend, B. P. & Shrout, P. E. (1985). "Hassles" in the conceptualization and measurement of life stress variables. *American Psychologist, 40*, 780–785.

Eckenrode, J. (1984). Impact of chronic and acute stressors on daily reports of mood. *Journal of Personality and Social Psychology, 46*, 907–918.

Eysenck, H. J. & Eysenck, S. B. G. (1968). *Manual for the Eysenck Personality Inventory.* San Diego, CA: Educational and Industrial Testing Service.

Folkman, S., Lazarus, R. S., Gruen, R. J. & DeLongis, A. (1986). Appraisal, coping, health status, and psychological symptoms. *Journal of Personality and Social Psychology, 50,* 571–579.

Folger, R. & Belew, J. (1985). Nonreactive measurement: A focus for research on absenteeism and occupational stress. *Research in Organizational Behavior, 7,* 129–170.

Fuller, J. L. & Thompson, W. R. (1978). *Foundations of behavior genetics.* St. Louis, MO: Mosby.

Goldberg, E. L. & Comstock, G. W. (1976). Life events and subsequent illness. *American Journal of Epidemiology, 104,* 146–158.

Hackman, R. C. (1969). *The motivated working adult.* New York: American Management Association.

Herzberg, F. (1966). *Work and the nature of man.* Cleveland: World.

Herzberg, F. (1976). *The managerial choice: To be efficient and to be human.* Homewood, IL: Dow-Jones-Irwin.

Herzberg, F., Mausner, B. & Snyderman, B. S. (1959). *The motivation to work.* New York: Wiley.

Holmes, T. H. & Rahe, R. H. (1967). The Social Readjustment Rating Scale. *Journal of Psychosomatic Research, 11,* 213–218.

Horowitz, M. J. (1976). *Stress response syndromes.* New York: Jacob Aronson.

Jenkins, C. D., Rosenman, R. H. & Friedman, M. (1967). Development of an objective test for the determination of the coronary-prone behavior pattern in employed men. *Journal of Chronic Diseases, 20,* 371–379.

Kanner, A. D., Coyne, J. C., Schaefer, C. & Lazarus, R. S. (1981). Comparison of two modes of stress measurement: Daily hassles and uplifts versus major life events. *Journal of Behavioral Medicine, 4,* 1–39.

Kasl, S. V. (1978). Epidemiological contributions to the study of work stress. In C. L. Cooper & R. Payne (Eds.), *Stress at work.* New York: Wiley.

Krug, S. E., Scheier, I. H. & Cattell, R. B. (1976). *Handbook for the IPAT Anxiety Scale* (rev. ed.). Champaign, IL: Institute for Personality and Ability Testing.

Lazarus, R. S., DeLongis, A., Folkman, S. & Gruen, R. (1985). Stress and adaptional outcomes: The problem of confounded measures. *American Psychologist, 40,* 770–779.

Leon, G. R., Gillum, B., Gillum, R. & Gouze, M. (1979). Personality stability and change over a 30-year period—middle age to old age. *Journal of Consulting and Clinical Psychology, 47,* 517–524.

Lykken, D. T. (1982). Research with twins: The concept of emergenesis. *Psychophysiology, 11,* 249–270.

Maslow, A. H. (1954). *Motivation and personality.* New York: Harper.

Maslow, A. H. (1968). *Toward a psychology of being* (2nd ed.). Princeton: Van Nostrand.

Mason, J. W. (1975). A historical view of the stress field. *Journal of Human Stress, 1,* 22–36.

Monroe, S. M. (1983). Major and minor life events as predictors of psychological distress: Further issues and findings. *Journal of Behavioral Medicine, 6,* 189–205.

Moriwaki, S. Y. (1974). The Affect Balance Scale: A validity study with aged samples. *Journal of Gerontology, 29,* 73–78.

Pearlin, L. I. (1983). Role strains and personal stress. In H. B. Kaplan (Ed.), *Psychosocial stress: Trends in theory and research* (pp. 3–32). New York: Academic Press.

Pearlin, L. I., Lieberman, M. A., Menaghan, E. G. & Mullan, J. T. (1981). The stress process. *Journal of Health and Social Behavior, 19,* 2–21.

Pennebaker, J. W. (1982). *The psychology of physical symptoms.* New York: Springer-Verlag.

Pennebaker, J. W. & Watson, D. (1986). *Blood pressure perception among normotensives and hypertensives.* Manuscript submitted for publication.

Rabkin, J. G. & Struening, E. L. (1976). Life events, stress, and illness. *Science, 194,* 1013–1020.

Rahe, R. H. (1974). The pathway between subjects' recent life changes and their near-future illness reports: Representative results and methodological issues. In B. S. Dohrenwend &

B. P. Dohrenwend (Eds.), *Stressful life events: Their nature and effects* (pp. 73–86). New York: Wiley.

Rossi, A. S. & Rossi, P. E. (1977). Body time and social time: Mood patterns by menstrual cycle phase and day of the week. *Social Science Research, 6*, 273–308.

Sanders, J. L. & Brizzolara, J. (1982). Relationship between weather and mood. *Journal of General Psychology, 107*, 155–156.

Scarr, S., Webber, P. L., Weinberg, R. A. & Wittig, M. A. (1981). Personality resemblance among adolescents and their parents in biologically related and adoptive families. *Journal of Personality and Social Psychology, 40*, 885–898.

Schroeder, D. H. & Costa, P. T. (1984). Influence of life event stress on physical illness: Substantive effects or methodological flaws? *Journal of Personality and Social Psychology, 46*, 853–863.

Selye, H. (1976). *The stress of life*. New York: McGraw-Hill.

Smith, T. W. (1979). Happiness: Time trends, seasonal variations, intersurvey differences, and other mysteries. *Social Psychology Quarterly, 42*, 18–30.

Spielberger, C. D., Gorsuch, R. L. & Lushene, R. E. (1970). *Manual for the State-Trait Anxiety Inventory*. Palo Alto, CA: Consulting Psychologists Press.

Staw, B. M., Bell, N. E. & Clausen, J. A. (1985). *The dispositional approach to job attitudes: A lifetime longitudinal test*. Manuscript submitted for publication.

Staw, B. M. & Ross, J. (1985). Stability in the midst of change: A dispositional approach to job attitudes. *Journal of Applied Psychology, 70*, 469–480.

Stone, A. A., Hedges, S. M., Neale, J. M. & Satin, M. S. (1985). Prospective and cross-sectional reports offer no evidence of a "Blue Monday" phenomenon. *Journal of Personality and Social Psychology, 49*, 129–134.

Taylor, J. A. (1953). A personality scale of manifest anxiety. *Journal of Abnormal and Social Psychology, 48*, 285–290.

Tellegen, A. (1982). *Brief manual for the Differential Personality Questionnaire*. Unpublished manuscript, University of Minnesota, Minneapolis.

Thayer, R. E. (1978). Toward a psychological theory of multidimensional activation (arousal). *Motivation and Emotion, 2*, 1–34.

Watson, D. (1986). *Negative Affectivity and its implications for mood, stress and symptom reporting over time*. Unpublished manuscript, Southern Methodist University.

Watson, D. & Clark, L. A. (1984). Negative Affectivity: The disposition to experience aversive emotional states. *Psychological Bulletin, 96*, 465–490.

Watson, D., Clark, L. A. & Tellegen, A. (1984). Cross-cultural convergence in the structure of mood: A Japanese replication and a comparison with U.S. findings. *Journal of Personality and Social Psychology, 47*, 127–144.

Watson, D. & Tellegen, A. (1985). Toward a consensual structure of mood. *Psychological Bulletin, 98*, 219–235.

Zevon, M. A. & Tellegen, A. (1982). The structure of mood change: An idiographic/nomothetic analysis. *Journal of Personality and Social Psychology, 43*, 111–122.

PART IV: ORGANIZATIONAL STUDIES OF STRESS

Machine Pacing and Shiftwork: Evidence for Job Stress

Joseph J. Hurrell, Jr.
Michael J. Colligan

SUMMARY. Machine-paced work and shiftwork are highly prevalent working conditions commonly believed to have adverse individual and organizational consequences. This article examines the empirical evidence for such effects, and acknowledges the conceptual and methodological problems which have clearly plagued pacing and shiftwork researchers. The literature on pacing while suggestive of overall health and performance effects indicates that the magnitude of such effects are in all likelihood situationally and individually determined. Very little is known, however, about such interactions. Similarly, the shiftwork literature is contradictory and inconclusive. Shiftwork appears to affect both the quality and quantity of sleep and to disrupt a wide range of physiological and behavioral circadian rhythms. The long-term consequences of these effects are still not known.

Joseph J. Hurrell, Jr. and Michael J. Colligan are affiliated with the National Institute for Occupational Safety and Health, Division of Biomedical and Behavioral Sciences, Cincinnati, OH.

Almost from inception, machine-paced work and shiftwork have been implicated as risk factors in the development of a variety of psychological and physical disorders. Both figure prominently in current job stress models as potent stressors capable of producing adverse individual and organizational strain consequences. Yet, in spite of these allegations, machine-paced work and shiftwork continue to flourish seemingly as a result of their economic advantages. Indeed, it has been estimated that there are over 50 million people worldwide in machine-paced jobs (Salvendy, 1981) and that over 20 percent of the working population in Europe and North America work some form of shift system (Tasto, Colligan, Skjei & Polly, 1978). This article will examine evidence for both the individual and organizational strain consequences of these highly prevalent working conditions.

MACHINE PACING

The Pacing Concept

The terms pacing, machine-pacing and forced paced work have been commonly used in the literature to refer to activity which requires a worker to perform a response or series of responses at a rate other than that which would be self-selected (Dudley, 1962; Franks, 1974; Murrell, 1963). Attempts to understand the relationship between paced work, health, and performance, however, have been hampered by a general lack of consistency among authors regarding definitions and descriptions of task structures. While several taxonomies have been proposed for the characterization and evaluation of paced work (Dainoff, Hurrell & Happ, 1981; Salvendy, 1981), they have not been widely used.

The extent to which the worker has control over the work process is clearly central to the concept of pacing. In paced work, control is manifested along two orthogonal dimensions: over the initialization of the task and over the duration of the work cycle (Dainoff et al., 1981). The extent to which the worker as opposed to the machine (or external environment) has control over either or both of these functions may be used to classify paced systems (Dainoff et al., 1981). Jobs in which the worker both initiates a task and controls the length of time it takes to complete it are clearly self-paced (sometimes called nonpaced or unpaced). Jobs in which a machine (or some element of the external environment) both initiates the task and controls its duration are typically referred to as paced or machine-paced. Though little studied, paced jobs also exist in which the worker initiates the task after which the machine (or external environment) controls its duration or the machine initiates the task after which the worker controls its duration.

Temporal parameters are also important in characterizing paced systems. Cycle time is generally defined as the amount of time between beginning work on successive units of work. Service time is the amount of time a worker actually takes when working on a unit and delay or operator waiting time is the difference between operator service time and cycle time. Tolerance time, a machine parameter, is generally defined (cf. Franks, 1974; Sury, 1967) as the amount of time that a unit is available for processing before it is missed. These three parameters — operator service time, delay time (these sum to cycle time) and tolerance time have been used by various researchers to describe the temporal characteristics of pacing.

Adding to the complexity, the nature of the work being paced may vary considerably with respect to both the physical and cognitive effort required to perform it. While most research on pacing has focused on assembly line tasks, the advent of computerized industrial and office systems in recent years has resulted in the creation of a new generation of paced jobs utilizing more of the workers' information processing rather than physical capability. Such jobs are usually short-cycled, repetitive, and involve search and discovery, recognition, decision and action components and unlike assembly line tasks, they often require different responses to each part or element being presented.

Thus, numerous varieties of pacing exist which require vastly different amounts and kinds of cognitive and motor activity from the worker. Unfortunately, as indicated above, studies concerned with the individual and organizational consequences of pacing have often failed to adequately document the control, temporal, and task characteristics of the system being studied. Thus, one often knows little more about the independent variable being considered except that it is something called pacing. The feature or features which produce an effect (e.g., type of control, temporal constraints, cognitive or motor demands, etc.) is (are) difficult to pinpoint. The following review is therefore largely limited to comparing the responses of workers in grossly defined paced systems of work to those of workers having non-paced jobs.

INDIVIDUAL CONSEQUENCES OF PACING

Physiological Effects

Physiological variables have been monitored in both laboratory and field studies to assess the demands of pacing. Cardiovascular parameters have generally received the greatest attention. Studies involving inspection (Koholova & Matoused, 1968), reaction time (Johansson & Lindstrom, 1975), and sorting tasks (Mackay, Cox, Watts, Thirlaway & Lazzerini, 1979) have reported higher mean heart rates (reflecting excess effort) for subjects in paced vs. self-paced conditions. Some evidence exists to suggest that pacing in such tasks may also be associated with elevations in blood pressure (Hokanson, Degood, Forrest & Brittain, 1971). No evidence for either elevated heart rate or blood pressure was found, however, in a study utilizing a paced marking-stapling task (Salvendy & Humphreys, 1979).

Decreases in heart rate variability are thought to reflect increases in mental load. Thus, if pacing places an additional load (above that imposed by self-paced work) on a worker's information processing capacity, it is believed that it should be reflected in decreases in variability. The evidence for such an effect, however, is mixed. While decreases in variability have been found in studies comparing paced vs. self-paced inspection (Coury, 1983; Drury, 1982), paced sorting and loading vs. minding (Mackay et al., 1979) and paced vs. self-paced marking-stapling (Salvendy & Humphreys, 1979), they were not found in a study of paced vs. self-paced light assembly (Manenica, 1977). The reasons for these discrepant findings are not clear.

A number of investigations have examined urinary catecholamine exertion rates (reflecting arousal) of paced and self-paced workers and experimental subjects. In the first of these, Frankenhaeuser and Gardell (1976) compared excretory rates of adrenaline and noradrenaline between fourteen workers engaged in paced jobs and ten workers in maintenance and other comparatively unrestricted work. Noradrenaline excretion was found to be highest among the paced workers while adrenaline excretion was found to be inversely related to the duration of the work cycle. Similar elevations in noradrenaline were reported by Mackay et al. (1979). Elevations in both adrenaline and noradrenaline for paced compared to self-paced sawmill workers have been reported by Johansson, Aronsson, and Lindstrom (1978). Reports of heightened feelings of arousal (Johansson et al., 1978) and irritation (Frankenhaeuser & Gardell, 1976) among paced workers are clearly consistent with these results.

More frequent health problems among paced workers have also been reported. In a Russian study of women engaged in a variety of paced and self-paced jobs (Samoilova, 1971), paced workers were found to have a higher incidence of cardiovascular disease, peripheral nervous system disorders and gastritis. These findings are consistent with the Frankenhaeuser and Gardells' (1976) results in which paced sawmill workers displayed a higher frequency of psychosomatic, cardiovascular, and nervous disorders than their self-paced controls. Findings of excess asthma and bronchitis among paced telegraphists (Ferguson, 1973) and angina among paced factory workers (Kritsikis, Heinemann & Eitner, 1968) have also been reported. It should also be noted that many paced jobs involve conditions (high demands accompanied by low control) found by Karasek (1981) to be predictive of cardiovascular diseases.

A number of studies (e.g., Luopajarvi, Kuorinka, Virolainen & Holmberg, 1979) have reported excess musculoskeletal complaints among paced workers. These complaints are likely a result of the repetitive movements associated with machine-paced tasks.

Psychological Effects

While it is commonly believed that paced work has adverse psychological consequences, surprisingly few studies have addressed the issue. In a large scale survey of over two thousand male workers in twenty-three occupations, Caplan, Cobb, French, Van Harrison, and Pinneau (1975) found levels of anxiety and depression among paced assemblers to exceed those of other workers engaged in less regimented work. More recently, Broadbent and Gath (1981) conducted an interview study of the mental health effects of pacing in a British auto assembly plant. The study was undertaken because medical records indicated that diagnoses of anxiety were highly prevalent among assembly line workers. The investigation is especially significant because of its attempt to differentiate the effects of pacing from those of repetition. Results of the study indicated that repetition was associated with job dissatisfaction but not increased anxiety. By contrast, pacing was associated with increased anxiety but not job dissatisfaction. Cycle time was also found to have no effect on either satisfaction or anxiety.

A recent study by Hurrell (1985) also found evidence of increased affective disturbances among paced workers. In this study, scores on measures of six mood states from over two thousand male and female operators of paced letter sorting machines were compared to those of male and female postal workers engaged in non-paced work. No instances were discovered in which either paced males or paced females, failed to report significantly higher scores than their self-paced counterparts.

ORGANIZATIONAL CONSEQUENCES OF PACING

Performance Effects

Unquestionably the greatest amount of research conducted in the area of pacing has been concerned with performance. This research seems to have been given its original impetus by an extensive yet largely descriptive field study conducted by Wyatt and Langdon (1938). This study showed that when machine speeds were progressively changed in paced work, an optimum work rate could be found which differed from worker to worker. In the ensuing years, researchers have attempted to identify factors influencing this optimum work rate.

Conrad (1955, 1960) was the first investigator to systematically consider individual performance in a variety of paced and self-paced tasks. In these studies, it was found that when the tolerance time is relatively long, paced work may yield the same output as unpaced work. But, when the tolerance time is more restricted, there are periods when the subject is unprepared to respond and the unit either waits or is not processed. Periods when subjects were ready too soon were also found.

Expanding upon these studies, Dudley (1962, 1963) examined the distribution of work cycle times of experienced operators in several paced tasks. In general, self-paced workers displayed a positive skewing toward longer cycle times. By contrast, in paced work, there was a strong tendency toward a much more nearly normal distribution of cycle times. These findings suggest that performance decrements associated with pacing may be a consequence of workers having to accommodate a few longer cycles within tolerance time (Belbin & Stammers, 1972).

Other laboratory and field studies comparing paced and self-paced performance have consistently shown less output and/or more errors in the paced condition. Tasks examined here include: testing electrical parts (Murrell, 1963), conveyor line assembly (e.g., Franks, 1974), card sorting (Salvendy, 1972), stapling-marking (Salvendy & Humphreys, 1979), timber grading (Seppala & Nieminen, 1981) and mail sorting (Bertelson, Boons & Renkin, 1965). Reaction times have also been found to be faster for self-paced subjects (Beck, 1963).

There is some evidence that the effects of pacing on performance may be mediated by individual worker characteristics. Brown (1957), for example, found that the pace set for men in their twenties on a grid matching task could not easily be maintained by men in their forties and fifties. These results are consistent with reports that older workers tend to move away from paced jobs (e.g., Belbin & Stammers, 1972; Chase, 1974). Other studies, however, have found that older workers are more energy efficient under paced conditions and less prone to nontask-related movements (Salvendy, 1972). These discrepancies suggest that the mediating effects of age (and quite likely other individual characteristics) are task dependent.

Personality characteristics also appear to mediate paced performance on certain tasks. Eskew and Riche (1982), for example, found that paced subjects displaying an internal locus of control performed more poorly in an inspection task than those displaying an external locus of control. Individuals who are trusting, introverted, less intelligent, more tense, and possessing a high tolerance for boredom have also been found to be more suited to various kinds of paced work (Salvendy & Humphreys, 1979; Stagner, 1975).

Job Satisfaction

Investigations considering job satisfaction among paced and self-paced workers have yielded mixed findings. While a number of studies have found increased dissatisfaction among paced workers (Caplan et al., 1975; Hurrell, Smith, Burg & Hicks, 1985; Walker & Marriott, 1952), others (Broadbent & Gath, 1981; Kalimo, Leppanen, Verkasalo, Peltomaa & Seppala, 1981; Khaleque, 1979) have found no differences. The reasons for these discrepant results are unclear but may apart from pacing be due to difficulties in controlling differences in the jobs being compared. In the Kalimo et al. (1981) study, for example, the authors could not control for differences in the wages paid to paced and self-paced workers. A prospective study of paced letter sorters (Arndt, Hurrell & Smith, 1981), however, has found progressive decreases in satisfaction following job entry.

Studies of differences in absenteeism and job turnover between paced and self-paced workers have produced more consistent findings. Fried, Weitman and Davis (1972) studied absentee rates in a paper products factory. Pacing, independent of wage, was found to be significantly related to frequency of absence. Likewise, Ferguson (1973) in a study utilizing two-year attendance records from seven hundred paced telegraphists and eight hundred self-paced workers serving as controls, found significantly higher absence among the telegraphists. Similarly, Chase (1974) in a survey of ninety-five large manufacturing companies found the highest turnover rates among paced employees.

Remarkably consistent findings exist concerning potential sources of job dissatisfaction in paced work. Monotony was the most frequently reported complaint among paced workers in studies by Frankenhaeuser and Gardell (1976), Ferguson (1973), and Walker and Marriott (1952). Likewise, Caplan et al. (1975) found that paced assemblers reported greater levels of boredom than the twenty-two other occupations represented in their study. Another consistently reported (Frankenhaeuser & Gardell, 1976; Ferguson, 1973) and objectively verified (Faunce, 1958) complaint among paced workers is the inability to interact with fellow workers. Consistent findings (Caplan et al., 1975; Ferguson, 1973; Hurrell et al., 1985) also exist with respect to paced workers feeling that their skills and abilities are underutilized.

CONCLUSIONS CONCERNING PACING

In addition to the conceptual problems noted earlier many of the studies reviewed here have limitations which further inhibit overall inferences about pacing. The field studies comparing paced and self-paced work are generally retrospective and self-report in nature and fail to control for a host of potentially confounding variables such as age, pay, shiftwork, length of employment, socioeconomic status and others. The laboratory studies, while giving a somewhat clearer picture of performance consequences, are of short duration and in many ways unrealistic. The extent, magnitude, and long-term health consequences of physiological changes in response to pacing are likewise unclear. Adding to this confusion, some of the effects of pacing appear to be task and individually specific. It seems trite to say that more research is needed but such is clearly the case. Prospective studies controlling for the aforementioned confounding factors are particularly needed. What else can then be said? From the studies reviewed above, it is clear that while the effects of pacing on individuals and organizations are not in all cases negative, they are seldom positive. When a choice is possible, the best choice appears to be self-paced work.

SHIFTWORK

Shiftwork, by requiring that individuals work at times which are contrary to their customary diurnal activity patterns, poses a potential threat to a wide range of physiological, psychological, and behavioral functions. Processes as diverse as respiration and heart rate, blood pressure, urine excretion, cell mitosis, enzyme production, reaction time, vigilance, and memory have been shown to follow a 24-hour (i.e., "circadian") rhythm in relation to the diurnal activity cycle (Luce, 1970). Shiftwork, and particularly night work, imposes on the worker an alteration or inversion of the normal activity cycle by obliging him or her to be alert and active during the night time hours while attempting to rest or sleep during the day. The ease with which an individual can adjust to various shifts is obviously a complicated matter. It can depend not only on the adaptability of the activity cycle to change in accord with the demands of the work schedule, but also on the ability of the numerous circadian processes to maintain their phase relationship with the altered activity cycle and with each other. To get a clearer picture of the issues involved in the adaptation process, it might be helpful to examine the research into the relationship between activity and body temperature.

Body Temperature and Activity

Body temperature evidences a relatively stable and predictable circadian pattern, falling to its ebb or low point at around 4 am during nocturnal sleep, rising rapidly to about 6-8 am when the individual normally awakens. It then gradually increases over the course of the day as the individual becomes more alert and active, reaching its peak at about 6 pm (Aschoff, 1981). The relationship between temperature and activity is more parallel than causal, however, as can be seen when the activity cycle is experimentally altered. Aschoff (1981) has summarized the results of a number of studies in which individuals were either kept active during their normal nocturnal sleep period or kept at bed rest during their normal daytime activity period and body temperature recorded. The effect in both cases was a general flattening of the temperature curve, but for different reasons. For the sleep-deprived individuals, body temperature remained slightly higher than normal throughout the night, whereas for the daytime-rested individuals, body temperature tended to be slightly lower than normal throughout the day. These studies suggest that whereas alterations in the sleep-rest cycle may influence body temperature, they do not produce a homologous phase shift in the temperature cycle. This appears to be the case even after 21 successive days on a night shift (Knauth & Rutenfranz, 1976). The implication, then, is that shiftwork disturbs not only the independent periodicity of the numerous circadian processes, but their interdependent synchrony as well. Given the number of processes involved and the fact that they are likely to be differently affected by a phase shift in the activity cycle, it seems improbable that shiftworkers ever completely adjust to the demands of their work schedule. The implications of this for the individual's health and performance are the topics of the following sections.

Individual Effects of Shiftwork

As one might expect, the most consistent effect of shiftwork on individual adjustment has been an impairment in the quality and quantity of sleep. Thus Tepas, Walsh, and Armstrong (1981) compared the reported sleep of groups of permanent and rotating shiftworkers and found that afternoon shift workers got significantly more sleep (averaging 7-1/2 hours per day) than any other shift while nightworkers got the least (averaging about 6 hours per day). Individuals working a day schedule fell in between, reporting about 7 hours of sleep per night. These findings replicated the results of a national sample of approximately 2000 shiftworkers previously reported by Tasto et al. (1978).

In addition to receiving less sleep than day workers, there is evidence that the quality of sleep of shiftworkers is poorer than that of day workers. As noted by Walsh, Tepas, and Moss (1981) and Weitzman and Kripke (1981), the general picture emerging from the research literature is that daytime sleep, as practiced by someone who must work at night, produces shorter rapid eye movement (REM) latency, fewer absolute minutes of REM sleep, less total sleep time, a greater percentage of slow wave sleep, less absolute stage 1 sleep, greater fragmentation of the sleep stages, and more frequent awakenings toward the end of the sleep cycle. The conclusion is that shiftwork does produce quantitative and qualitative changes in sleeping patterns. This has been related to feelings of fatigue and lethargy similar to that resulting from marginal sleep deprivation (Walsh et al., 1981). Still not understood are the long-range consequences, if any, these altered sleep patterns might have for long-range health and adjustment.

Research into the more general effects of shiftwork on individual physical well-being has produced results which are confusing and inconclusive. In part, this may be attributed to the methodological problems which beset the shiftwork researcher (Colligan, 1980). Field studies have tended to use cross-sectional designs extracting data from existing record sources (e.g., visits to company health clinics, health insurance claims, sickness absence) or self-report surveys to assess worker health. In addition to the deficiencies inherent in these data sources (e.g., reporting biases, validity), most cross-sectional studies suffer from selective attrition, that is, night shift workers who can't adjust to their work schedule may either quit or transfer to a different shift such that the shiftworkers sampled represent only the survivors. Obviously, well-controlled prospective studies are required which would provide a picture of the long-term effects (if any) of shiftwork on specific parameters of worker health.

Recognizing the shortcomings of the available literature, it appears that the most prevalent health consequence of shiftwork involves disorders of digestion and the gastrointestinal tract. This is presumably due to the fact that the diet and eating habits of the shiftworker are made irregular as a result of the work schedule, and that eating times may be out of phase with digestion-related circadian functions. Thus, Thiis-Evensen (1958) reported that 30% of the workers transferring from nondaytime to day schedules complained of gastritis. Digestive disorders were a frequent reason for sickness absence among night workers in a study by Walker and De La Mare (1971), and the results of other investigations (e.g., Thiis-Evensen, 1958, 1969; Wesseldijk, 1961) suggest that the incidence of ulcers may be 2-8 times higher among shiftworkers than among day workers. Still other studies (e.g., Mott, Mann, McLoughlin & Warwick, 1965; Dirken, 1966) have failed to replicate these findings.

The evidence linking shiftwork to other specific illnesses is inconclusive or nonexistent. Rutenfranz et al. (1977) surveyed the literature and concluded that shiftwork has no effects on the incidence of cardiovascular and nervous diseases. Harrington (1978) concluded that there were no dramatic health effects associated with shiftwork following his extensive review of the literature, and Dirken (1966) found that although shiftworkers reported more fatigue and general malaise, there was no clear symptom profile which would distinguish them from day workers.

ORGANIZATIONAL CONSEQUENCES OF SHIFTWORK

Safety and Performance Effects

Much of the research into the effects of shiftwork on safety and productivity suffers from the same methodological limitations cited above. Cross-sectional field comparisons of safety performance or efficiency across shifts are usually contaminated by extraneous differences in the nature and conditions of work being performed. Nevertheless, there is some evidence that industrial accidents tend to occur with greater frequency at certain times of the day, perhaps because worker performance is readily affected by disruption in circadian rhythms (Morgan, Brown & Alluisi, 1974). Although it is difficult to generalize across industries, Menzel (1950) found that most accidents in shift work systems seemed to occur between 10:00 pm and 2:00 am. Studies by Browne (1949) and Bjerner, Holm, and Swensson (1955) of telephone operators and gas meter readers, respectively, demonstrated that there were clear circadian patterns in the frequency of mistakes, with the greatest number tending to occur during late afternoon and early morning hours. In a more recent study, Colquhoun (1971) experimented with shift worker performance on simple tasks and found that performance was worse on night than on day shifts and that, once the sleep-wake cycle has been disrupted, there was a sharp drop in worker efficiency during the first few days, which tended to level off after about one week. Circadian periodicity in performance efficiency has consistently been demonstrated in the laboratory. Thus, Colquhoun (1976) has demonstrated that efficiency of signal detection, reaction time, and arithmetic calculations vary directly with the body temperature rhythm, peaking at about 4 pm and ebbing at roughly 9 am. Subsequent research (Folkard, Knauth, Monk & Rutenfranz, 1976; Monk & Folkard, 1983) has qualified this finding by suggesting that whereas basic motor responses may be directly related to temperature, cognitive performance such as memory may show an inverse relationship to body temperature. Rutenfranz and Colquhoun (1979) have interpreted this to mean that there may be two types of performance rhythms: one involving immediate information processing operations, which is directly related to body temperature and arousal, and the other involving information storage which may be inversely related to the temperature rhythm. A fruitful area of future research might be to clarify the effects of various work schedules on performance as a function of task demands. The design of optimal work schedules may require tailoring to the specific nature of the work and the characteristics of the workforce. The best approach, therefore, is an empirical one in which both labor and management develop a willingness to implement, and evaluate the efficacy of various schedules in terms of a set of agreed upon criteria.

REFERENCES

Arndt, R., Hurrell, J.J. & Smith, M.J. (1981). Comparison of biochemical and survey results of a four-year study of letter sorting machine operators. In G. Salvendy & M.J. Smith (Eds.), *Machine Pacing and Occupational Stress*, London: Taylor & Francis Ltd.

Aschoff, J. (1981). Circadian rhythms: Interference with and dependence on work-rest cycles. In L.C. Johnson, D.I. Tepas, W.P. Colquhoun & M.J. Colligan (Eds.), *The Twenty-Four Hour Workday: Proceedings of a Symposium on Variations in Work-Sleep Schedules*. DHHS (NIOSH) Publication 81–127. Washington, D.C.: U.S. Govt. Printing Office.

Beck, C.H.M. (1963). Paced and self-paced serial simple reaction time. *Canadian Journal of Psychology, 17*, 90–98.

Belbin, R.M. & Stammers, D. (1972). Pacing stress, human adaptation and training in car production. *Applied Ergonomics, 3*(3), 142–146.

Bertelson, P., Boons, J.P. & Renkin, A. (1965). Self pacing and forced pacing in a task simulating mechanical sorting of mail. *Ergonomics, 8*, 3–22.

Bjerner, B., Holm, A. & Swensson, A. (1955). Diurnal variation in mental performance: A study of three shift workers. *British Journal of Industrial Medicine, 12*, 103–110.

Broadbent, D.E. & Gath, D. (1981). Symptom levels in assembly line workers. In G. Salvendy & M.J. Smith (Eds.), *Machine Pacing and Occupational Stress*. London: Taylor & Francis Ltd.

Brown, R.A. (1957). Age and "paced" work. *Occupational Psychology, 31*, 11–20.

Browne, R.C. (1949). The day and night performance of teleprinter switchboard operators. *Occupational Psychology, 23*, 121–126.

Caplan, R.D., Cobb, S., French, J.R.P., Van Harrison, R.V., Pinneau, S.R. (1975). *Job Demands and Worker Health*. Contract No. HSM–99–72–61, U.S. Department of Health, Education, and Welfare, HEW Publication No. 75–160 (NIOSH). Washington, D.C.: U.S. Government Printing Office.

Chase, R.B. (1974). Survey of paced assembly lines. *Industrial Engineering, 6*(2), 14–18.

Colligan, M.J. (1980). Methodological and practical issues related to shiftwork research. *Journal of Occupational Medicine, 22*, 163–166.

Colquhoun, W.P. (Ed.) (1971). *Biological Rhythms and Human Performance*. London: Academic Press, 1971.

Colquhoun, W.P. (1976). Accidents, injuries, and shiftwork. In P.C. Rentos & R.D. Shepard (Eds.), *Shiftwork and Health: A Symposium*. DHEW Publication No. (NIOSH 76–203). Washington, D.C.: U.S. Govt. Printing Office.

Conrad, R. (1955). Comparison of paced and unpaced performance at a packing task. *Occupational Psychology, 29*, 15–24.

Conrad, R. (1960). Letter sorting machines-paced, "lagged," or unpaced? *Ergonomics, 3*, 149–157.

Coury, B.G. (1983). *The Impact of Extended Work Periods on Performance and Response in Paced Conditions*. Final report NIOSH Contract No. 821591. Cincinnati, OH: National Institute for Occupational Safety & Health.

Dainoff, M.J., Hurrell, J.J., Jr. & Happ, A. (1981). A taxonomic framework for the description and evaluation of paced work. In G. Salvendy & M.J. Smith (Eds.), *Machine Pacing and Occupational Stress*. London: Taylor & Francis, Ltd.

Dirken, J.M. (1966). Industrial shift work: Decrease in well-being and special effects. *Ergonomics, 9*, 115–124.

Drury, C.G. (1982). Improving inspection performance. In G. Salvendy (Ed.), *Handbook of Industrial Engineering*. New York: John Wiley & Sons.

Dudley, N.A. (1962). The effects of pacing on operator performance. *International Journal of Production Research, 2*, 60–68.

Dudley, N.A. (1963). Work time distributions. *International Journal of Production Research, 2*, 137–145.

Eskew, R.T. & Riche, C.V. (1982). Pacing and locus of control on quality-control inspection. *Human Factors, 24*(4), 411–415.

Faunce, W. (1958). Automation in the auto industry: Some consequences for in-plant social structure. *American Sociological Review, 23*, 401–407.

Ferguson, D. (1973). A study of occupational stress and health. *Ergonomics, 16*(5), 649–663.

Folkard, S., Knauth, P., Monk, T.H. & Rutenfranz, J. (1976). The effect of memory load on the circadian variation in performance efficiency under a rapidly rotating shift system. *Ergonomics, 19*, 479–488.

Frankenhaeuser, M. & Gardell, B. (1976). Underload and overload in working life: Outline of a multidisciplinary approach. *Journal of Human Stress, 2*(3), 35–46.

Franks, I.I. (1974). Some characteristics of conveyor-based operator performance. *Work Study and Management Services, 18*(7), 432–436.

Fried, J., Weitman, M. & Davis, M.K. (1972). Man-machine interaction and absenteeism. *Journal of Applied Psychology, 56*(5), 428–429.

Harrington, J.M. (1978). *Shiftwork and Health: A Critical Review of the Literature.* London: Her Majesty's Stationery Office.

Hokanson, J.E., Degood, D.E., Forrest, M.S. & Brittain, T.M. (1971). Availability of avoidance behaviors in modulating vascular stress responses. *Journal of Personality and Social Psychology, 19*, 60–68.

Hurrell, J.J. (1985). Machine-paced work and the Type A behaviour pattern. *Journal of Occupational Psychology, 58*, 15–25.

Hurrell. J.J., Smith, M.J., Burg, J.R. & Hicks, K.M. (1985). *Job Demands and Worker Health in Machine-Paced Mail Sorting Operations.* National Institute for Occupational Safety and Health, Cincinnati, Ohio.

Johansson, G., Aronsson, G. & Lindstrom, B.O. (1978). Social psychological and neuroendocrine stress reactions in highly mechanized work. *Ergonomics, 21*, 583–599.

Johansson, G. & Lindstrom, B. (1975). Paced and unpaced work under salary and piece-rate conditions. Report No. 459 from the Department of Psychology, University of Stockholm.

Kalimo, R., Leppanen, A., Verkasalo, M., Peltomaa, A. & Seppala, P. (1981). Mental strain in machine-paced and self-paced tasks. In G. Salvendy & M.J. Smith (Eds.), *Machine Pacing and Occupational Stress.* London: Taylor & Francis Ltd.

Karasek, R. (1981). Job decision latitude, job demands and cardiovascular disease: A prospective study of Swedish men. *American Journal of Public Health, 71*(7), 694–705.

Khaleque, A. (1979). Performance and job satisfaction in short-cycled repetitive work. In R. Sell & P. Shipley (Eds.), *Satisfaction in Job Design.* London: Taylor & Francis Ltd.

Knauth, P. & Rutenfranz, J. (1976). Experimental shift work: studies of permanent night and rapidly rotating shift work systems. *International Archives of Occupational and Environmental Health, 37*, 125–137. Cited by Aschoff, J. (1981). Circadian rhythms: Interference with and dependence on work-rest cycles. In L.C. Johnson, D.I. Tepas, W.P. Colquhoun & M.J. Colligan (Eds.), *The Twenty-Four Hour Workday: Proceedings of a Symposium on Variations in Work-Sleep Schedules.* DHHS (NIOSH) Publication 81–127. Washington, D.C.: U.S. Govt. Printing Office.

Koholova, I. & Matousek, O. (1968). Changes of autonomic functions during mental activity in laboratory conditions. *Cslka Psychology, 1*, 49–54.

Kritsikis, S.P., Heinemann, A.L. & Eitner, S. (1968). Die Angina Pectoris im Aspektibrer Korrelation mit Biologischen Disposition, Psychologischen und Soziologischen Enflussfaktoren. *Deutsch Gesundheit, 23*, 1878–1885.

Luce, G.G. (1970). *Biological Rhythms in Psychiatry and Medicine.* U.S. Public Health Service Publication No. 2088, Washington, D.C.: U.S. Govt. Printing Office.

Luopajarvi, T., Kuorinka, I., Virolainen, M. & Holmberg, M. (1979). Prevalence of tenosynovitis and other injuries of the upper extremities in repetitive work. *Scandinavian Journal of Work Environment and Health, 5*, 48–55.

Mackay, C.J., Cox, T., Watts, C., Thirlaway, M. & Lazzerini, A.J. (1979). Psychological correlates of repetitive work. In C. Mackay & T. Cox (Eds.), *Response to Stress.* Guildford: IPC Science and Technology Press.

Manenica, I. (1977). Comparison of some physiological indices during paced and unpaced work. *International Journal of Production Research, 15*, 261–275.

Menzel, W. (1950). Zur physiologic und pathologic des nacht und schichtarbeiters. *Arbeitsphysiologie, 14*, 304–318. Cited by Tasto, D.L., Colligan, M.J., Skjel, E.W. & Polly, S.J. (1976). *Health Consequences of Shiftwork.* (NIOSH Publication No. 78–154) Washington, D.C.: U.S. Government Printing Office.

Monk, T.H. & Folkard, S.G. (1983). Circadian rhythms and shiftwork. In G.R.J. Hockey (Ed.), *Stress and Fatigue in Human Performance.* London: Wiley.

Morgan, B.B. Jr., Brown, B.B. & Alluisi, E.A. (1974). Effects on sustained performance of 48 hours of continuous work and sleep loss. *Human Factors, 16,* 406–414.

Mott, P.E., Mann, F.C., McLoughlin, Q. & Warwick, D. (1965). *Shift Work: The Social, Psychological, and Physical Consequences.* Ann Arbor, MI: Univ. of Michigan Press.

Murrell, K.F.H. (1963). Laboratory studies of repetitive work I: Paced work and its relationship to unpaced work. *International Journal of Production Research, 2,* 169–185.

Rutenfranz, J., Colquhoun, W.P., Knauth, P. & Ghata, J.N. (1977). Biomedical and psychosocial aspects of shiftwork: A review. *Scandinavian Journal of Work and Environmental Health, 3,* 165–182.

Rutenfranz, J. & Colquhoun, W.P. (1979). Circadian rhythms in human performance. *Scandinavian Journal of Work Environment and Health, 5,* 167–177.

Salvendy, G. (1981). Classification and characteristics of paced work. In G. Salvendy & M.J. Smith (Eds.), *Machine Pacing and Occupational Stress,* London: Taylor & Francis Ltd.

Salvendy, G. (1972). Physiological and psychological aspects of paced and unpaced performance. *Acta Physiologica, 42*(3), 267–275.

Salvendy, G. & Humphreys, A.P. (1979). Effects of personality, perceptual difficulty, and pacing of a task on productivity, job satisfaction and physiological stress. *Perceptual and Motor Skills, 49,* 219–222.

Salvendy, G. & Pilitsis, J. (1971). Psychophysiological aspects of paced and unpaced performance as influenced by age. *Ergonomics, 14,* 703–711.

Samoilova, A.J. (1971). Morbidity with temporary loss of working capacity of female workers engaged in monotonous work. *Sovetskia Zdravakhranenie, 30,* 41–46.

Seppala, P. & Nieminen, K. (1981). Workers' behavioral and physiological responses and the degree of machine pacing in the sorting of sawmill products. In G. Salvendy & M.J. Smith (Eds.), *Machine Pacing and Occupational Stress.* London: Taylor & Francis Ltd.

Stagner, R. (1975). Boredom on the assembly line: Age and personality variables. *Industrial Gerontology, 2,* 23–44.

Sury, R.J. (1967). Operator performance in conveyor based working. *Work Management Services,* 12–15.

Tasto, D.I., Colligan, M.J., Skjei, E.W. & Polly, S.J. (1978). *Health Consequences of Shiftwork.* (NIOSH Publication No. 78–154) Washington, D.C.: U.S. Govt. Printing Office.

Tepas, D.I., Walsh, J.K. & Armstrong, D.R. (1981). Comprehensive Study of the Sleep of Shiftworkers. In L.C. Johnson, D.I. Tepas, W.P. Colquhoun & M.J. Colligan (Eds.), *The Twenty-Four Hour Workday: Proceedings of a Symposium on Variations in Work-Sleep Schedules.* DHHS (NIOSH) Publication 81–127. Washington, D.C.: U.S. Govt. Printing Office.

Thiis-Evensen, E. (1958). Shift work and health. *Industrial Medicine and Surgery, 27,* 493–497.

Thiis-Evensen, E. (1969). Shift work and health. In A. Swenson (Ed.), *Proceedings of the First International Symposium on Night and Shift Work.* Stockholm: Institute of Occupational Health, 81–85.

Walker, J. & De La Mare, G. (1971). Absence from work in relation to length and distribution of shift hours. *British Journal of Industrial Medicine, 28,* 36–44.

Walker, S. & Marriott, R. (1952). A study of some attitudes to factory work. *Occupational Psychology,* March, 181–191.

Walsh, J.K., Tepas, D.I. & Moss, P.D. (1981). The EEG sleep of night and rotating shift workers. In L.C. Johnson, D.I. Tepas, W.P. Colquhoun & M.J. Colligan (Eds.), *The Twenty-Four Hour Workday: Proceedings of a Symposium on Variations in Work-Sleep Schedules.* DHHS (NIOSH) Publication 81–127. Washington, D.C.: U.S. Govt. Printing Office.

Weitzman, E.D. & Kripke, D.F. (1981). Experimental 12-hour shift of the sleep-wake cycle in man: Effects on sleep and physiologic rhythms. In L.C. Johnson, D.I. Tepas, W.P. Colquhoun & M.J. Colligan (Eds.), *The Twenty-Four Hour Workday: Proceedings of a*

Symposium on Variations in Work-Sleep Schedules. DHHS (NIOSH) Publication 81-127. Washington, D.C.: U.S. Govt. Printing Office.

Wesseldijk, A.T.G. (1961). The influence of shiftwork on health. *Ergonomics, 4*, 281-282.

Wilkes, B., Stammerjohn, L. & Lalich, N. (1981). Job demands and worker health in machine-paced poultry inspection. *Scandinavian Journal of Work Environment and Health, Suppl. 4*, 12-19.

Wyatt, S. & Langdon, J.N. (1938). The machine and worker, IFRB report number 82.

Managers and Professionals in Business/Industrial Settings: The Research Evidence

Steven P. Glowinkowski
Cary L. Cooper

SUMMARY. This article reviews some of the research that has been carried out on managerial and executive stress. It indicates that there are a number of potential problem areas: factors intrinsic to the job, role based stress, relationships, career development factors, organizational structure and climate, and the work : family interface. It appears that the area of career development is severely under-researched.

The pressures on professionals in business and industry, particularly managers has been growing over the last decade (Cooper, 1983). This is due in part to the enormous change that is taking place in organizations throughout the western economies, technological as well as social change. This article reviews the research on the sources of managerial and professional stress in business and industry.

SOURCES OF MANAGERIAL STRESS

Research has identified at least six major sources of managerial stress (Cooper & Marshall, 1978; Schuler, 1982; Cooper, 1982). These sources of stress are probably applicable to the labor force as a whole. Briefly they include:

Steven P. Glowinkowski and Cary L. Cooper are affiliated with the Department of Management Sciences, University of Manchester Institute of Science and Technology.

1. *Stress in the job itself*. This includes factors such as repetitive work, time pressures and work overload.
2. *Role based stress*, such as role ambiguity, role conflict and responsibility for others.
3. *Relationships* with subordinates, colleagues and superiors.
4. *Career development factors*, such as fear of redundancy, obsolescence, and under/over promotion.
5. *Organizational structure and climate*, including such factors as office politics, communication, participation and organizational trust.
6. *The work : family interface*, which refers to the relationship between work-demands and family/social demands.

These categories of stressors are often blurred. However, they do represent a convenient structure in which to examine sources of managerial stress. The following section provides a more detailed picture of these issues in terms of past and current research.

STRESS FROM THE JOB ITSELF

Stressors intrinsic to the job itself dominated early research (Cooper & Marshall, 1978). The majority of studies examined working conditions. In a classical study of industrial workers, Kornhauser (1965) found unpleasant working conditions related to poor mental health. Shephard (1971) and Cooper and Smith (1985) showed that physical health was adversely affected by repetitive and dehumanizing work environments. Excessive travel, deadlines and the pressures of mistakes have also been shown as potential sources of stress (Cooper, 1982).

Indeed, Cooper and Marshall (1978) suggested that most job descriptions include factors that at some time can be sources of stress. Thus, intrinsic stress sources will be defined by the nature of the job in question. A recent study by Leatt and Schnick (1985) examined stress with nurses. They found traumatic emotional experiences, psychogeriatric workload and physician-nurse relationships were major sources of stress. Crump et al. (1980) identified "equipment failure" and "poor controllers ability" as major sources of stress with air traffic controllers.

Managerial work, however, is much less easy to define. Nevertheless, an important stress source for managers is work overload. French and Caplan (1973) view work overload as being either quantitative (i.e., too much to do) or qualitative (i.e., work that is too difficult). In theoretical terms overload corresponds to a condition of excess demand.

These authors found that managers with more phone calls, office visits and meetings per unit of work time, smoked significantly more cigarettes. Russek and Zohman (1958) also found a strong association between overload and CHD. Margolis et al. (1974) in a large scale study, found overload to be associated with low work motivation, lowered self-esteem and escapist drinking.

More recent studies confirm these relationships (Cooper, 1983). Cooper and Roden (1985) examined a representative group of British tax inspectors. They found that qualitative and quantitative overload predicted high levels of anxiety and depression. Indeed, French et al. (1985) indicated that qualitative and quantitative overload have been associated with at least nine psychological and physiological responses: job dissatisfaction, job tension, lower self-esteem, threat, embarrassment, high cholesterol levels, increased heart rate, skin resistance and increased smoking.

The condition of work overload has also been linked to ill-health (Cox, 1981). Despite limited research, the concept has usually been associated with boring repetitive "blue collar" environments. However, recent research suggests that underload can be a major problem for managerial groups.

Davidson and Cooper (1983) identify women managers as a major group "at risk" from work underload. These authors suggest that due to under-promotion women are more likely to be clustered at the lower levels of most organizations. In an empirical study (Davidson & Cooper, 1983), they found that women were considerably more qualified than their male counterparts of similar management level. Thus women may represent a large group of underutilized managers.

Another group likely to suffer underload are graduate recruits. Following a stimulating university environment, graduates often enter managerial life with high expectations. Several studies have shown that early experiences often fail to live up to initial expectations. The associated problems tend to be low job satisfaction, poor motivation and high staff turnover (Hall, 1976). A recent study by Keenan and Newton (1984) looked at graduate engineers in industry. They found that qualitative underload was a strong predictor of job dissatisfaction.

With managers one would expect qualitative underload to be a major stress source. Also, it would be interesting to observe possible interaction effects with quantitative workload. For example, with highly ambitious and talented managers, the most stressful situation could be a mixture of qualitative underload and quantitative overload.

ROLE BASED STRESS

A great deal of research has concentrated on the managerial role as a source of stress. This has assumed that certain requirements and assumptions of the role can lead to the experience of stress. Before examining the empirical evidence, it is worth considering the notion of role from a managerial perspective.

Gowler and Legge (1975) point out that any social position or role, carries specific rights and duties. Also, that these rights and duties may influence the individuals behavior, values and feelings. Indeed, the manager is often faced with a range of different role relationships or role sets. These authors suggest that this range of role sets will have their own unique requirements and expectations. Stress will occur when the requirements of one specific role set are inhibited or prevented. This could be due to the complexity of the role itself, or through conflict with the requirements of a different role set. Gowler and Legge (1975) suggest three such possible situations:

1. *Conflict between different role sets.* This may occur when the demands of one role set (e.g., the work environment) prohibit specific required action in another role set (e.g., the home environment). In this situation, the duties of at least one social role will be neglected.
2. *Conflict may occur within a role set.* An individual may be faced with a range of mutually exclusive (or at least conflicting) demands within his role as a manager. For example, he may feel a duty to ensure job security for his subordinates. At the same time he may also have to consider the organizations need for rationalization. These are just two examples from an infinite number of situations that can result in role conflict.

3. *Lack of clarity regarding role requirements*. A manager who experiences a lack of clarity about what is expected may be unable to accomplish his role requirements. This role ambiguity is not only a source of stress in itself, but also prohibits any clear path to good performance and perceived success.

These situations are likely to become stressful when the individual manager feels unable to cope with the specific role demands. This might lead to either an actual or perceived decline in performance and subsequent decline in job satisfaction. Numerous studies have examined the work and health effects of role ambiguity and conflict. We now briefly examine the empirical evidence.

ROLE AMBIGUITY

Kahn et al. (1964) found that role ambiguity was associated with lower job satisfaction and job related tension. French and Caplan (1970) conducted a study with engineers, scientists and administrators. They found that role ambiguity was associated with low job satisfaction and feelings of job related threat to individual well-being. Margolis et al. (1974) investigated a representative national U.S. sample of 1496 employed persons, 16 years of age or older. They found significant relationships between symptoms of physical and mental ill-health and role ambiguity.

ROLE CONFLICT

Kahn et al. (1974) found that men suffering role conflict had lower job satisfaction and higher job related tension. They also found that the greater the status of the individuals "sending" the conflicting messages, the stronger the relationship between role conflict and job dissatisfaction. Several studies have also related role conflict to physical health outcomes (e.g., French & Caplan, 1970). Shirom et al. (1973) collected data on 762 Kibbutz members from a broad range of occupational groups. For the white collar workers only, they found a relationship between role conflict and CHD. Cooper and Marshall (1978) suggest that it is managerial and professional occupations that are more likely to suffer negative effects from such role based stressors.

More recent studies have confirmed these relationships (e.g., Vrendenburgh & Trinkaus, 1983; Keenan & Newton, 1984; Martin, 1984). Kemery et al. (1985) applied sophisticated path analysis to data from a sample of accountants. The analysis showed role ambiguity and conflict to have a direct influence on job related tension, job satisfaction and propensity to leave an organization.

Several other factors have also been cited as potential sources of role based stress for the manager. These include responsibility for others (too much or too little), lack of managerial support, rapid technological change and so on (Cooper, 1982). In terms of empirical research, however, these factors have been relatively neglected. However, some studies have shown a relationship between "responsibility for others" and CHD risk-factors (e.g., Pincherie, 1972).

Nevertheless, unlike ambiguity and conflict, these factors are rather more structural than psychological. Thus, they are more likely to act as moderators or even precursors of role ambiguity and conflict itself.

For example, the greater the responsibility the manager has, then the greater may be the potential for role conflict situations. Also, support from senior management is likely to alleviate the conflict situations. Specific occupational groups may also be more prone to conflict situations. Davidson and Cooper (1983) found female managers to suffer considerable conflict between work and home demands. Lower and middle managers have also been cited as "at risk" (Cooper, 1982). Glowinkowski and Nicholson (1984) conducted a study of British police inspectors. This group of officers traditionally operate as a link between the senior police management and the operational ("on the beat") policeman. These officers expressed considerable conflict between the demands and expectations of the organizational hierarchy and the realities of the "street."

Role ambiguity might also be moderated by these factors. New developments through technology require continuous updating of skills. Indeed, Gowler and Legge (1975) suggest that managers will mostly experience role ambiguity when entering new roles. This can be through promotion, a change of company or even organizational change. The problem may be manifest for new graduate recruits. Such individuals neither know the job, the organization, nor even the experience of work itself.

Despite this extensive research into role based stressors, the relationships with stress outcomes are often rather small. Kasl (1978) reported, that at best, only moderate correlations with various components of job satisfaction have been observed. The relationships with mental health tend to be weak—with physical health indices, they are often negligible. These criticisms also apply to the work overload measures reported earlier. Indeed, Payne et al. (1982) suggest that the majority of studies often account for less than 20% of the variance in the dependent stress variable.

A relevant factor in this regard is that a certain amount of stress might be of benefit to the individual (Bernard, 1968). The foregoing discussion implied that work underload or even too little responsibility may be sources of managerial stress.

Most studies using the traditional Likert type rating scales, at least implicitly, require the individual to rate negative pressure. They leave little room to accommodate the individual who feels under pressure, but at the same time derives satisfaction from that pressure. For some people, a reduction in "job clarity" may mean an increase in "autonomy" yet for others represent a taxing burden of ambiguity. Indeed, Payne (1981) found that managers rated 9 out of 43 items to have both "demand" and "satisfaction."

A recent approach to this problem is that of Person/Environment Fit. This has primarily been associated with the stress research team at the University of Michigan (Caplan et al., 1975; French et al., 1982).

THE APPROACH OF PERSON/ENVIRONMENT FIT

The approach operationalizes stress by calculating the discrepancy between what an individual perceives and desires from various aspects of the work environment. Stress or "misfit" is defined by either demand exceeding a persons capability or desired level (i.e., the excess demand view of stress) and capability exceeding the demand (i.e., the excess resource view of stress). This latter situation of misfit refers to when the work environment fails to supply the needs of the individual. Qualitative underload would clearly fall into this category.

The Michigan research team (French et al., 1982) used this approach in a large scale study involving over 2,000 people from 23 different occupations. The researchers found relatively strong correlations between several measures of "work role fit" and various job affect variables (including, job dissatisfaction, workload dissatisfaction, and boredom), the results with mental and physical health were rather small. Indeed, with physical health indices they were often non-significant.

Despite the relative success of this study there are severe conceptual problems with the misfit or discrepancy approach in general. For example, an individual's appraisal of a situation (i.e., perception of demand) is blurred by their affective evaluation (Shirom, 1982). Indeed, Shirom argues that the measurement of "insufficient opportunities from the work environment" corresponds essentially to the nature of job satisfaction. There is also the problem that discrepancy, in terms of both excess resource and excess demand, can count as equal levels of misfit. These situations, however, are surely different psychological states (Glowinkowski & Cooper, 1985).

A further point to consider is that the emphasis on role based stress and work over/underload may well be inappropriate. When Kahn et al. (1964) originally proposed the concepts of role ambiguity and conflict, industrial society was enjoying economic growth. The late seventies and early eighties, however, are characterized by recession.

It is more likely that manager's major concerns will stem from the threat of redundancy or obsolescence due to changing technology. Highly competitive markets may also have their impact. Thus, fear of mistakes, relationship with the organization and its members, performance of superiors or even competition within organizations for individual survival, may be "high pressure" points.

RELATIONSHIPS AT WORK

Relationships with superiors, colleagues and subordinates have been suggested to be a potential source of managerial stress (Cooper, 1982). Mintzberg (cited by Cooper & Marshall, 1978) conducted an intensive study with a small sample of chief executives. In a large organization, Mintzberg found that only 22% of time was spent in desk work. The remaining time was spent in scheduled meetings (59%), unscheduled meetings (10%), telephone calls (6%) and other activities (3%). Even in smaller organizations, Mintzberg found that managers spent up to 40% of their time in face to face contacts.

Despite the obvious importance of interpersonal relations, relatively few studies have provided any substantive results (Cooper, 1983). French and Caplan (1970), however, did find that poor relationships were positively associated with role ambiguity. These authors suggested that this led to inadequate communications between people, low job satisfaction and job related threat.

Without longitudinal investigation, the exact temporal relationship between ambiguity and relationships is unclear. Poor relationships with superiors might be expected to precipitate role ambiguity. With colleagues, however, one might expect current ambiguity to be compounded, or even precipitate poor relationships.

Role ambiguity is often an intrinsic aspect of managerial work. Role conflict on the other hand, depends on discrepancies in role relationships. Therefore, one might expect interpersonal relations to have a major impact on the occurrence of role conflict.

Relationships are also important in establishing strong social support (social support is discussed in more detail below). For managers, one would expect support from colleagues and subordinates to be integral for good performance (Cooper & Marshall, 1978). Indeed, Payne (1980) makes the point that heterogenous groups such as "sales and marketing" are characterized by high rates of exchange. Thus, members of such groups will rely heavily on continuous support in the normal routine of work.

Surprisingly, research into this important aspect of managerial life (i.e., relationships) is relatively scarce. Future studies need to examine the temporal causal networks between work relationships and role ambiguity and conflict. Also, as suggested above, the significance of relationships for different occupational groups needs further examination.

THE ORGANIZATION

A major source of managerial stress can arise from the organization itself. These factors include, lack of participation in decision making, low organizational trust, office politics, poor communications or even restrictions on behavior. The main thrust of research in this field has tended to concentrate on lack of participation and stress related outcomes.

In the French and Caplan (1970) study mentioned earlier, it was found that greater participation was related to higher job satisfaction, low job related threat, and higher self-esteem. Buck (1972) found that managers and workers most under pressure tended to have more autocratic leadership. Margolis et al.'s (1974) national U.S. sample found that non-participation was a significant predictor of several negative health indices. These included, poor physical health, escapist drinking, low job satisfaction, low motivation, propensity to leave the organization and absenteeism. Wall and Clegg (1981) provide evidence from longitudinal data that when substantial increases in group autonomy and work identity were achieved, they were followed by increased work motivation, performance, job satisfaction and mental health. The authors discounted a Hawthorne effect because the changes were maintained over a period of at least 18 months. Also, while performance and motivation increases occurred quickly, the job satisfaction and mental health improvements took several months to appear. This study strongly suggests a causal effect of "increased participation" on subsequent psychological strain.

Despite the studies mentioned above, most research into participation has emphasized blue collar groups. However, it was suggested earlier that a manager's relationship with the organization may have become a highly significant source of stress. Some recent studies support this assumption.

A study of senior managers by Cooper and Melhuish (1980) factor analyzed a broad range of stressors. They found that the "relationship with the organization," "job insecurity" and "poor organizational climate" were all factors predictive of lower mental health and physical health among executives. This study showed that "poor organizational climate" were no longer the preserve of blue collar workers. Also, they found the absence of "role based stress" in the stress outcome equation. A study from the career development field by Alban-Metcalfe and Nicholson (1984) found similar results. Among a sample of British managers, "challenge," "creative work" and "good quality management" were valued as highly important. Clearly specified work roles were rated as relatively unimportant.

A further point to consider is that movement toward greater worker participation (within society as a whole) can in itself become a source of stress. Donaldson and Gowler (1975) pointed to four main factors which can make participation a source of stress for managers:

1. mis-match of formal and actual power
2. the manager may resent the erosion of his formal role
3. increased role conflict due to the need to be both participitative and achieve high production
4. subordinates may refuse to participate.

The reaction of managers to increases in their subordinates "participation" is extremely under-researched. Future studies need to consider this issue in more detail.

THE MANAGERIAL CAREER

The idea of career progression is often of overriding importance to the individual manager. However, the managerial career has several dimensions and consequent sources of stress. Cooper and Marshall (1978) identified two main clusters of potential career stressors:

1. Lack of job security, fear of redundancy and obsolescence due to changing technology.
2. Status incongruity. This refers to under/over promotion or frustration at having reached one's career ceiling.

Numerous studies have shown these factors to have deleterious health consequences (Cooper, 1983). Studies have also suggested the dysfunctional effects on organizations. This is particularly the case with status incongruity (Hall, 1976).

Recent studies also point to the importance of "the career" in terms of stress outcomes. Martin (1984) found with hospital workers that, "inability to leave" was related to acute and chronic mental health problems. Keenan and Newton (1984) found that "frustration in organizations" was frequently reported by young graduate engineers in industry. These authors reported frustration as related to a variety of stress outcome variables such as job dissatisfaction and work related anxiety. Despite these studies, the significance of the career as a life long developmental process has been neglected. Sources of stress will be contingent on this process.

Indeed, career development research has identified at least three distinctive career stages (Hall, 1976) that are relevant to the experience of stress: (1) establishment, (2) advancement, and (3) maintenance. The *establishment* stage refers to the early years of the career. Hall and Nougain (1964) found in a study of young managers, that in the first year of employment there were strong needs for "safety," "gaining recognition" and "establishing oneself" in the organization. By the end of the fifth year, however, the need for safety had declined significantly.

The next stage they found was one of *advancement*. The individual is less concerned with "fitting in" than with moving up and mastering the organization. Once established, however, there follows a leveling off period, eventually reaching a managerial plateau. In short, the manager reaches a point of *maintenance*, often adopting a guidance role for new organizational entrants (Hall, 1976).

While perhaps of more relevance to managerial and professional workers, the central point is that different career stages may emphasize different stressors. In the early years, "relationships," particularly with superiors, may be of paramount concern. This will relate to both feelings of security and also provision of information about the company and the employee's own performance. The individual experiences "reality shock," moving through a socialization process by learning and acquiring the values and orientations of the organization (Van Maanen & Schein, 1979). Indeed, role ambiguity could also be a major stressor during this phase. Hall and Nougain (1964) found early experiences to affect a manager's future attitudes, expectations and performance.

During the stage of *advancement*, "promotion" and "personal future plans" may begin to dominate. Also, since individuals may have gained higher status, the need for support from colleagues and subordinates may be vital for good performance. Thus, stable positive relationships with these "support agencies" may be crucial.

Another potential stress source at this stage is from the work : family interface. Preoccupation with the job during advancement years is likely to have disruptive effects on family life during important developmental years (Cooper, 1982).

At the stage of *maintenance*, different factors may become sources of stress. Career frustrations, fears of obsolescence or even negative organizational attitudes could dominate his/her concerns. A study of police inspectors (a rank equivalent to a first line manager) by Glowinkowski and Nicholson (1984) found the middle aged group to hold considerable negative attitudes towards the organization (i.e., the constabulary), in terms of their own careers. They also revealed a series of superstitious beliefs and feelings of uncertainty, regarding the workings of the promotion system itself. These authors emphasized the importance of the culture of the organization, which encouraged the idea of promotion as a reward system, and yet provided no feedback or guidance regarding promotion chances.

Future research needs to examine the relationship between career stage, sources of stress and health outcomes. While stressors may exist for all individuals, they may not have the same valence and subsequent health outcomes for all career groups.

EXTRA-ORGANIZATIONAL SOURCES OF STRESS

Extra organizational sources of stress refer to the myriad of interfaces between work and family life that put pressure on the manager (Cooper & Marshall, 1978). These include family problems, financial difficulties, the disruptive effects of managerial relocation and so on (Cooper, 1982). However, the major areas of interest have centered around two main issues, (1) the relationship between work and family life, and (2) stressful life events.

The Work : Family Relationship

The relationship between work and family is usually viewed in terms of the family as "the social support team." Gowler and Legge (1975), for example, have stressed the importance of the managerial wife, coining the term "hidden contract." Handy (1975) endorses this view, suggesting the necessity of the family bond to career success. However, this relationship is infinitely more complex and has not been effectively integrated within the stress : strain paradigm.

From largely outside the stress literature, three general hypotheses to explain the work : family relationship have been proposed; (1) *Spillover*, where the events of one environment affect the other; (2) *Compensation*, where the individual attempts to compensate in one environment for what is lacking in the other, and (3) where both environments are said to be *independent*.

Kabanoff (1980) in an empirical review suggested that evidence supports all three hypotheses. However, in a managerial study, Evans and Bartolome (1980) found the largest proportion of their sample described their own circumstances as one of unidirectional spillover from the work to the home environment. More recently, these authors found several moderating relationships (Evans & Bartolome, 1984). Spillover into family life occurred mainly from negative work feelings. Also, when work was important to an individual, conflict between the two environments was more likely than when work was less important. The latter tended to result in an "independent attitude." They also suggested a mediating role; when work is not important, there will be less spillover of negative work outcomes.

The topic of the work : family relationship raises a number of research issues. First, is there a relationship between career stage and the work : family relationship? The advancement years of an employee may result in conflict and create a spillover effect, particularly in the case of the ambitious manager or other white collar worker. Mid-career stages, however, are more likely to be characterized by compensatory attitudes, particularly if the individual feels frustrated at reaching his/her career limit. In order to cope, the relationship might change to one of instrumentality or independence if the individual psychologically withdraws from his work.

Second, how do women perceive the work : home interface? Several studies have shown the work : family interface to be a major source of stress for female managers and professionals (e.g., Davidson & Cooper, 1983). However, research has neglected to provide more detailed data (both experimental and experiential) into the *nature* and *process* of this relationship. In addition, the work that has been done has almost totally neglected the problems and occupational stressors among blue collar women (Cooper & Smith, 1985).

IMPLICATIONS OF RESEARCH FOR MANAGERS

Different job and organizational stressors require different solutions, and only when companies are willing to accept their responsibility and contemplate carrying out specific organizational "stress audits" will we begin to deal effectively with managerial stress. In the meantime, there are several direct implications of much of this research for organizations. First, the health and well-being of employees depends on managers who are flexible and participative. Training must begin to take place to engender a "real" rather than "espoused" participative style of management at work. Second, corporate personnel policies must begin to change to acknowledge the coming of age of the "dual career family." Company relocation policies, career development plans and reward structures within organizations must be adapted to the constraints of two earner managerial families. Third, more effort should be taken to ensure that the "right manager" is fit to the "right job." Managerial selection should be more comprehensive, with thorough assessment centers, psychometrics and family circumstance taken into account. And finally, "stress" within organizations, must cease to be a "four letter word." We must help executives in trouble rather than encourage the corporate Rambo or Business Amazon mentality. Stress counselling for executives (and others for that matter) should be a high priority.

CONCLUSION

Many of the problems and stressors facing professionals in business and industry are not new or "earth shattering," but do require organizational action. Setting up appropriate personnel policies to support, encourage and develop professionals in industry is what we ought to be aiming for. Twenty years ago, Kornhauser (1965) reflected on what individuals at work need not only to survive the "9 to 5" but to positively enjoy it:

Mental health is not so much a freedom from specific frustrations as it is an overall balanced relationship to the world, which permits a person to maintain a realistic, positive belief in himself and his purposeful activities. Insofar as his entire job and life situation facilitate and support such feelings of adequacy, inner security, and meaningfulness of his existence, it can be presumed that his mental health will tend to be good. What is important in a negative way is not any single characteristic of his situation but everything that deprives the person of purpose and zest, that leaves him with negative feelings about himself, with anxieties, tensions, a sense of lostness, emptiness, and futility.

REFERENCES

Alban-Metcalfe, B. & Nicholson, N. (1984). *The career development of british male and female managers*. London: British Institute of Management.

Bernard, J. (1968). The eudaemonists. In S.Z. Klausner (Ed.), *Why man takes chances*. Garden City, New York: Anchor (Doubleday).

Buck, V. (1972). *Working under pressure*. London: Staples Press.

Caplan, R.D., Cobb, S., French, J.R.P. Jr., Van Harrison, R. & Pinneau, S.R. Jr. (1975). *Job demands and worker health*. National Institute of Safety and Health, US Department of Health. Washington, DC: US Government Printing Office.

Cooper, C.L. (1982). *Executive families under stress*. New Jersey: Prentice Hall.

Cooper, C.L. (1983). *Stress research: Issues for the 80s*. New York: John Wiley.

Cooper, C.L. & Marshall, J. (1978). Sources of managerial and white collar stress in *Stress at work*, Cooper, C.L. & Payne, R. (Eds.). Chichester, New York: John Wiley & Sons.

Cooper, C.L. & Melhuish, A. (1980). Occupational stress and the manager. *Journal of Occupational Medicine*, 22, 588–592.

Cooper, C.L. & Roden, J. (1985). Mental health and satisfaction among tax officers. *Social Science and Medicine*, 21, 747–751.

Cooper, C.L. & Smith, M.J. (1985). *Job stress and blue collar work*. New York: John Wiley & Sons.

Crump, J.H., Cooper, C.L. & Smith, M. (1980). Investigating occupational stress: A methodological approach. *Journal of Occupational Behaviour*, 1, 191–204.

Cox, T. (1981). *Stress*. London: Macmillan Press.

Davidson, M.J. & Cooper, C.L. (1983). *Stress and the woman manager*. Oxford: Martin Robertson Publishers.

Evans, P. & Bartolome, F. (1980). The relationship between professional and private life. In C.B. Durr (Ed.), *Work, family and career*. New York: Praeger, 281–317.

Evans, P. & Bartolome, F. (1984). The changing picture of the relationship between career and family. *Journal of Occupational Behaviour*, 5, 9–21.

French, J.R.P. & Caplan, R.D. (1970). Psychosocial factors in coronary heart disease. *Industrial Medicine*, 39, 383–397.

French, J.R.P. & Caplan, R.D. (1973). Organisational stress and individual strain. In A.J. Marrow (Ed.), *The failure of success*.

French, J.R.P., Caplan, R.D. & Van Harrison, R. (1982). *The mechanisms of job stress and strain*. Chichester, New York: John Wiley & Sons.

Glowinkowski, S.P. & Nicholson, N. (1984). The promotion pathology: A study of british police inspectors. Memo 659, MRC/ESRC SAPU, University of Sheffield.

Glowinkowski, S.P. & Cooper, C.L. (1985). Current issues in organizational stress research. *Bulletin of the British Psychological Society*, 38, 212–216.

Gowler, D. & Legge, K. (1975). Stress and external relationships: the 'hidden' contract. In D. Gowler & K. Legge (Eds.), *Managerial Stress*. Aldershot, Hants: Gower Publishing.

Hall, D.T. (1976). *Careers in organisations*. New York: Goodyear.

Hall, D.T. & Nougain, K. (1964). An examination of Maslow's need hierarchy in an organisational setting. *Organisational Behaviour and Human Performance*, 3, 12–35.

Handy, C. (1975). Difficulties in combining family and career. *The Times*. London, 22nd September, p. 16.

Kabanoff, B. (1980). Work and non-work: A review of models, methods and findings. *Psychological Bulletin*, 88, 60–77.

Kahn, R.L., Wolfe, D.M., Quinn, R.P., Snock, J.D. & Rosenthall, R.A. (1964). *Organisational stress*. New York: John Wiley & Sons.

Kasl, S.V. (1978). Epidemiological contributions to the study of work stress. In C.L. Cooper & R. Payne (Eds.), *Stress at work*. Chichester, New York: John Wiley & Sons.

Keenan, A. & Newton, T.J. (1984). Frustration in organizations: Relationships to role stress, climate and psychological strain. *Journal of Occupational Psychology*, 57, 57–65.

Kornhauser, A. (1965). *Mental health of the industrial worker*. New York: John Wiley & Sons.

Leatt, P. & Schneck, R. (1985). Sources and management of organisational stress in nursing sub-units in Canada. *Organisation Studies*, 6, 55–78.

Margolis, B.L., Kroes, W.H. & Quinn, R.P. (1974). Job stress: An unlisted occupational hazard. *Journal of Occupational Medicine*, 16, 654–661.

Martin, T.N. (1984). Role stress and inability to leave as predictors of mental health. *Human Relations*, 37, 969–983.

Payne, R. (1980). Organisational stress and social support. In C.L. Cooper & R. Payne (Eds.), *Current concerns in occupational stress*. Chichester, New York: John Wiley & Sons, pp. 269–278.

Payne, R., Jick, T.D. & Burke, R.J. (1982). Whither stress research? An agenda for the 1980's. *Journal of Occupational Behaviour*, 3, 131–145.

Pincherle, G. (1972). Fitness for work. *Proceedings of the Royal Society of Medicine*, 65, 321–324.

Russek, H.I. & Zohman, B.L. (1958). Relative significance of hereditary diet, and occupational stress in CHD of young adults. *American Journal of Medical Science*, 235, 266–275.

Schuler, R.S. (1982). An integrative transactional process model of stress in organisations. *Journal of Occupational Behaviour*, 3, 5–19.

Shirom, A., Eden, D., Silberwasser, S. & Kellerman, J.J. (1973). Stresses and risk factors in coronary heart disease among occupational categories in Kibbutzim. *Social Science and Medicine*, 7, 875–892.

Shirom, A. (1982). What is organisational stress? A facet analytic conceptualisation. *Journal of Occupational Behaviour*, 3, 21–38.

VanMaanen, J. & Schein, E.H. (1979). Toward a theory of organisational socialisation. In B.M. Staw (Ed.), *Research into organisational behaviour*, 1, 209–264.

Vredenburgh, D.J. & Trinkaus, R.J. (1983). An analysis of role stress among hospital nurses. *Journal of Vocational Behaviour*, 23, 82–95.

Wall, T.D. & Clegg, C.W. (1981). A longitudinal field study of group work design. *Journal of Occupational Behaviour*, 2, 31–49.

Professionals in Medical Settings: The Research Evidence in the 1980s

Cynthia Lee

SUMMARY. Selected literature is reviewed to illustrate the causes and effects of stressors in various medical professional groups. In general, the common stressors faced by medical professionals appear to result from the interdependent nature of the jobs in the hospital or medical settings, the individual's sociocultural background and personality. Individual characteristics moderated the relationship between stressors and stress symptoms. Job and role-related stressors were consistently related to distress, or negative consequences, while positive work relationships and social support appeared to decrease distress. Directions for future research areas are discussed.

The major studies of stress came from the experimental research conducted by Hans Selye in the 1930s. Stress is the natural adaptive response to job and organizational demands, constraints or opportunities, mediated by individual characteristics. Stress stimuli are "stressors" which have both beneficial and destructive consequences. The positive consequences are called "eustress." Although we are very concerned with the negative effects of stress, or "distress," identification of "eustress" may help individuals to cope with their everyday stressors.

Colligan, Smith and Hurrell (1977) have identified six of the hospital/health care occupations (health technologists, practical nurses, clinical laboratory technicians, nurses' aides, health aides and registered nurses) in the state of Tennessee which exhibited the

Cynthia Lee, Temple University School of Business Administration, Philadelphia, PA.
The author thanks Gary Blau and Randall S. Schuler for their helpful comments on this paper.

195

highest incidence of mental health disorder admissions. It may be that particular stressors present in the hospital environment are conducive to the development of mental disorders or distress. The purpose of this paper is to present a review of writings which addressed "stressors" and "distress" only in the medical settings in the 1980s. Studies in the medical settings prior to 1980 are excluded from this review. The term "writing" is used because of the variety of research methods used in the studies reviewed. Descriptive studies, narrative studies and studies which presented descriptive statistics (frequencies, rank-order of the stressors) are used to identify stressors unique to the medical professionals. Comparative studies will be used as supportive findings. The next section of this paper will review the stressors and effects of stress from a variety of health care professional studies employing correlational, quasi-experimental and experimental designs. In this section, studies which did not measure both stressors and eustress or distress are excluded. The last section will suggest a general framework to guide needed research in the medical settings.

The major stressors and distress categories have been discussed by Cooper (1983) and Ivancevich and Matteson (1980). The stressors are *activators* from an individual's internal or external environmental events which change the individual's present state and activates his/her defense mechanisms. Such *reaction* to the stressful events is the symptoms of stress. Successful initial coping may return the individual's current stressful state to equilibrium. However, if the stressful events continue over a period of time and if the initial defense mechanisms do not work, the individual's adaptive mechanisms collapse and the consequences will be in the form of mental or physical ill-health.

STRESS PROFILE AMONGST
MEDICAL PROFESSIONALS

The following review on each medical professional group will be based on empirical studies since 1980. Since the stressors faced by medical students, interns, residents, physicians, medical technologists and nurses are somewhat different, the following review will summarize their stressors individually. Only the top ten ranked of those stressors with the highest frequencies are considered. This section will be followed by a more general discussion summarized from empirical studies on the combined medical professionals' stressors and symptoms of stress. Empirical studies on the effects of stress for the dentists are scarce. The dentists' stressors identified by O'Shea, Corah and Ayer (1984), Sword (1984) and Wilson (1984) are similar to those faced by medical residents. Given this overlap, dental studies were dropped from this review.

1. Medical Students

(a) Preclinical years: the first and second year medical students spend most of their time in and out of classes. Their stressors come from being in medical school and the adjustments to medical life. Examples of stressors are student/faculty relationships, evaluations and curriculum activities, heavy class schedules; too much material to learn with too little time, unable to meet high self-expectations and the competitive nature of classmates. Medical students also felt that they are powerless in family, social and life crises (Bjorksten, Sutherland, Miller & Stewart, 1983; Folse, DaRose & Folse, 1985; Gaensbauer & Mizner, 1980; Huebner, Roger & Moore, 1981; Strayhorn, 1980a).

(b) Clinical years: during the third year medical students begin taking responsibility for patients, have to deal with death and the dying of patients, interact with other medical personnel and also receive pressure from patients, as well as other medical personnel. Other stressors come from overwork, the lack of effective consultation from faculty, advisors, or counselors. Some students also reported having mental and financial difficulties as well as concerns for their future such as internship (Gaensbauer & Mizner, 1980; Heubner et al., 1981; Linn & Zeppa, 1984). Rosenberg and Silver (1984) reported both medical students and physicians agreed that during the clinical years, medical students are generally abused and humiliated. In particular, third-year medical students are called "mullets" by interns, residents and attendings.

The sample of medical students is predominately male (over 70%). Of the studies which reported demographic differences in their perception of stress, Huebner et al. (1981) found females and older students to experience significantly higher stress especially during preclinical years. In addition, Gaensbauer and Mitzner

(1980) reported that female medical students feel stressed from their role identities as being a physician and also as a woman.

Strayhorn (1980a,b) examined the stressor differences between black and white first year medical students. He found that blacks perceived significantly higher stress levels than whites. In addition to the course work related stress, blacks felt that academically they were underprepared for medical school, that understanding role models were unavailable and medical school personnel were insensitive to their cultural background.

In addition to the age, gender and race differences reported above, Huebner et al. (1981) and Mitchell, Matthews, Grandy and Lupo (1983) reported that the perception of stress was significantly higher during the clinical years than the preclinical years of medical school. Heins, Fahey and Leiden (1984), in a comparative study between medical, law, psychology and chemistry graduate students, found that the second and third year medical students experienced lower levels of stress than the law students, but their stress level was higher than the Psychology and Chemistry students. However, when compared to other health sciences students (dental, allied health, pharmacy and nursing), the medical students (of all four years) reported higher stress levels than the other student samples (Bjorksten et al., 1983). The difference in stress levels between law and medical students may be that the law students go through a completely different process than the medical students.

In general, the stresses which medical students face are mostly developmental, caused by the demands and the competitive nature of medical school environment and the adaptive capacities of the students (Gaensbauer & Mizner, 1980).

2. Interns

Medical interns reported similar stressors as the clinical year medical students, that is, the responsibility for patients, managing the dying patients, making decisions in the face of uncertainty about proper diagnosis and treatment, anger at group leaders, attendings and physicians, the lack of control over one's life as a result of hospital bureaucracy, having social problems, and the lack of adequate support systems (Adler, Werner & Korsch, 1980; Ziegler, Kanas, Strull & Bennet, 1984). Adler et al. (1980), in a study of four successive cohorts of pediatric interns, found significantly higher levels of stress during the first year of internship and also found significantly lower levels of stress during the last year of internship. They also found significantly higher stress levels at the beginning of the last year of internship than at the end of the same year. From the analysis of 34 female and 60 male interns, they did not find any gender differences in the level of stress experienced. More studies on interns are necessary before drawing any conclusions from the above.

3. Residents

This group reported similar stressors as the interns, but added that general medicine was the most stressful rotation with excessive work load and responsibility, extremely long hours, and the lack of supervision. Professional socialization, conflicts between personal and professional commitments and time demand from others were among the stressors described by the residents (Rudner, 1985; Wolfe & Jones, 1985; Ziegler et al., 1984).

Rudner (1985) in examining 43 female family practice residents (out of a sample of 78 residents), found that female residents felt they must accommodate to subtle forms of sexism, be more professional than their male counterparts, and have responsibility for both home and career. In addition, Wolfe and Jones (1985), using cases and literature review to illustrate, found abortions to be a solution among some pregnant residents. Other female residents found taking care of an infant and being a resident stressful. Other gender related stressors reported by Wolfe and Jones (1985) were in the areas of sexual harassment and discrimination.

Rotbart, Nelson, Krantz and Doughtery (1985), in a 3-year study of pediatric residents, found nearly all residents reported experiencing emotional stress during residency. They also found a uniform trend of increasing happiness and fulfillment as one progressed through residency. This may be a result of knowing that they are finally at the end of a long involved professional socialization and training and that they will have exciting choices to make.

4. Physicians

Other than unrealistic work schedule and work load, patients and patients' family demands, physician stressors included physical threat by patients (especially psychiatrists), lengthy on-call hours and prolonged sleep deprivation, death or suicide of patients, being held responsible for substandard work performed by others, staff conflicts and disagreements, resource deficiencies, heavy medical insurance and unnecessary paperwork (Clarke, Maniscalco, Taylor-Brown, Roghmann, Shapiro & Hannon-Johnson, 1984; Dawkins, Depp & Selzer, 1984; Krakowski, 1982; Schaff & Hoekelman, 1981). In addition, Walker (1981) also reported that there is a general tendency for physicians to feel insecure, have higher demands from parents, have higher need for approval and the fear of failure.

Although the stressors described by the physicians should also be found among residents, interns and medical students, stressors such as sleep deprivation, lengthy on-call hours are to be expected for students, interns and residents. However, as physicians, these stressors are expected to be less problematic and less severe. Krakowski (1982), in a comparative study between physicians and the general population, found physicians to fare better in withstanding physical illness than the general population, but not psychiatric illness of alcoholism and drug addiction. Krakowski (1982) also found physicians to be higher in coronary artery disease. It may be that since college, physicians were socialized and grew up in "Type A" environments which have been found to be related to coronary heart disease.

The stressors described by the medical students, interns, residents and physicians are probably related to many of the Type A personality qualities discussed by Friedman and Rosenman (1974). They described Type A individuals as "aggressively involved in a chronic, incessant struggle to achieve more and more in less and less time." From the stress profile just described above, the medical professionals reported stressors such as overwork, time pressure, pressure from self and others which may be a result of their Type A personality.

Glass (1977), in an attempt to explain why Type A individuals work hard to succeed and conduct their activities at a rapid pace, suggested that these behaviors represent an attempt to maintain control over the stressful aspect of their environment. The jobs in a hospital setting are typically interdependent, where performance of one individual depends on the successful performance of others. Thus, the successful release of a patient depends on the decisions and performance of many medical personnel. Medical professionals may feel that they have little or no control over the quality of treatment given to their patients. As a result, the above stress profile contained stressors such as anger at group leaders and attending physicians, lack of supervision, pressure from patients and other medical personnel, and interpersonal stress. Hendrix, Ovalle and Troxler (1985) have suggested that perceived control over work can decrease job stress and this assertion was supported by Jackson's findings (1983). Hospital administrators may design programs to increase medical personnel's sense of control over their work environment as a means for reducing their job stress.

In addition, the stress profile indicated that developmental or learning stress occur in different forms among medical students, interns and residents. The competitive nature of medical school, the socialization which these medical professionals went through tend to reinforce Type A Behavior Pattern (Russek, 1974). Unfortunately, such behavior has been found to be a major cause of coronary heart disease (Friedman & Rosenman, 1974). Russek and Russek (1976) found family physicians who reported higher stress levels tend to suffer more heart attacks as they approach fifty years of age. Future studies should examine ways to decrease the apparent predisposition of physicians to heart disease as a probable result of their stressful job environment.

The stress profile also suggests that black and female medical professionals experienced more stressful events due to social and cultural mobility. Russek and Russek (1976) reported the risk of coronary heart disease increases with major changes in residency, occupation and discrepancies between culture of origin and the current culture situation. For example, the rates of heart diseases increase as individuals move into unfamiliar social circumstances or into a social environment which the individuals have not previously been prepared. Programs should be designed to help both blacks and females to cope with their social and cultural mobility stressors.

5. Technicians and Nurses

The majority of writings on these two professional groups primarily concern nurses, with the exception of Griffin and Klun (1981); Ivancevich and Matteson (1986) and Matteson and Ivancevich (1982b,c). They described the stressors facing medical technologists as a result of shift work, time pressure for immediate and accurate results, constant interruption, fear of making mistakes, equipment failure, work overload, lack of communications and interpersonal conflict with physicians and medical staff, lack of advancement opportunities and the lack of support from supervisors. Such stressors are similar to those faced by nurses. However, nurses, unlike technicians, have direct patient contact. As a result, some of the nurses' stressors are similar to those of the interns and residents. They are the death of patients, uncertainty about patient treatment, inability to meet patient needs and expectations, looking after dying babies, facing the shortage of skilled labor, communication and interpersonal problems with medical staff and supervisors, having family and life crises, poor self-esteem and insecurity about one's knowledge and competence and fear of failure (Anderson & Basteyns, 1981; Bailey, Steffen & Grout, 1980; Barstow, 1980; Boxall & Garcia, 1983; Cronin-Stubbs & Velsor-Friedrich, 1981; Fountain, 1984; Gray-Toft & Anderson, 1981; Ivancevich & Matteson, 1980; Marcus & Popovic, 1985; Parkes, 1985).

Carter (1982), in a comparative study of 206 senior female students (with 103 nurses and 103 liberal arts students), did not find any significant differences between these two student groups among 18 emotional distress items. Psychoticism was the only distress item which the liberal arts students reported a significantly higher level than the nursing students. In support of Carter (1982), Parkes (1980) found no evidence that student nurses had higher level of distress when compared to a large scale community survey.

In the studies which were designed to compare across hospital wards, Parkes (1980; 1982) found that medical wards gave rise to higher level of distress than surgical wards while surgical wards nursing students showed higher level of eustress. On the other hand, Ivancevich, Matteson and Preston (1982) found no significant differences in physiological responses from operating room and medical-surgical registered nurses even though the medical-surgical nurses reported higher levels of quantitative work overload and time pressure. In comparing emergency wards with trauma or clinic wards, Brosnan and Johnson (1980) found no differences between groups on eustress but clinic nurses had significantly higher amount of role tension. On the other hand, Brunt (1984) found that although trauma ward first-year nursing students showed higher levels of anxiety than their emergency ward counterparts, the third year nursing students' anxiety levels between these two wards were reversed. In another study, Cavagnaro (1983) compared the stress factors of critical care registered nurses with other units, and found critical care nurses suffered significantly higher stress levels than anesthetic nurses. However, Maloney (1982) found non-intensive care unit nurses reported more state and trait anxiety, more somatic complaints and a greater workload dissatisfaction than the intensive care nurses. Further, Keanne et al. (1985) did not find any significant differences in burnout reported by intensive care unit (ICU) versus non-ICU nurses. In another study, Stewart, Meyerowitz, Jackson, Yarkin and Harvey (1982) compared the stressors and distress among cancer, cardiac, operating room and ICU nurses. They found that cancer nurses experienced significantly more mood swings, relational problems, and greater difficulty in discussing the patient's condition than nurses from the other units.

In another comparative study of nine specialties of 153 headnurses, Leatt and Schneck (1980) found no significant differences in age and experience on the five stressors studied. Of the five stressors, role-based stress (the administrator role of the headnurse) was the only factor that did not make a difference in the nine units. It may be that the administrative role is universally defined and accepted by all the headnurses. However, patient-based stress was highest in ICU, medical and auxiliary units but lowest in obstetrical and psychiatry units. Task ambiguity stress was higher in auxiliary and psychiatry units while staff-movements or problems were higher in pediatrics but lower in auxiliary units. Finally the lack of physician contact was "lower in auxiliary, rural and rehabilitation, but higher in all the other units (medical, surgical, pediatrics, psychological, obstetrical and ICU).

The above comparative studies do not reveal any consistency in suggesting which nursing unit is most stressful (Gentry & Parkes, 1982). Future studies should examine the structural characteristics of units that affect the form and degree of stress nurses experience, and individual characteristics which may attract nurses to specific units (Gray-Toft & Anderson, 1981). The studies reviewed do suggest that nursing students (mostly females) may not be the most stressed student group, but they also experience learning or knowledge stress as the medical students (mostly males).

There appears to be a common core of stressors for the health care professionals due to the interdependent nature of the jobs in the medical settings which may result in the perceived lack of control over one's life, individual characteristics such as sociocultural background and personality. However, some stressors may be more potent in some wards for a certain group than the others. More systematic research in examining the differences in job demands, responsibilities and hospital procedural restriction as well as the current changes in patient care procedures on the type and degree of stress on different health care professionals of various job types and wards are needed.

CAUSES AND SYMPTOMS OF STRESS IN MEDICAL SETTINGS

The following section examines the effects of stress from correlational, quasi-experimental and experimental studies on medical professionals. Studies which did not measure stressors and symptoms are excluded. The effects of individual, job and hospital, and relationships at work are summarized in the following.

Individual Stressors

a. Physiological Symptoms

Eden (1982), in a study on the effects of critical job events (time-bounded peak of performance demands made on the individual as an integral part of the job) from 39 first year nursing students, found critical job events (CJE), or measures of objective stress (first comprehensive patient care or CJE1, and final exam or CJE2) to be related to physiological symptoms. Eden (1982) found that systolic blood pressure, pulse rate and serum uric acid increased significantly before CJE1 from the baseline level and decreased again after CJE1. Similarly, just before CJE2, the student nurses' systolic and diastolic blood pressure, pulse rate and serum uric acid levels increased and decreased after CJE2. According to the student nurses, CJE1 was stressful because of their apprehension about touching the patient's body, caring for a naked person, exposure to contagious diseases, inflicting pain on the patient, and witnessing other persons' suffering.

In another study, Ivancevich et al. (1982) found Type A nurses to report higher levels of serum cholesterol and systolic blood pressure. They also found that for Type A individuals, quantitative work overload was positively related to serum cholesterol and systolic blood pressure, while time pressure and role conflict were positively related to serum cholesterol.

The above studies suggest that objective and subjective stress are related to physiological symptoms either directly or indirectly. Student nurses' stress or (CJE1) was related to learning stress identified earlier, while nurses' stressors' relationship to physiological symptoms were moderated by individual characteristics. More systematic research on the physiological effects of stressors on various professional groups are needed before we can draw any conclusions to suggest any effective coping mechanisms for each professional group.

b. Psychological/Behavioral Symptoms

Of the possible demographic variables, nursing experience was negatively related to burnout (Stone, Jebsen, Walk & Belsham, 1984), psychological symptoms (Norbeck, 1985a), and propensity to leave the hospital (Decker, 1985). While Norbeck (1985a) found a positive association between experience and satisfaction, Decker's (1985) study failed to support such a finding. In addition, Decker (1985) found education to be unrelated to satisfaction, but positively related to propensity to leave. Keanne et al. (1985), on the other hand, found burnout to be positively associated with education but negatively related to age.

The studies above did not show that demographic variables are directly related to stress symptoms. It is possible that demographic and personality variables moderate the stressors and symptoms relationship (Ivancevich & Matteson, 1980). For example, Lester and Brower (1981) failed to find any relationship between Type A Personality with job satisfaction and other symptoms such as fatigue, overeating and irritability. Ivancevich et al. (1982) found that Type B nurses were higher in intrinsic job satisfaction. However, they did not find any difference between Type As and Type Bs on extrinsic satisfaction. They further discovered that time pressure lowered intrinsic satisfaction of the Type A nurses. In another study of nursing employees, Mossholder, Bedeian and Armenakis (1982) found that peer group interaction lowered job tension and propensity to leave among the low self-esteem individuals.

Further evidence on the moderating effects of personality of environmental stressors and the stress symptoms can be found in Matteson and Ivancevich's (1982a) study of medical technologists.

They found that Type A individuals working in Type A organizations reported more negative health symptoms. On the other hand, the Type B individuals working in Type B organizations indicated they had fewer mental and physical health symptoms.

Environmental or Hospital Stressors and Symptoms

In a study of three intake groups of student nurses, Parkes (1982) found job discretion or autonomy to be positively related to work satisfaction and negatively related to affective symptoms such as depression, anxiety and somatic complaints. However, in another study, Posner and Randolph (1980) found perceived influence to be negatively associated with job satisfaction and unit effectiveness of nurses and respiratory therapists. By employing a Solomon's four group design to study hospital employees (registered nurses, clerical workers, nurses aides, and technicians) Jackson (1983) found participation in decision making (as manipulated) did not directly relate to emotional stress, job satisfaction, absence frequency and turnover intentions. However, the hospital employees' perceived influence was directly and positively related to job satisfaction and turnover intentions. According to Price and Mueller (1981), better trained nurses were more likely to report intentions to leave. Jackson (1983) suggested that perhaps the better trained nurses have more informal influence and that superior training may have confounded such a finding.

Jackson (1983) also found a positive and direct relationship between role ambiguity and conflict with emotional stress. In addition, the negative relationships between job satisfaction and role ambiguity and conflict were because of the indirect effect of emotional stress. Posner and Randolph's (1980) study also supported Jackson's results. They also found role ambiguity and conflict to be negatively associated with job satisfaction, unit effectiveness among nurses and respiratory therapists. Role ambiguity was also found to have a negative relationship with individual performance. Similarly, Decker (1985) also found person-role conflict to have a negative association with job satisfaction. Jamal (1984) also found role ambiguity, role conflict, role overload and resource inadequacy to be negatively related to employee effectiveness but positively related to tardiness, absenteeism and anticipated turnover among nurses. Martin (1984), in a study of nurses, nurses aides, support employees, technical specialists, office and management employees in two hospitals, found role overload and inability to leave to be positively related to mental health problems in both hospitals while role ambiguity positively affected mental health in one of the two hospitals. White and Wisdom (1985), and Wisdom (1984) also found quantitative overload to be positively related to mental ill-health. In addition, Wisdom (1984) found difficulty of work, consequence of decisions and inadequate influence to be positively associated with physical ill-health.

In a study of hospital employees (executives, nurses, technicians and blue collar workers), Arsenault and Dolan (1983) found job content stress such as contact with patients, urgent decisions or job participation to be negatively associated with absenteeism on technicians and blue collar workers but unrelated to performance in all the occupational groups. Job context stress such as restrictions on behavior, skills underutilization or career ambiguity, on the other hand, was positively related to absenteeism on executives and blue collar workers but negatively related to performance of all the occupational groups.

In general, there appears to be a negative relationship between job, role and organizational stress with job satisfaction (Gray-Toft & Anderson, 1981; Norbeck, 1985; Rogers, 1983). The effects from job discretion, participation or perceived influence, and role stress suggest that the individual's belief of control results in reduced feelings of threat, and may lower the negative effects of stress. Hendrix et al. (1985) found that job stress was increased if the organization increased its control over the individuals, and stress was decreased if the control was given to the individuals through realistic job goals, role clarification and more job autonomy. Future studies should be designed to examine the effects of perceived control on the individual's psychological/behavioral and health status.

Work Relationship Stressors and Symptoms

While role-related stress showed consistent negative effects across occupational groups, positive work relationships may be related more to eustress. For example, Decker (1985) found that positive work relationships with head nurses and coworkers increased job satisfaction and decreased staff nurses' propensity to leave the hospital. Similarly, Mossholder et al. (1982) found peer group interaction decreased job tension and the low self-esteem nursing employees' propensity to leave the hospital. In another study, Norbeck (1985b) found social support to be associated with lower levels of stress, lower levels of dissatisfaction and psychological symptoms among female critical care unit nurses. However, Norbeck (1985b) did not find the interaction of stress and social support to be related to satisfaction or psychological symptoms in married critical care unit nurses.

Using a quasi-experimental design, Gray-Toft and Anderson (1983) found the use of support groups reduced perception of work load stress for both the day shift and night and evening shift hospice nurses. They also found that the use of support groups was positively related to satisfaction in the evening shift but not in the day shift hospice nurses. Martin (1984) was the only study which examined the effects of group support and cohesiveness on health symptoms. Martin (1984) found low group support and cohesion predicted mental health problems in one of the two hospital employee groups.

Although the above studies demonstrated the general positive effect of social support, these studies did not reveal whether it is the number of unavailable others to whom one can turn to in times of need, and/or the degree of satisfaction with the available support which reduce stress and health problems. In general, the studies reviewed suggest that social support can reduce the negative effects of stress. Norbeck (1985b) found that the unmarried female critical care unit nurses received more support from friends and less support from relatives than the married nurses. It is possible that the married nurses have more relatives than the unmarried nurses. Norbeck (1985b) also found that it was only the support from relatives that was effective for the unmarried nurses. It may be that friends reflect changes in value across generations while the role of family and kin provide long term support (Litwak & Szelenyi, 1969). Since coping with job stress is an experience not tied to generational values, support from relatives for the unmarried nurses may explain why they perceived less job stress. The interaction between perceived job stress and support from relatives was found to reduce psychological symptoms only for the unmarried nurses. Future studies should explore the types or sources of support systems that can reduce stress and symptoms for other medical professionals, of various ages, gender, cultural and personality.

CONCLUSIONS AND SUGGESTIONS

Ivancevich and Matteson (1980) have proposed using a multidisciplinary research approach to advance our understanding regarding stressors, reactions and consequences of stress. Such an approach includes both the behavioral and medical science disciplines to draw the connections between stress, physiological, psychological and health reactions. From the studies reviewed above, with the exception of Eden (1982), Hendrix et al. (1985), and Ivancevich and associates, most studies either focused on health symptoms or psychological/behavioral symptoms. Furthermore, most of the cited studies focused their efforts on psychological/behavioral symptoms exclusively.

The studies on the stressors and effects of stress reviewed have used methodologically more rigorous designs such as quasi-experimental and experimental but these were few in number (Eden, 1982; Gray-Toft & Anderson, 1983; Jackson, 1983; Parkes, 1982). Most of the studies reviewed were correlational, relying on a single approach for studying the effects of stress. Moreover, the stressors studied were pre-selected and were not based on the respondent-generated stressors which are relevant and stressful to the respondents. Further, most of these studies did not examine the stressors and their effects on each health care professional group even though the sample was represented by a variety of groups and job types. Studies using these approaches may miss important information on how the health care professionals become stressed and react to such stressors. Ivancevich and Matteson (1986) suggested that the studies of health care professionals can be improved with focused, systematic research effort employing self-report, interview, historical and personal observation modes of data collection. Further, researchers should describe and define the stressors and type of stress they are studying, identify the moderators as well as the short-term and long-term consequences.

The negative consequences of role-related stressors found among the health care professionals support Jackson and Schuler's (1985) meta-analysis findings. Jackson and Schuler (1985) recommended studying the effects of role ambiguity and role conflict using moderator variables and causal designs. The identification of moderating variables can help health care professionals learn more about what they can do to reduce role-related stress. Causal designs, on the other hand, allow researchers to examine behavioral and health changes before and after the stressful event(s), and why or how an event becomes stressful in the first place. Such research endeavours would permit the compilation of lists of potential stressors that have a reasonable probability of being stressful in specific settings among specific occupational groups or job types (Ivancevich & Matteson, 1986).

In addition to compiling the list of potential stressors to medical professionals, intervention programs should be designed to reduce the specific stressors identified for each health care professional group. For example, Gray-Toft and Anderson (1983) designed a hospital staff support program to reduce role-related stress experienced by hospice unit nurses. The first part of the support program consisted of group discussions designed to reduce role conflict and ambiguity by developing greater self-awareness concerning nurses' reactions to the stressful incident, insight into the behavior of the patient, the patient's family or physician, and in exploring alternative ways of coping with the nurses' report on any stressful incident.

The second part of the group discussion session involved either an in-depth discussion of the stressful situation as described, or introduced structured exercise (such as role-playing) designed to provide nurses with coping skills to the reported stressful incident. Such multiple group, time-series program was found to result in lower stress levels, higher coworker satisfaction and lower turnover among hospice nurses (Gray-Toft & Anderson, 1983). Such a support program focused on identifying stress areas prior to group discussions, collecting pre- and post-program scores on instruments to evaluate the effectiveness of the program should be replicated to other health care professionals in various wards or units.

REFERENCES

Adler, R., Werner, E.R. & Korsch, B. (1980). Systematic study of four years of internship. *Pediatrics*, 66, 1000–1008.

Anderson, C.A. & Basteyns, M. (1981). Stress and the critical care nurse reaffirmed. *The Journal of Nursing Administration*, January, 31–34.

Arsenault, A. & Dolan, S. (1983). The role of personality, occupation and organization in understanding the relationship between job stress, performance and absenteeism. *Journal of Occupational Psychology*, 56, 227–240.

Bailey, J.T., Steffen, S.M. & Grout, J.W. (1980). The stress audit: identifying the stressors of ICU nursing. *Journal of Nursing Education*, 19, 15–25.

Barstow, J. (1980). Stress variance in hospice nursing. *Nursing Outlook*, December, 751–754.

Bjorksten, O., Sutherland, S., Miller, C. & Stewart, T. (1983). Identification of medical student problems and comparison with those of other students. *Journal of Medical Education, 58,* 759–767.

Boxall, J. & Garcia, J. (1983). Stress and the nurse in neonatal units. *Midwives Chronicle & Nursing Notes,* December, 407–410.

Brosnan, J. & Johnson, M. (1980). Stressed but satisfied: organizational change in ambulatory care. *Journal of Nursing Administration,* November, 43–46.

Brunt, C. (1984). Assessing anxiety levels. *Nursing Times,* February, 37–38.

Carter, E.W. (1982). Stress in nursing students: dispelling some of the myth. *Nursing Outlook,* April, 248–252.

Cavagnaro, M.A. (1983). A comparison study of stress factors as they affect CRNAs. *Journal of the American Association of Nurse Anesthetists,* June, 290–294.

Clarke, T.A., Maniscalco, W.M., Taylor-Brown, S., Roghmann, K.J., Shapiro, D.L. & Hannon-Johnson, C. (1984). Job satisfaction and stress among neonatologists. *Pediatrics, 74,* 52–57.

Colligan, M.J., Smith, M.J. & Hurrell, J.J. (1977). Occupational incidence rates of mental health disorders. *Journal of Human Stress,* September, 34–39.

Cooper, C.L. (1983). Identifying stressors at work: recent research developments. *Journal of Psychosomatic Research, 27,* 369–376.

Cronin-Stubbs, D. & Velsor-Friedrich, B. (1981). Professional and personal stress: a survey. *Nursing Leadership, 4,* 19–26.

Dawkins, J., Depp, F.C. & Selzer, N. (1984). Occupational stress in a public mental hospital: the psychiatrist's view. *Hospital and Community Psychiatry, 35,* 56–60.

Decker, F.H. (1985). Socialization and interpersonal environment in nurses' affective reactions to work. *Social Science Medicine, 20,* 499–509.

Eden, D. (1982). Critical job events, acute stress, and strain: a multiple interrupted time series. *Organizational Behavior and Human Performance, 30,* 312–329.

Folse, M.L., DaRosa, D.A. & Folse, R. (1985). The relationship between stress and attitudes toward leisure among first-year medical students. *Journal of Medical Education, 60,* 610–617.

Fountain, D.B. (1984). Job stress on an oncology nursing unit. *Hospital Topics,* January/February, 26–28.

Friedman, M. & Rosenman, R. (1974). *Type A Behavior and Your Heart.* New York: Knopf.

Gaensbauer, T.J. & Mizner, G.L. (1980). Developmental stresses in medical education. *Psychiatry, 43,* 60–70.

Gentry, W.G. & Parkes, K.R. (1982). Psychologic stress in intensive care unit and non-intensive care unit nursing: a review of the past decade. *Heart and Lung, 11,* 43–47.

Glass, D.C. (1977). *Behavior Patterns, Stress, and Coronary Disease.* Hillsdale, NJ: Erlbaum.

Gray-Toft, P. & Anderson, J.G. (1981). The nursing stress scale: development of an instrument. *Journal of Behavioral Assessment, 3,* 11–23.

Gray-Toft, P. & Anderson, J.G. (1983). A hospital staff support program: design and evaluation. *International Journal of Nursing Studies, 20,* 137–147.

Griffin, P. & Klun, C.L. (1981). Laboratory stress: what causes it? *American Journal of Medical Technology, 46,* 490–494.

Heins, M., Fahey, S.N. & Leiden, L.I. (1984). Perceived stress in medical, law and graduate students. *Journal of Medical Education, 59,* 169–179.

Hendrix, W.H., Ovalle, N.K. & Troxler, R.G. (1985). Behavioral and physiological consequences of stress and its antecedent factors. *Journal of Applied Psychology, 70,* 188–201.

Huebner, L.A., Royer, J.A. & Moore, J. (1981). The assessment and remediation of dysfunctional stress in medical school. *Journal of Medical Education, 56,* 547–558.

Ivancevich, J.M. & Matteson, M.T. (1980). *Stress and work: a managerial perspective.* Glenview, IL: Scott, Foresman and Company, p. 44.

Ivancevich, J.M. & Matteson, M.T. (1980). Nurses & stress: time to examine the potential problem. *The Journal for Nursing Leadership and Management*, June, 17–22.

Ivancevich, J.M., Matteson, M.T. & Preston, C. (1982). Occupational stress, Type A behavior, and physical well being. *Academy of Management Journal, 25*, 373–391.

Ivancevich, J.M. & Matteson, M.T. (1986). Medical technologists and laboratory technicians: sources of stress and coping strategies. In R. Payne & J. Firth (Eds.), *Stress in the Health Professions*, John Wiley and Sons.

Jackson, S.E. (1983). Participation in decision making as a strategy for reducing job-related strain. *Journal of Applied Psychology, 68*, 3–19.

Jackson, S.E. & Schuler, R.S. (1985). A meta-analysis and conceptual critique of research on role ambiguity and role conflict in work settings. *Organizational Behavior and Human Decision Processes, 36*, 16–78.

Jamal, M. (1984). Job stress and job performance controversy: an empirical assessment. *Organizational Behavior and Human Performance, 33*, 1–21.

Keanne, A., Ducette, J. & Adler, D.C. (1985). Stress in ICU and non-ICU nurses. *Nursing Research, 34*, 231–236.

Krakowski, A.J. (1982). Stress and the practice of medicine – the myth and reality. *Journal of Psychosomatic Research, 26*, 91–98.

Leatt, P. & Schneck, R. (1980). Differences in stress perceived by headnurses across nursing specialties in hospitals. *Journal of Advanced Nursing, 5*, 31–46.

Lester, D. & Brower, E.R. (1981). Stress and job satisfaction in a sample of pediatric intensive care nurses. *Psychological Reports, 48*, 738.

Linn, B.S. and Zeppa, R. (1984). Dimensions of stress in junior medical students. *Psychological Reports, 54*, 964–966.

Litwak, E. & Szelenyi, I. (1969). Primary group structures and their functions: Kin, neighbors, and friends. *American Sociological Review, 34*, 465–481.

Maloney, J.P. (1982). Job stress and its consequences on a group of intensive care and nonintensive care nurses. *Advances in Nursing Science*, January, 31–42.

Marcus, A.L. & Popovic, S. (1985). Managing stress in the OR. *AORN Journal, 41*, 723–729.

Martin, T.N. (1984). Role stress and inability to leave as predictors of mental health. *Human Relations, 37*, 969–983.

Matteson, M.T. & Ivancevich, J.M. (1982a). Type A and B Behavior Patterns and self-reported health symptoms and stress: examining individual and organizational fit. *Journal of Occupational Medicine, 24*, 585–589.

Matteson, M.T. & Ivancevich, J.M. (1982b). Stress and the medical technologist: I. a general overview. *Focus, 48*, 163–168.

Matteson, M.T. & Ivancevich, J.M. (1982c). Stress and the medical technologist: II. Sources and coping mechanisms. *Focus, 48*, 169–176.

Mitchell, R.E., Matthews, J.R., Grandy, T.G. & Lupo, J.V. (1983). The question of stress among first-year medical students. *Journal of Medical Education, 58*, 367–371.

Mossholder, K.W., Bedeian, A.G. & Armenakis, A.A. (1982). Group process-work outcome relationships: a note on the moderating impact of self-esteem. *Academy of Management Journal, 25*, 575–585.

Norbeck, J.S. (1985a). Perceived job stress, job satisfaction, and psychological symptoms in critical care nursing. *Research in Nursing & Health, 8*, 253–259.

Norbeck, J.S. (1985b). Types and sources of social support for managing job stress in critical care nursing. *Nursing Research, 34*, July/August, 225–230.

O'Shea, R.M., Corah, N.L. & Ayer, W.A. (1984). Sources of dentists' stress. *Journal of American Dental Association, 109*, 48–51.

Parkes, K.R. (1980). Occupational stress among student nurses–1: a comparison of medical and surgical wards. *Nursing Times, 76*, October, 113–116.

Parkes, K.R. (1982). Occupational stress among student nurses: a natural experiment. *Journal of Applied Psychology, 67*, 784–796.

Parkes, K.R. (1985). Stressful episodes reported by first-year student nurses: a descriptive account. *Social Science Medicine, 20,* 945–953.

Posner, B.Z. & Randolph, W.A. (1980). Moderators of role stress among hospital personnel. *Journal of Psychology, 105,* 215–224.

Price, J.L. & Mueller, C.W. (1981). A causal model of turnover for nurses. *Academy of Management Journal, 24,* 543–565.

Quick, J.C., Dalton, J.E., Nelson, D.L. & Quick, J.D. (1985). Health administration can be stressful . . . but not necessarily distressful. *Hospital & Health Services Administration,* September/October, 101–111.

Rogers, D.A. (1983). Stress and job satisfaction of clinical laboratory scientists. *American Journal of Medical Technology, 49,* 183–188.

Rosenberg, D.A. & Silver, H.K. (1984). Medical Student Abuse: an unnecessary and preventable cause of stress. *The Journal of the American Medical Association, 251,* 739–742.

Rotbart, H.A., Nelson, W.L., Krantz, J. & Doughty, R.A. (1985). The developmental process of residency education. *AJDC, 139,* 762–765.

Rudner, H.L. (1985). Stress and coping mechanisms in a group of family practice residents. *Journal of Medical Education, 60,* 564–566.

Russek, H.I. (1974). Behavior patterns, stress, and coronary heart disease. *American Family Physician, 9,* April, 117–122.

Russek, H.I. & Russek, L.G. (1976). Is emotional stress an etiologic factor in coronary heart disease? *Psychosomatics, 17,* 63–67.

Schaff, K.A., Hockelman, R.A. (1981). Medical education: at what expense? *Journal of Medical Education, 56,* 433–435.

Stewart, B.E., Meyerowitz, B.E., Jackson, L.E., Yarkin, K.L. & Harvey, J.H. (1982). Psychological stress associated with outpatient oncology nursing. *Cancer Nursing,* October, 383–387.

Stone, G.L., Jebsen, P., Walk, P. & Belsham, R. (1984). *Western Journal of Nursing Research, 6,* 201–211.

Strayhorn, G. (1980a). Perceived stress and social supports of black and white medical students. *Journal of Medical Education, 55,* 618–619.

Strayhorn, G. (1980b). Social supports, perceived stress, and health: the black experience in medical school – a preliminary study. *Journal of the National Medical Association, 72,* 869–881.

Sword, R.O. (1984). Psychological aspects of dentistry. *Dental Management,* December, 55–62.

Walker, J.I. (1981). Coping with the stress of medical practice. *Connecticut Medicine, 45,* 593–596.

White, D.D., Wisdom, B.L. (1985). Stress and the hospital administrator: sources and solutions. *Hospital & Health Services Administration,* September/October, 112–119.

Wilson, B. (1984). Stress in dentistry: national survey. *Dental Management,* July, 14–19.

Wisdom, B.L. (1984). Primary sources of hospital administrator stress. *Journal of Occupational Behavior, 5,* 229–232.

Wolfe, E.S. & Jones, H.W. (1985). Problems experienced by residents in internal medicine training. *The Western Journal of Medicine,* April, 570–572.

Ziegler, J.L., Kanas, N., Strull, W.M. & Bennet, N.E. (1984). A stress discussion group for medical interns. *Journal of Medical Education, 59,* 205–207.

PART V: STRESS MANAGEMENT INTERVENTIONS

A Review of Organizational Stress Management Research: Methodological Considerations

Lawrence R. Murphy

SUMMARY. Evaluation studies of worksite stress management training (SMT) are reviewed and methodological considerations are offered regarding (1) program orientation, (2) experimental design, (3) worker participants, (4) outcome measures, and (5) duration of training effects and worker compliance. Suggestions for additional research include the need to (1) employ additional comparison groups in order to detect training-specific effects, (2) evaluate SMT in blue-collar settings, (3) expand the scope of outcome measures to include employee behaviors, and (4) assess long term effects of SMT and factors associated with worker maintenance of learned skills. It is concluded that SMT has value as a prevention activity in work settings but its use as a treatment strategy for troubled workers is not supported conceptually or empirically. Companies and practitioners

Lawrence R. Murphy, PhD, is affiliated with the Department of Health and Human Services, Centers for Disease Control, National Institute for Occupational Safety and Health, Applied Psychology and Ergonomics Branch, Division of Biomedical and Behavioral Science.

Address reprint requests to Lawrence R. Murphy, NIOSH, 4676 Columbia Parkway, Cincinnati, Ohio 45226 (USA).

are encouraged to view SMT not as an isolated activity but as one component of occupational health and safety activities. A holistic approach which incorporates stress management into company health and safety philosophies is viewed as the optimal strategy.

Since the early 1970s, occupational stress has increasingly been the focus of media attention and scientific research. The topic remains highly visible even today but with an added dimension: worker compensation claims for stress-related illness. The number of such claims and their associated costs has increased dramatically in the 1980s (National Council on Compensation Insurance, 1985) to the point where stress on the job ". . . has become a legal obligation" for companies (Ivancevich, Matteson & Richards, 1985, p. 60). Along with interest in identifying job stressors and their consequences has come attendant interest in strategies for preventing and reducing job stress. Approaches to the problem can be roughly classified into three main categories, (1) *organizational change* (eliminating the source(s) of stress by altering features of the organization or job tasks) (2) *job enrichment* (making the work activity more challenging and interesting), and (3) *individual-oriented techniques* (teaching workers how to prevent or reduce distress).

In a review of the literature in 1979, Newman and Beehr noted the paucity of well-designed job stress reduction studies. Since this review, a number of job stress prevention/reduction studies have appeared in the literature. The bulk of these more recent studies have evaluated the merits of individual-oriented techniques for preventing or reducing worker distress (Murphy, 1984a). Accordingly, these are the topics of the present paper.

Stress management training (SMT) is an umbrella term connoting a variety of techniques including biofeedback, muscle relaxation, meditation, imagery, and cognitive-behavior modification. Many techniques were borrowed from clinical practice where they have been used successfully for treating psychophysiological and psychosomatic disorders (Pomerleau & Brady, 1979; Meichenbaum, 1977). The popularity of individual-oriented relative to organizational change approaches is due to both logistic and conceptual factors. For example, individual-oriented programs (1) are inexpensive and can be established and evaluated quickly without major disruptions of work routines, (2) focus on the worker not the workplace as targets for change, (3) address the issue of individual differences in the perception of and reaction to stress, and (4) can be readily incorporated into existing employee assistance and other company training programs.

The workplace represents an ideal site for implementing SMT programs because of access to large numbers of individuals with social support networks already in place. Participation in programs offered at the worksite is facilitated among individuals with significant familial or social commitments which would otherwise compete for available time. To illustrate the popularity of worksite SMT, Figure 1 charts the frequency of SMT studies published from 1974 to 1984. While published accounts underestimate SMT activity in organizational settings, it is clear that interest in SMT has grown over the last 10 years and dramatically so in more recent years.

The purpose of this paper is to review the existing literature and raise some methodological issues in this young research area. Five features of studies will be examined which reflect considerations of (1) program orientation, (2) experimental design, (3) worker participants, (4) outcome measures, and (5) duration of training effects.

SMT ORIENTATION

Rather than gearing worksite SMT toward treatment and targeting distressed or troubled workers as participants, 75% of the published studies (Figure 2) offered stress management to all workers as a prevention activity. The prevention vs. treatment issue is an important one since the orientation adopted presumes different degrees of clinical expertise among program providers. Workers with manifest clinical problems (e.g., chronic anxiety, recurring headaches, alcohol/drug abuse) require treatment by trained professionals in a therapeutic atmosphere. Targeting troubled workers and providing a brief worksite stress management program is inappropriate. Also, the effects of SMT as a treatment for stress are less well documented. Programs adopting a treatment orientation convey the belief that the worker, not the workplace, is the appropriate focus for occupational stress reduction efforts. This is particularly evident in cases where SMT is the only company activity dealing with stress. In situations where organizational stress is high and no concurrent stressor reduction efforts are underway or planned, the in-

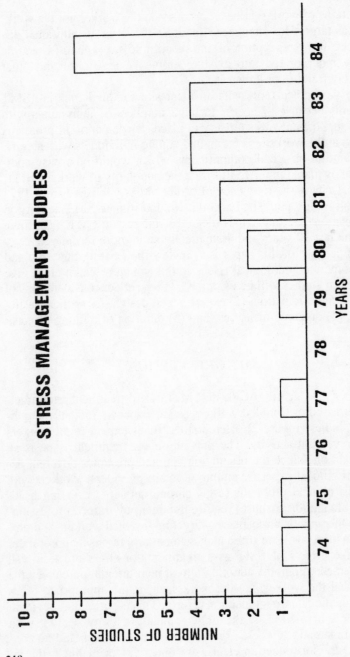

FIGURE 1. Frequency of worksite stress management training (SMT) studies from 1974-1984.

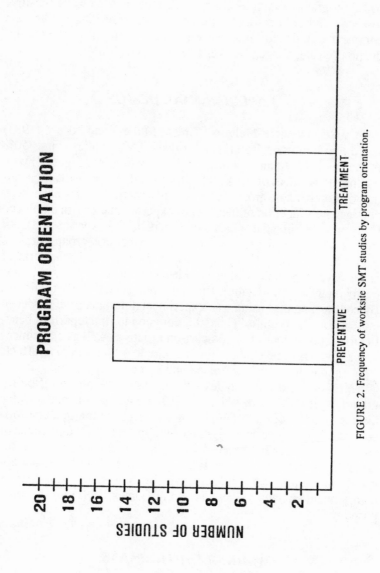

FIGURE 2. Frequency of worksite SMT studies by program orientation.

troduction of a brief stress management program may generate more anxiety, frustration, and anger than it relieves. Unlike community-based programs, practitioners in work settings need to be sensitive to social and political aspects of work and prevailing worker and company attitudes toward occupational stress and its prevention/reduction (Neale, Singer, Schwartz & Schwartz, 1982).

EXPERIMENTAL DESIGN

In a recent review, McLeroy, Green, Mullen, and Foshee (1985) noted two important features of worksite SMT studies. First, 50% of the studies used an experimental level design (see Figure 3) with random assignment of workers to groups and the inclusion of a control or comparison group. Second, differential results have been obtained as a function of the level of experimental design employed (i.e., pre-experimental, quasi-experimental, and experimental). *All* studies which used pre-experimental (no control group) designs (Cook & Campbell, 1976) reported positive results in the form of lower psychophysiological arousal levels, reduced stress symptoms (psychological and somatic), and enhanced relaxation after training. By contrast, studies using true experimental designs have produced more ambiguous results. Thus, it is common to find reports of beneficial effects in control or comparison groups as well as experimental groups. In some studies, the magnitude of post-training effects were equally large among trained and comparison groups.

This state of affairs suggests the operation of nonspecific program factors (Kazdin & Wilcoxin, 1976). Such factors may involve discrete aspects of the training program (e.g., sitting in a comfortable chair) or may reflect a Hawthorne-type effect. The presence of these factors suggests the need for additional control groups in future studies in order to isolate training-specific effects. Another approach to the problem would involve component analyses of stress management strategies (West, Horan & Games, 1984) for the same purpose.

WORKER PARTICIPANTS

It has been noted elsewhere (Murphy, 1984a) that while most studies reported significant post-training effects in normative

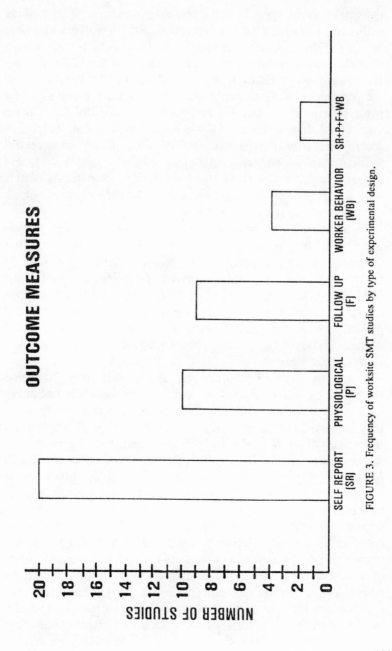

FIGURE 3. Frequency of worksite SMT studies by type of experimental design.

(group) analyses, not all participants may have learned the training skills. My experience has been that about 30% of workers who were taught biofeedback or progressive muscle relaxation were unsuccessful at lowering forehead muscle tension levels by 25% of baseline (an arbitrary criterion). While most studies have not mentioned the percentage of participants who acquired the training skills by some criterion, a similar percentage of unsuccessful participants would probably be found. In this regard, it would be helpful to identify and compare characteristics of successful vs. unsuccessful participants along sociodemographic, personality, job/life stress levels, and health belief variables. Necessarily, comparisons of this type will require larger group sizes than has been typical in stress management studies.

In addition to examining successful vs. unsuccessful participants, some efforts are needed to characterize workers who do not volunteer for these programs and those who volunteer but either do not attend training sessions or drop-out of training. Since all of the SMT studies have employed some form of muscle relaxation exercise and *relaxation-induced* anxiety has been reported in about 10% of the population (Heide & Borkovec, 1984), practitioners also need to acknowledge potential counterproductive effects of SMT for some participants.

Stress management programs are usually offered in "carpeted floor" as opposed to shop floor settings. Although only one study has been conducted with blue collar workers, stress management may be particularly beneficial for these workers given the interactive effects of stress (and lifestyle factors) and exposure to physical and chemical agents (Cohen, 1984; House, Wells, Landerman, McMichael & Kaplan, 1979). At the same time, application of these programs in blue collar settings would benefit from a careful examination of performance as well as health effects as the former can impact safe work behavior. For example, does a relaxation break taken at work result in restored vigor and lowered fatigue so that worker performance improves, *or* does such a break create feelings of drowsiness and inattention leading to reduced performance, or worse, a predisposition toward unsafe behaviors? Does relaxation increase or decrease worker vigilance? One might suspect the former in each case, but there is a need to consider competing (though unappealing) hypotheses and determine relative merit.

OUTCOME MEASURES

Outcome measures in stress management studies most commonly included self-reports of psychological and somatic complaints, and about half additionally used a psychophysiological indicator like muscle tension or blood pressure (Figure 4). Two types of outcomes have not been assessed, one from the stress coping literature and the other from the employee behavior literature. Regarding the former, stress management may improve participants' psychological resources such as self-esteem and mastery. Since people draw upon these resources to formulate coping behaviors during stressful encounters (Pearlin & Schooler, 1978), they represent important factors to assess after training.

Regarding employee behaviors, no controlled evaluations of absenteeism, productivity, or work accidents after SMT have appeared in the literature. This in contrast to the popular press and marketplace brochures which explicitly state or strongly imply direct effects of SMT on such measures. Conceptually, one might predict positive behavior change following SMT as function of increased stress awareness (decreased ambiguity) and enhanced physiological and subjective relaxation. Two as yet unpublished studies have tested these predictions. One recorded absenteeism, productivity, and job satisfaction in clerical workers for a year before and after SMT. Absenteeism decreased and productivity increased during the post-training period but the effects were evident for *both* trained and control groups. On the other hand, job satisfaction *decreased* in the trained group after training relative to controls (Riley, Fredericksen & Winett, 1984).

A second study compared organizational records of absenteeism, performance ratings, work accidents and injuries for 2-1/2 years before and 2 years after biofeedback or muscle relaxation training in highway maintenance workers (Murphy, 1984b). Regression analyses indicated significant improvements in attendance ratings and reductions in total hours absent and Monday-Friday absences in the muscle relaxation group relative to biofeedback or comparison groups. The effects were small and accounted for 4-6% of the variance after controlling for prior absenteeism. No differences among groups were found for absence frequency, hour absent, performance ratings, equipment accidents, or work injuries (Murphy & Soren-

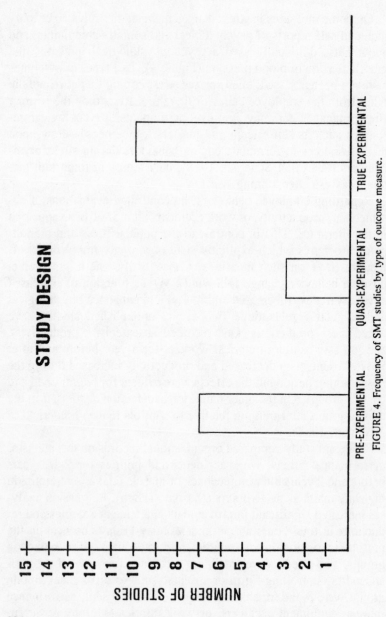

FIGURE 4. Frequency of SMT studies by type of outcome measure.

son, 1986). Clearly additional studies are needed to explore effects on these and other employee behaviors before more definitive statements are possible.

DURATION OF TRAINING EFFECTS

Looking again at Figure 4, follow-up evaluations have been conducted in nearly half of the published studies but none of these extended to a full year. The evidence indicates that post-training effects will decay over time in the absence of programmed training sessions. Lack of worker practice may underlie such decay. The few studies which did assess practice rate reported moderate to low compliance and little or no relationship between practice rate and stress reduction.

Factors which influence practice rate and the maintenance of training skills have not been examined in great detail. An exception is the work of Peters (1981) who found that practice rate during a 6 month follow-up were higher among participants who reported more noticeable benefits during meditation/relaxation training. However, even those who stopped practicing after training maintained some benefits over time. The best predictor of perceived benefit of training was whether participants taught the technique they learned to someone else (e.g., a spouse or close friend). Finally, Peters (1981) noted that practice rate in the first month after training was a good predictor of practice rate 6 months later. The implication of a "critical period" immediately after training warrants more indepth study.

SUMMARY

This paper reviewed organizational stress management studies and offered methodological considerations for future research. Most studies adopted a preventive orientation and evaluated programs in terms of individual level outcomes (e.g., blood pressure, subjective psychological states, etc.). Studies have demonstrated the efficacy of SMT but additional research is necessary to (1) isolate training-specific effects, (2) evaluate the relative merits of training techniques, (3) elaborate factors associated with worker compliance, and (4) evaluate potential effects of SMT on employee behaviors.

Conceptually, stress management represents a "band-aid" approach if used as the sole stress reduction strategy when job/organization-focused approaches should be attempted (Ganster, Mayes, Sime & Tharp, 1982). Efforts to deal with occupational stress solely through individual-oriented methods invoke a psychological fallacy of assuming that " . . . since the organization is made up of individuals, we can change the organization by changing its members" (Katz & Kahn, 1978). On the other hand, the overwhelmingly positive response of employees and the significant post-program changes found in all studies (specific and nonspecific effects) suggest that stress management programs have value within organizational stress prevention/reduction programs.

Organizations need to maintain a realistic attitude about the kind of outcomes which can be expected after stress management programs. Though marketplace brochures promise everything from fewer headaches to reductions in absenteeism, turnover, and medical care costs, the available evidence supports expectations of small to moderate changes on subjective well-being and psychophysiological arousal. Too few studies have evaluated effects of stress management on direct outcome measures like absenteeism and health care costs to draw any conclusions.

Ideally, stress management represents one component of an organization's employee health activities. Its incorporation into company health and safety philosophies reflects the kind of holistic approach which should facilitate program success and benefit employees and employers alike.

REFERENCES

Alderfer, C.P. (1976). Change processes in organizations. In *Handbook of Industrial and Organizational Psychology*. M.D. Dunnette (Ed). Chicago, Illinois: Rand McNally College Publishing Co.

Cohen, A. (1984). Health Promotion/Hazard Protection at the Workplace: A Position and Planning Guide. Proceedings of Society of Prospective Medicine, Atlanta, Georgia.

Cook, T.D. & Campbell, D.T. (1976). The design and conduct of quasi-experiments and true experiments in field settings. In M.D. Dunnette (Ed.), *Handbook of Industrial and Organizational Psychology*. Chicago, Illinois: Rand McNally College Publishing Company, pp. 223–326.

Ganster, D.C., Mayes, B.T., Sime, W.E. & Tharp, G.D. (1982). Managing occupational stress: A field experiment. *Journal of Applied Psychology, 67*, 533–542.

Heide, F.J. & Borkovec, T.D. (1984). Relaxation-induced anxiety: Mechanisms and theoretical implications. *Behavior Research and Therapy, 22*, 1–12.

House, J.S., Wells, J.A., Landerman, L.R., McMichael, A.J. & Kaplan, B.H. (1979). Occupational stress and health among factory workers. *Journal of Health and Social Behavior, 20*, 139–160.

Ivancevich, J.M., Matteson, M.T. & Richards, E.P. (1985). Who's liable for stress on the job? *Harvard Business Review*, March-April, 60–72.

Katz, D. & Kahn, R.L. (1978). *The Social Psychology of Organizations*. New York: John Wiley & Sons.

Kazdin, A.E. & Wilcoxin, L.A. (1976). Systematic desensitization and non-specific treatment effects: A methodological evaluation. *Psychological Bulletin, 83*, 729–756.

McLeroy, R.R., Green, L.W., Mullen, K.D. & Foshee, V. (1984). Assessing the effects of health promotion in worksites: A review of the stress program evaluations. *Health Education Quarterly, 11*, 379–401.

Meichenbaum, D.T. (1977). *Cognitive-Behavior Modification*. New York: Plenum Press.

Murphy, L.R. (1984a). Occupational stress management: A review and appraisal. *Journal of Occupational Psychology, 57*, 1–15.

Murphy, L.R. (1984b). Stress management in highway maintenance workers. *Journal of Occupational Medicine, 26*, 436–442.

Murphy, L.R. & Sorenson, S. (1986). Employee behaviors before and after stress management training. *Journal of Applied Psychology*, under review.

National Council on Compensation Insurance (1985). *Emotional Stress in the Workplace – New Legal Rights in the Eighties*. New York: National Council on Compensation Insurance.

Neale, M.S., Singer, J.A., Schwartz, G.A. & Schwartz, J. (1982). Conflicting perspectives on stress reduction in occupational settings: A systems approach to their resolution. *Report to NIOSH on P.O. # 82–1058*. Cincinnati, Ohio 45226 (USA).

Newman, J.D. & Beehr, T. (1979). Personal and organizational strategies for handling job stress: A review of research and opinion. *Personnel Psychology, 32*, 1–43.

Pearlin, L.I. & Schooler, C. (1978). The structure of coping. *Journal of Health and Social Behavior, 19*, 2–21.

Peters, R.K. (1981). *Daily Relaxation Response Breaks: Follow-up of a Work-Based Stress Management Program*. Springfield, Virginia: National Technical Information Service Document No. PB 83–175364.

Pomerleau, D.F. & Brady, J.P. (1979). *Behavioral Medicine, Theory and Practice*. Baltimore, Maryland: Williams and Wilkins.

Riley, A.W., Fredericksen, L.W. & Winett, R.A. (1984). Stress management in the workplace: A time for caution in health promotion. *Report to NIOSH on P.O. 84–1320*. Cincinnati, Ohio 45226 (USA).

West, D.J., Horan, J.J. & Games, P.A. (1984). Component analysis of occupational stress inoculation applied to registered nurses in an acute care facility. *Journal of Counseling Psychology, 31*, 209–218.

Organizational Level Stress Management Interventions: A Review and Recommendations

John M. Ivancevich
Michael T. Matteson

SUMMARY. The popular press has informed the public that stress can be efficiently managed with a diverse array of techniques and programs. Unfortunately, these claims have not been scientifically tested or evaluated. In fact, organizational based stress management intervention programs which incorporated well designed evaluations have rarely even been attempted. This paper provides a stress management framework and then reviews the literature to determine what can be done to increase researcher interest and dedication to scientifically designing, implementing, and evaluating organizational level stress management intervention programs.

There has been a dramatic increase in medical care expenditures in the United States from $26.9 billion in 1960 (5.3 percent of Gross National Product) to a projected $462.4 billion in 1985 (9.9 percent of GNP) (Murphy, 1984). This significant increase in expenditures has generated an increase in strategies, programs, and techniques to improve the health and well being of individuals. The 1979 Surgeon General's report, *Healthy People*, identified fifteen priority prevention areas for improving the health and well being of Americans. A companion publication identified specific objectives to be accomplished by 1990 (Promoting Health/Preventing Disease, 1980). Stress was recognized throughout the list of objectives. For example, the report stated that:

John M. Ivancevich and Michael T. Matteson are affiliated with the Department of Management, University of Houston.

229

- By 1985, a methodology should have been developed to rate the major categories of occupation in terms of their environmental stress loads.
- By 1990, the existing knowledge base through scientific inquiry about stress effects and stress management should be greatly enlarged.
- By 1990, of the 500 largest U.S. firms, the proportion offering work-based stress reduction programs should be greater than 30%.

The geometric increase in popular press articles on stress and its health, organizational, and life consequences and recommendations on how to reduce its negative impact continues unabated. Unfortunately, most of the popular press presentations are non-empirically based, not grounded in sound theory, based on anecdotal claims, and incorporate numerous inaccurate assumptions.

It is now generally accepted that stress is a significant part of performing in a job for an employer or even for oneself (an entrepreneur). Furthermore, empirical evidence points toward the notion that excessive job stress is associated with health consequences (Cousins, 1983; Eliot & Breo, 1984; Maier & Laudenslager, 1985). Despite the general acceptance about the pervasiveness of stress and the growing empirical evidence, there is a limited amount of research available that rigorously evaluates the effectiveness of stress management programs within organizations. The following highlights the paucity of evaluative research:

> Perhaps the most glaring impression we received from the review was the lack of evaluative research in this domain. Most of the strategies reviewed were based on professional opinions and related research. Very few have been evaluated directly with any sort of scientific rigor. In spite of this weak empirical base, many personal and organizational strategies for handling stress have been espoused. Although some of these strategies seem to glow with an aura of face validity, there remains the extremely difficult task of validating their effectiveness; until this is done, practitioners have little more than their common sense and visceral instincts to rely on as they attempt to develop badly needed preventive and creative stress management programs. (Newman & Beehr, 1979, p. 35)

Since this quote was made in 1979 there has been very few research reported investigations of what can be designated as an organizational level stress management intervention program; that is, a program that has as its purpose the reduction or minimization of stress that focuses primarily on organizationally specific stressors. The present paper will examine organizational level stress management intervention in terms of available research and will then provide some suggested strategies for filling the empirical gap that so obviously exists.

STRESS MANAGEMENT PROGRAMS

What is an organizational level stress management intervention? Answering this question is the first problem we encounter in examining the effectiveness of programs. There is not only confusion surrounding the topic of "stress" and what we mean by the word, but there is also uncertainty about what should be classified as a "stress management intervention" in an organization. In this paper we have elected to not add to the confusion and to simply state that organizational level stress management intervention programs are any effort initiated by the management of an organization that focuses on job specific stressors (e.g., intrinsic to the job, structure) intended to reduce any assumed negative outcomes and consequences associated with stress. This definition includes programs that attempt to remove stressors from the work environment and those that attempt to match an individual's needs, goals, aspirations, skills, and abilities with job tasks and environment.

Murphy (1984, 1986) has published a series of comprehensive reviews of what are referred to as stress management training (SMT) programs in work settings. The majority of studies he reviewed have adopted an individual or preventive health oriented approach as opposed to one that focuses on the treatment of organizationally based stress related problems. Meditation, muscle relaxation, biofeedback, and cognitive/behavioral techniques have been used as the individually oriented intervention strategies in the studies reviewed by Murphy (1984, 1986).

The majority of SMT programs contained a relaxation procedure for individuals to follow in order to lower arousal level. Also most programs included some type of stress awareness and understanding training or learning module for participants. The assessment of outcomes immediately after training and after a brief follow-up period were also common SMT practices. Other common features of the studies reviewed by Murphy (1984, 1986) were:

— The majority used white-collar employees only as participants.
— The formats varied from one training session to fifteen training sessions that lasted from one to sixteen hours.
— No studies included a long-term or longitudinal follow-up design that tracked job satisfaction and/or absenteeism before and after the program.
— The studies that used less rigorous research designs (no control groups) reported more positive attitude and affective results when compared to studies using more elegant designs (one or more control/comparison groups).

Murphy's (1984, 1986) reviews of the literature have pointed out a number of important points. First, most of what he refers to as SMT is individually focused. His review includes no studies that attempt to correct, fix, or modify the work or organizational environment that may or may not be a major source of the workplace stress. Second, no theoretical or conceptual model is used by researchers to systematically guide their assessments of the effects of programs on relevant outcomes. Consequently, there is no programmatic effort being undertaken by researchers that addresses well thought out evaluation concerns. Third, long-term effects, if any, of interventions intended to reduce or control stress are not being monitored. Therefore, immediate or short-term benefits of stress management interventions are being used to justify the time and expense. Fourth, white-collar male employees are for the most part the participant group involved in stress management interventions. The physical, chemical, and work environment stressors generally found in blue-collar work environments appear to be ideal targets for stress management interventions. Fifth, the overemphasis on individually oriented stress management interventions has slowed down efforts by organizations to alter work conditions that contribute to stress. Although this argument has been expressed again and again by labor unions it has not been taken seriously by most practitioners who are concerned about the economic, personal, and legal costs of uncontrolled, sustained workplace stress (Neal, Singer, Schwartz & Schwartz, 1984).

A STRESS FRAMEWORK

Practicing managers intuitively believe that unchecked stress among their subordinates can reduce performance, create morale problems, and may even contribute to turnover. However, when managers think about stress they generally do not include in their analyses a view of genetic properties, cognitive appraisal mechanisms, physiological responses, or cause and effect linkages. The manager's concept of stress is more personal, less scientifically based, and much more work related. He or she has developed a personal set of beliefs about stress at work and what can be done about it by listening, observing, and talking with colleagues and other employees.

If managers are to play a more active role in the diagnosis, implementation, and evaluation phases of any intervention program they need to have a framework that is rigorous enough to guide actions, but practical enough to be meaningful. The framework presented in Figure 1 is designed specifically to stimulate managerial thinking in terms of suggesting organizational level stress management interventions primarily in some of the crucial work related stressor areas.

Figure 1 emphasizes that stress is an individual perceptual phenomenon. Stress is a part of a complex and dynamic system of transaction between the person and his or her work and non-work environment. The framework illustrates that a feedback loop links stressors and outcomes which illustrates a cyclical rather than a linear stress system.

The sample of variables presented as stressors serve to highlight rather than exhaust the possibilities. Five categories, each a candidate for intervention, of organizational stressors are presented — intrinsic job, organizational structure and culture, reward system, human resource system, and leadership system. Each of these categories is important and warrants special consideration when considering organizational level interventions. The entry and processing of a stimulus is what we mean by cognitive appraisal perception. Perception is the intake of the stressor (e.g., a lack of performance feedback) and the cognitive processing of it by the individual. In the model perception is a process that involves thought, cognition or interpretation which is why the term cognitive appraisal perception is used. This interpretation combines the notion of sensory in-

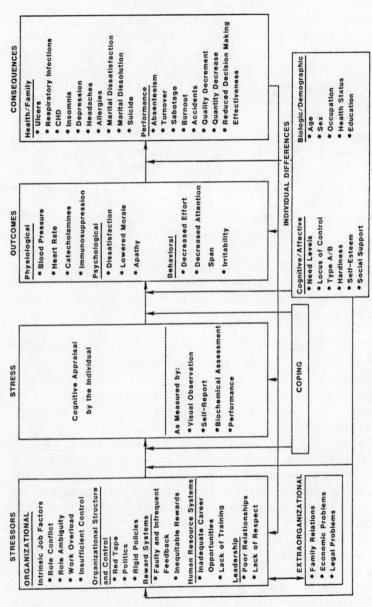

FIGURE 1. Organizational Stress Framework.

234

take and appraisal. Cognitive appraisal is the process of interpreting an event as good or bad, threatening or nonthreatening, boring or exciting.

Many factors influence a person's cognitive appraisal perception. Some of these include his or her need levels, cultural upbringing and attitudes, self esteem, experience, education, and personal behavior patterns. These and other individual differences are shown as potential moderators in Figure 1. Since we all have different personal histories and infinitely diverse appraisal patterns, the same stressors can be interpreted quite differently. This is why, for example, a reward-type stressor may be a major factor for one individual and have no meaning or intensity at all for another person.

When a person appraises an event as a stressor that is meaningful (stressful) then an outcome or combination of outcomes is triggered. Physiological, psychological, and behavioral outcomes can each be a response. Individual differences affect which outcomes do or do not occur.

The outcomes lead to health/family and/or performance consequences. The potential consequences claimed to be linked to the stress process or aggravated in some way by stress are based on limited research findings. The framework presented in Figure 1 suggests that a person that experiences chronic stress eventually will suffer consequences. Exactly what a person's stress tolerance level or competency is depends upon individual differences and coping skills.

Coping is also shown as a moderator in the framework and is considered to be a cognitive act of analyzing the environmental stressors in order to tolerate, reduce, master, or manage them. While many different typologies of coping have been introduced (Bruhn & Philips, 1984; Lazarus & Folkman, 1984), they generally fit into one of three coping categories: (a) modify the stressful event/situation (i.e., stressor) through direct action; (b) control the meaning of the stressful situation; and (c) manage the outcome.

AVAILABLE RESEARCH ON ORGANIZATIONAL LEVEL STRESS MANAGEMENT INTERVENTIONS

Since working and living in society is inevitably stressful, and if too much stress can result in health/family and performance consequences, it is important to learn to better manage stress. The individually oriented strategies such as relaxation and meditation, bio-feedback, exercise, and cognitive restructuring are intended to inoculate individuals against the effects of stressors and to cope better with situations. On the other hand, organizational intervention strategies would address one or some combination of the five main work stressor categories presented in Figure 1 — intrinsic job, organizational structure and culture, reward system, human resource systems, leadership systems.

A review of the behavioral medicine, health psychology, applied organizational behavior, stress, management, and organizational development literature indicates that very few studies are reported that examine the effectiveness of organizational level stress management intervention programs. In most reports the researcher has used a weak or no scientific methodology to trace and examine how or why a particular intrinsic job related intervention is linked to stress, outcomes, and consequences. Can the increase in control of resources reduce cognitively appraised stress and physiological responsivity, and eventually result in improved absenteeism rates? Can an improved performance feedback system reduce stress and improve morale to the extent that individual health problems are improved? To date we can only speculate about what, if anything, organizational level stress management interventions can do in addition to and instead of individual based stress management interventions. The lack of available published research does not even permit researchers and practitioners to propose combinations of individual and organizational intervention programs that may be more powerful or effective than any single level (i.e., individual or organizational) program.

If the management of work related stress is to advance, researchers need to adhere to a more systematic program of applied research. The framework which is detailed in Figure 1 is designed to offer a common starting place for guiding an increase in much needed research. Some of the questions that the framework attempts to raise in helping to fill the organizational stress management intervention effectiveness knowledge gap are these:

1. What are some of the relevant factors within the work environment that are potentially stressful?
2. Why do work related stressors affect some employees negatively and not others?
3. What are the consequences of prolonged, unmanaged stress?

4. What type of diagnosis would be the best starting point for the intervention?
5. What kind of organizational interventions would be the most effective?

The lack of available organizational level stress management intervention research and the model suggest that much more serious work on diagnosing stress is needed before any type of intervention, individual or organizational, is initiated. Diagnosis is critical because an invalid assessment could mean a waste of energy, resources, and time correcting a problem that really is not significant. Two types of problems need to be searched out in diagnosing work stress: (1) those related to the individual in terms of physical, psychological, and behavior outcomes and health and family consequences; and (2) those related to the organization in terms of excessive absenteeism and turnover rates and performance decrements. Both problems need to be assessed simultaneously because of their significant interdependence. Perhaps both kinds of problems also need to be corrected by a combination individual/organizational intervention approach. We simply do not know what kind of intervention strategy is likely to be the most effective within any organization or for any occupation groups because of the empirically based knowledge void in the literature.

RELATED RESEARCH: STRENGTHS AND WEAKNESSES

Since little available research has examined organizational level stress management intervention programs a review of individual level interventions, preventive health programs, and organizational behavior reviews on stress management issues was conducted. This was done to determine if knowledge is available in tangential areas of inquiry that could serve as examples or models for needed intervention research.

Jackson (1983) proposed and tested a causal model to examine the effect of participation in decision making on perceived influence, role conflict, role ambiguity, personal and job-related communications, social support, emotional strain, overall job satisfaction, absenteeism, and turnover intention. Data were collected from employees of an outpatient facility affiliated with a university hospital. A Solomon four-group design was modified to include two posttests (three and six months after intervention) rather than one.

Participants were randomly assigned to the intervention or no intervention conditions, where the intervention was the introduction of frequently held staff meetings. This intervention remained in effect throughout the course of the study. The analysis of the six months postintervention data indicated that participation had a significant negative effect on two specific stressors, role conflict and role ambiguity. These two stressors, in turn, were positively related to emotional strain and negatively related to job satisfaction. Emotional strain was positively related to absence frequency and turnover intention. Jackson (1983) concludes that participation in decision making (a management intervention as defined in the present paper) appears to be an important causal determinant of role strains.

The Jackson (1983) study used a much needed longitudinal design. In fact, the differences between intervention and control participants were quite small at the three month post-intervention data point. It would have been interesting and insightful to trace the effects of the intervention for a period longer than six months as was done in the study. The Jackson (1983) study also failed to examine specific performance outcomes which is a universal problem associated with all forms of stress management evaluations. However, Jackson (1983) attempted to institute a rigorous research design, to conduct a longitudinal investigation, and proposed a theoretical model that guided the empirical testing.

Ganster, Mayes, Sime and Thorp (1982) conducted a fairly rigorous study of individual level stress management training. These researchers selected a training strategy that had a strong a priori potential for success. They also wanted to test a stress management program that had some degree of generalizability to other organizational settings. Thus, they studied employees of a public agency. One group of employees was exposed to 16 hours of training in recognition of stress-inducing cognitions, work on systematically evaluating the consequences of events as work, and how to utilize muscle relaxation procedures. The control group employees were not exposed to the 16-hour training package.

Three types of variables were assessed: psychological, physiological, and somatic complaints. The treatment employees exhibited lower epinephrine and depression levels than did controls at the posttest and also at the four-month follow-up assessment point. The researchers raise some important points about limitations of their study. They state that although some significant findings are found to support the treatment effects, the actual size of the treatment group versus control group differences are not dramatic. Ganster et al. (1982) also raise the point that training employees (individual intervention) to better tolerate poorly designed organizations (organizational intervention) may be a questionable strategy. In essence, they suggest that organizational interventions should be but are not in most cases, given higher priority than individual interventions such as the type used in the study.

The experimental design used in the Ganster et al. (1982) study should be lauded by those interested in evaluating the effects of stress management interventions. Unfortunately, the study did not examine or compare organizational level interventions, nor did it incorporate any performance based outcome variables. Furthermore, the generalizability of public agency based results to other organizational settings is questionable. Despite these limitations the Ganster et al. (1982) research is the type that is badly needed in assessing organizational level stress management interventions.

A study by Carrington, Collings, Benson, Robinson, Wood, Lehrer, Wollfolk and Cole (1980) used a comparison design strategy to examine the effects of three individual level meditation/relaxation techniques on symptoms of employees over a five and a half month period. A total of 154 employee volunteers, self-selected on the basis of perceived stress and screened to eliminate persons with previous experience in meditation/relaxation were randomly assigned to one of four groups:

1. Clinically standardized meditation (CSM)
2. Respiratory One Method (ROM) meditation
3. Progressive muscle relaxation (PMR)
4. Control group, receiving no intervention

The results of the study were very revealing. Compliance with meditation/relaxation practice was higher than anticipated. At the end of the study, 81 percent of the CSM, 76 percent of the ROM, and 63 percent of the PMR subjects were still following a practice regimen. Also, the participants in the three treatment groups taken as a whole showed symptom reduction. However, when the three meditation/relaxation techniques were examined separately in terms of degree of symptom reduction the methods were found to differ in their effectiveness. The progressive muscle relaxation (PMR) group showed no more improvement than controls, but the two meditation groups (CSM and ROM) were significantly better.

Again this study, like the Jackson (1983) and Ganster et al. (1982) investigations, used a highly recommended experimental design. However it, like the other studies, failed to examine any performance outcomes, it covered a relatively short time frame of only five and a half months, and it focused solely on comparisons of individual level interventions.

The designs, variables studied, and methodologies incorporated in the three sample studies just presented provide insights on the type of intervention research that is needed. Each of the studies illustrate that although longitudinal designs were used the time period mentioned after the intervention was relatively short. The need to extend the postintervention period is obvious even in what should be considered fairly rigorous stress management intervention research. There is also the need to pay more specific attention to managerial needs. The discussions attached to each study fail to address any particular managerial concern or objective.

ORGANIZATIONAL INTERVENTIONS: MANAGERIAL ACTIONS

Figure 1 presented five organizational level targets for managerial action: intrinsic job, organizational structure and culture, reward systems, human resource systems, and leadership systems. An important managerial based objective of organizational interventions is to have a direct effect on the stressor(s). Table 1 lists some potential organizational strategies that practitioners could incorporate in combatting stress. Again, like Figure 1, the descriptions in Table 1 are certainly not exhaustive. The list only serves to illustrate the kind of intervention procedures that could be developed and evaluated if stress were diagnosed.

A crucial first step in taking any form of managerial initiated action is to determine which categories are creating the stress. That is, a formal diagnosis (needs diagnosis) that defines the scope, magnitude, and duration of the stress problem is needed. Diagnosis should be conducted with observation methods which at a minimum are standardized, permit assessment of factors and magnitude of changes, are nonreactive to repeated measuring, and have checks for manipulation. Thus, before practitioners even consider a partic-

Table I

Managerial Intervention Actions
on Organizational Stressors

Category	Stressor	Managerial Action To Be Developed, Implemented, and Evaluated
Intrinsic to Job	Work Overload	Redesign job to match individual's skills, energy, needs.
Intrinsic to Job	Insufficient Control of Resources	Initiate, through participation, involvement, and discretion in job related events.
Organizational Structure and Culture	Red Tape	Simplify reporting requirements and relationships between levels in the hierarchy.
Organizational Structure and Culture	Lack of Mission and Strategy	Document and circulate the mission and strategy being used by the firm (department or unit).

TABLE 1 (continued)

Reward System	Lack of Feedback	Institute goal setting program with a number of formal and informal feedback sessions.
Reward System	Inequitable Rewards	Conduct survey to determine points of concern and correct problems that can be reasonably changed.
Human Resource Systems	Lack of Training	Institute training programs that can improve a person's self confidence, performance, and/or commitment.
Human Resource Systems	Lack of Job Security	Specify position of firm about employment security and work with employees to develop a fair plan in case layoffs are required.
Leadership Systems	Poor Relationships	Institute team building program that would involve leaders and followers.
Leadership Systems	Lack of Respect	Improve selection process for hiring or promoting leaders so that most talented individuals hold these positions.

ular form of intervention it is important to conduct a needs diagnosis (more on this will be discussed later) which is perhaps the critical as well as the most difficult step in the management of stress. Certainly, it is necessary for any needs diagnosis to be valid and reliable before a positively contributory applied research program is even attempted.

APPLIED RESEARCH: SOME GUIDELINES

The ideal study of individual or organizational stress management interventions has yet to be designed. It is probably accurate to conclude that were such a study designed it would be impossible to execute in an organizational setting. Thus, instead of presenting ideal suggestions we will offer what seem to be reasonable courses to take in investigating organizational level stress management interventions.

Needs Diagnosis

As already suggested, the first step in organizational level stress management is to conduct a needs diagnosis. What is the prevalence of stress among employees? Are organizational stressors contributing to these stress levels? Which stressors can be efficiently modified to reduce or minimize the stress? The needs diagnosis is intended to verify that a stress problem exists. In a workplace setting, a needs diagnosis could also examine the incidence and distribution of health/family and performance consequences. Is there a particular unit or group in which excessive health/family and performance consequences are occurring?

The next phase of a needs diagnosis is to establish corrective managerial action goals. Specific quantifiable outcome and consequence measures of any corrective action should be discussed, debated, and established. The establishment of goals will aid in the development of research designs that can be used to evaluate the impact of the specific intervention program.

Experimental Designs

As noted in this paper there have been very few reported studies that have evaluated organizational level stress management interventions. The ideal design would be a true experiment. The one true experimental design to consider is the pre-intervention-post-intervention group comparison (Campbell & Stanley, 1966).

$$R \quad O_1 \quad X \quad O_2 \quad \text{Intervention Group}$$
$$R \quad O_3 \quad\quad\ \, O_4 \quad \text{Control Group}$$

The Rs refer to the randomization of participants (which may have to be used to designate units), the Os represent the observations or measurements, and X refers to the intervention (e.g., increased use of appraisal feedback or permitting employees greater control of resources, or increased job security provisions).

The true experimental design can only be used when the target population is much larger than the number of program participants. An appraisal feedback program designed for all employees cannot be properly evaluated by this design, because no employees will be available to be included in the control group. Also, in a small work setting, where intervention and control group participants are likely to interact, contamination of effects may result.

When the use of true experimental design is not possible, which may be most of the time, quasi-experimental design is the preferred nonequivalent control group design (Cook & Campbell, 1979). When randomizing volunteers (or units) to intervention and control groups is not possible, it is useful to find a nonrandomized comparison group. The nonequivalent control group design is

$$O_1 \quad X \quad O_2 \quad \text{Intervention Group}$$
$$O_3 \quad\quad\ \, O_4 \quad \text{Control Group}$$

A second quasi-experimental design is the time series design, which is

$$O_1 \quad O_2 \quad X \quad O_3 \quad O_4$$

When longitudinal measures are available, intervention participants can be used as their own controls. However, if another event occurs at the same time as the intervention (e.g., a change in the manager in charge), it is not possible to determine whether the intervention or the other event is causing the changes in outcomes and consequences.

Longitudinal Research

There is a void in the literature in the development of comprehensive theories of how to manage stress. Longitudinal data can provide the necessary empirical base for developing these needed comprehensive theories. Longitudinal organizational level stress management intervention research would permit the observation, description, and/or classification of stressors, stress, outcomes, and consequences in such a way that the stress process can be empirically documented as a dynamic phenomenon.

An appropriate question that stress researchers must raise is what constitutes longitudinal research. If we are studying the development of human intelligence, and if we believe that it is largely shaped in the first sixteen years of life, we do not want to collect data once every sixteen years. A more appropriate time span might be every year. Similarly, in the analysis of organizational stress, the nature of the problem and the nature of the theoretical framework (Figure 1) brought to bear on the problem should address the meaning of longitudinal.

Longitudinal studies of the management of organizational level stress requires a longer time frame than one week, one month, or three months. The time span must be of sufficient length to permit changes in outcomes and consequences to unfold. Since few available studies are now reported it is our intent to caution researchers about carefully specifying reasonable time spans for data collection. At least one year seems to be a reasonable starting point in tracking whether an organizational level intervention is having an impact on outcomes and/or consequences.

Outcome and Consequence Measures

Of paramount importance in organizational level stress management interventions is the improvement of outcome and consequence variables like those presented in Figure 1. Thus, research designs and methodologies need to incorporate multiple outcome and consequence measures. For example, if intervention research can demonstrate that absenteeism is reduced and that measurable changes in psychophysiological reactivity such as blood pressure or apathy are also occurring, then a more comprehensive understanding of intervention mechanisms can be achieved. Since the intervention-consequence mechanisms are not fully understood or known, then organizational level intervention research can be conducted as much to develop insights on mechanisms as to identify useful models of intervention.

Methods of Interventions

A major managerial decision involves whether to adopt a multi-modal or single method intervention strategy. The majority of individual level interventions use single method approaches, such as focusing on relaxation, exercise, or on cognitive restructuring. The single method is more precise, demands either theoretical or empirical reasons for selecting a specific intervention, but has a higher risk of lack of results for reasons other than the potency of the intervention. Research at the organizational level should use both approaches for the differing insights each offers: the multimodal method being more likely to provide information on the methodology for promoting improvements, the single method being more likely to test hypotheses about mechanisms.

A primary deficiency in individual level intervention research which must be addressed in organizational level intervention research is the lack of controls. The increasing media publicity about the desirability of managing stress may pose a contamination problem in any intervention research. When possible, controls should be incorporated into the research design. However, even when controls can't be incorporated into the research design it could be important to gather information about how individuals have been affected by their involvement with an organizational level stress management intervention. Even a no control group situation can document whether an intervention is having some affect. Although nothing definitive can be said about the intervention at least some demonstration of affect can be reviewed in terms of costs and benefits.

CONCLUDING NOTE

Strictly speaking, it is important for researchers to demonstrate the relationship between organizational level stress management intervention and outcome and consequence changes. Researchers must recognize the potential complexity of organizational level intervention. The list of interactive variables include individual differences, coping skills, and the type and duration of the intervention itself.

The current knowledge base on organizational level stress management intervention is almost non-existent. Individual level interventions should not be replaced by organizational level interventions because enough evidence to make such a decision is not available. As Ganster et al. (1982) have implied individual level interventions may need to be combined with organizational level interventions. However, before such a suggestion can be taken seriously more organizational level interventions must be conducted and evaluated. Certainly, the total elimination of stressors via intervention programs is beyond the ability of any manager. Organizational managers, however, will have to accept the idea of paying greater attention to organizational level stressors such as intrinsic job factors, organizational structure and culture, reward systems, human resource systems, and leadership systems. Eventually, as research and experience accumulates, this increased attention could result in the improvement in health/family and performance consequences.

REFERENCES

Bruhn, J.G. & Philips, B.V. (1984). Measuring social support: A synthesis of current approaches. *Journal of Behavioral Medicine, 7*, 151–170.

Campbell, D.T. & Stanley, J.C. (1966). *Experimental and quasi-experimental designs for research*. Chicago: Rand McNally.

Carrington, P., Collings, G.H. Jr., Benson, H., Robinson, H., Wood, L.W., Lehrer, P.M., Wollfolk, R.L. & Cole, J.W. (1980). The use of meditation relaxation techniques for the management of stress in a working population. *Journal of Occupational Medicine, 22*, 221–231.

Cook, T.D. & Campbell, D.T. (1979). *Quasi-experimentation: Design and analysis issues for field settings*. Chicago: Rand McNally.

Cousins, N. (1983). *The healing heart: Antidotes to panic and helplessness*. New York: Norton.

Eliot, R.S. & Breo, D.L. (1984). *Is it worth dying for?* New York: Bantam Books.

Ganster, D.C., Mayes, B.T., Simes, W.E. & Thorp, G.D. (1982). Managing occupational stress: A field experiment. *Journal of Applied Psychology, 67*, 533–542.

Jackson, S. (1983). Participation in decision making as a strategy for reducing job-related strain. *Journal of Applied Psychology, 68*, 3–19.

Lazarus, R.S. & Folkman, S. (1984). *Stress, appraisal, and coping*. New York: Springer.

Maier, S.F. & Laudenslager, M. (1985). Stress and health: Exploring the links. *Psychology Today, 19*, 44–49.

Murphy, L.R. (1984). Occupational stress management: A review and appraisal. *Journal of Occupational Psychology, 57*, 1–15.

Murphy, L.R. (1985). Evaluation of worksite stress management. *Corporate Commentary, 1*, 24–32.

Murphy, L.R. (in press). A review of organizational stress management research: Methodological considerations. *Journal of Organizational Behavior and Management*.

Neale, M.S., Singer, J.A., Schwartz, G.E. & Schwartz, J. (1984). Conflicting perspectives on stress reduction in occupational settings: A systems approach to their reduction. Cincinnati, OH: Report to NIOSH.

Newman, J.D. & Beehr, T. (1979). Personal and organizational strategies for handling job stress: A review of research and opinion. *Personnel Psychology, 32*, 1–43.

U.S. Department of Health and Human Services, Public Health Service (1980). *Promoting health/preventing disease: Objectives for the nation*. Washington, DC: U.S. Government Printing Office.

PART VI: CONCLUSION

The Present and Future Status of Stress Research

Ronald J. Burke

SUMMARY. Five research thrusts were identified in current stress research: replications and extensions of ISR's work environment and health model, Type A behavior, psychological burnout, social support, and the work-nonwork interface. However, one or more limitations were noted in stress research methodology which limited the value of much of this work. In addition to addressing these shortcomings, future stress researchers are encouraged to employ longitudinal designs and include measures of physiological symptoms. Stress researchers should concentrate on: stress as a process, blue and pink collar workers, work stress of women, sex differences in stress dynamics, and the work, family and societal interface. In addition, bridging the gap between the producers *and* consumers of stress research findings would achieve better informed research *and* practice. Although occupational stress has become a central variable in OB research, our understanding of stress phenomena remains rather limited. Increases in understanding will continue to come slowly.

About five years ago (Jick & Burke, 1982; Payne, Jick & Burke, 1982), my colleagues and I attempted to take stock of the progress

Ronald J. Burke is affiliated with York University.

Preparation of this manuscript was supported in part by the Faculty of Administrative Studies, York University. I would like to acknowledge the assistance of Betty Hagopian in preparing the manuscript and the helpful comments of Esther Greenglass and Gene Deszca.

that had been made in stress research and to critically examine key concepts, measurement techniques and major areas in need of more refined analysis. The field of occupational stress appeared to be a crossroads in which key choices would have to be made in the 1980s. We highlighted three choices: How should we study stress? Who do we want to study? And what problems should be studied?

We noted three methodological challenges: identifying the relative value of various methods used in stress research, examining the meaning and phenomenology of the stress experience, and examining the validity of measures in the hope of standardizing diagnostic instruments. We recommended that more care be devoted to the selection of subjects. Subjects who were strained (about ten percent of the population) should be selected noting whether the state was acute versus chronic. Researchers should concentrate on blue collar jobs which were demanding but of low discretion (Karasek, 1979), the long term unemployed, chronically threatened job incumbents, the wives of men who are themselves in stressful occupations, women in professional and executive roles, the wives of the unemployed, and single parent families in general. Stress problems worthy of study included: acute versus chronic states of stress, the role of the objective and subjective environment, the relationship between psychological strain and physiological mechanisms, coping behaviors, and the work, family and societal interface.

The objectives of this article are to describe the present status of stress research, to determine whether earlier recommendations and suggestions can be observed in current research, and to examine the future status of stress research.

INCREASING INTEREST IN OCCUPATIONAL STRESS

The volume of stress research continues to grow. Newman and Beehr (1979) noted that occupational stress first appeared as a key word in *Psychological Abstracts* in 1973, indicating that there was not enough published material prior to this time to warrant this heading. Pioneering stress researchers such as Jack French and his colleagues (French, Kahn & Mann, 1962; French & Caplan, 1972) and Alan McLean (1966) began their research programs twenty-five years ago. But it is only within the last ten years that a broad interest in occupational stress by academics has emerged (Beehr & Bhagat,

1985; Cooper, 1983; Cooper & Payne, 1978, 1980; Ivancevich & Matteson, 1980; Quick & Quick, 1984; Addison-Wesley Series, 1980). And academic research in occupational stress is currently being undertaken in various countries around the world. It is not an exaggeration to conclude that occupational stress has become a central topic in the field of organizational behavior (Staw, 1984).

CURRENT STRESS RESEARCH CONTENT

There are at least five important areas that can be identified in current stress research. These include: (1) replications and extensions of the work environment and well-being framework developed by the Institute for Social Research at the University of Michigan (Caplan et al., 1975), (2) studies of coronary-prone or Type A behavior (Friedman & Roseman, 1974; Chesney & Rosenman, 1980),[1] (3) investigations of burnout in work settings (Cherniss, 1980; Maslach, 1982), (4) examinations of various effects of social support on work stress and well-being (House, 1980) and (5) examination of the ways in which work stress and life stress influence each other and both individual and organizational outcomes (Bhagat, 1985; Burke & Bradshaw, 1981).

Work Stress and Individual Well-Being

Several studies have been conducted to establish links between various work stressors and several aspects of individual well-being. Most of these studies have used the person-environment fit model (or part of it) developed by ISR and many of ISR's measures (Caplan et al., 1975).

These investigations have included diverse samples, have examined a wide range of occupational stressors, and have included several different measures of emotional and physical well-being. These studies have consistently shown modest but statistically significant associations between measures of work stress and individual well-being. These studies, taken together, have served to keep the work stress-health relationship in the mainstream of organizational behavior research. They have also replicated and extended several findings reported previously (Caplan et al., 1975). Given the num-

---

[1]This research is reviewed in the article by Ganster in this issue.

findings reported previously (Caplan et al., 1975). Given the number of studies that have employed the same (or similar) measures the time has come to undertake a meta-analysis of their findings (see Jackson & Schuler, 1985).

Psychological Burnout in Work Settings

Another area of work stress interest deals with the concept of psychological burnout. Burnout has been defined in various ways by different researchers. The broadest definitions (Freudenberger, 1980) equate burnout with stress, connect burnout with an endless list of adverse health and well-being variables, and suggest it is caused by the relentless pursuit of success. Other definitions are narrower, relating burnout to human service professions with interpersonal stress as its cause (Maslach & Jackson, 1981); that is, emotional burnout is related to feelings experienced by people whose jobs require repeated exposure to emotionally charged interpersonal situations (Maslach, 1982).

DEVELOPING MODELS
OF PSYCHOLOGICAL BURNOUT

Although there are many significant and interpretable findings related to burnout, few research investigations have been guided by a comprehensive model or research framework. Pines, Aronson, and Kafry (1981) divide the work environment into internal and external variables. Maslach (1982) categorizes variables into those representing involvement with people, the job setting, and personal characteristics, but this clustering implies only a person-environment interaction (at the most general level) without specifying the central features of either.

The only comprehensive model has been offered by Cherniss (1980). This model proposes that individuals with particular career orientations and extra-work support and demands interact with particular work setting characteristics. The interaction of these factors results in the experience of specific sources of stress. Individuals cope with these stresses in different ways. Some employ techniques and strategies which might be termed active problem solving while others cope by exhibiting the negative attitude changes Cherniss identified in his concept of burnout. Burnout, for Cherniss, occurs over time—it is a process—and represents one way of adapting to, or coping with, particular sources of stress.

Several investigations were designed to validate the Cherniss model in a study of burnout among men and women in police work, and in teaching. Measures of his concepts had to be created for the research since none existed. The data (Burke, Shearer & Deszca, 1984a; Burke, Deszca & Shearer, 1984) provided considerable support for the model.

Examining Progressive Phases of Burnout

Golembiewski and his colleagues (Golembiewski, 1984; Golembiewski, Munzenrider & Stevenson, 1986; Golembiewski & Munzenrider, 1981) proposed the existence of eight progressive phases of burnout. They operationalized these phases using the three scales of the MBI. They hypothesized that Emotional Exhaustion was the most potent contributor to burnout, that Lack of Personal Accomplishment was less potent and that Depersonalization was the least potent contributor to burnout. Eight progressive phases of burnout were then created by dichotomizing scores on the three MBI scales. Individuals in the least advanced phase of burnout would score low (bottom half) on the three MBI subscales. Individuals in the most advanced phase of burnout would score high (top half) on the three MBI subscales. Individuals with other combinations of low and high subscale scores would represent phases of burnout somewhere between the two extremes.

Recent research (Golembiewski, Munzenrider & Carter, 1983; Golembiewski & Munzenrider, 1984; Burke, 1986; Burke, Shearer & Deszca, 1984b) has validated the notion of progressive phases of burnout by comparing individuals in the various phases of burnout on other measures. In general, these studies provide support for the proposition that individuals at different phases of burnout also differ on antecedents and consequences of burnout. This is particularly important since individuals may have the same *total* MBI score but fall into different phases of burnout.

Social Support and Work Stress

Considerable attention has been devoted to identifying factors within the individual or the environment that reduce the disease-promoting effects of stress. Social support has received considerable research attention as one such conditioning variable (Payne, 1980; House, 1980; Wells, 1984).

There is evidence that supervisor support is more likely to have direct effects on stress, strain and the stress-strain relationship than are co-worker support and spouse support (Caplan et al., 1975; LaRocco & Jones, 1978; LaRocco, House & French, 1980). There has been an increasing emphasis on examining facets of social support such as structural, informational and emotional (Ford, 1983, 1985; Karasek, Triantis & Chaudry, 1982). Finally, there is a suggestion (Fisher, 1985) that effects of social support may be stronger when researchers examine specific organizational transitions (e.g., starting a new job) rather than chronic stressors (e.g., role overload).

While these studies demonstrate the importance of social support, there still remains several unanswered questions (Ganster, Fusilier & Mayes, 1986). These include: definitions and measures of social support, an examination of possible functions of social support (direct, buffering, conditioning), appropriate data analyses of social support relationships, relevant sources of social support, and a consideration of other variables (e.g., personality hardiness, Maddi & Kabasa, 1984) that capture the complexity of the work stress and health relationship (House, 1980).

Work and Life Stress

I previously reviewed material in the area of work and life stress and the family (Burke & Bradshaw, 1981), and am currently preparing a chapter on work and family (Burke & Greenglass, 1987). A tremendous amount of material has been written on these topics during the past six years. Some of this material deals specifically with the stresses of dual career couples (Hall & Hall, 1980; Gupta & Jenkins, 1985). A larger amount deals with work and family conflict (Lee & Kanungo, 1984; Nieva, 1984; Nieva & Gutek, 1981; Larwood, Stromberg & Gutek, 1985; Kanter, 1977).

Greenhaus and Beutell (1985) provide an excellent review of the literature on conflict between work and family roles using the role conflict framework proposed by Kahn and his colleagues in their classic study of organizational stress (1964). Greenhaus and Beutell conclude that work-family conflict exists when *time* devoted to the requirements of one role makes it difficult to fulfill requirements of the other, *strain* from participating in one role makes it difficult to fulfill requirements of the other, and *behavior* required by one role makes it difficult to fulfill the requirements of the other.

CURRENT STRESS RESEARCH METHODOLOGY

Although research on work stress has been steadily increasing, most studies in this area have one or more of the following limitations: (1) they employ self-report data almost entirely, thus observed relationships may be artifacts of method similarity and content overlap in the measures of stress and health; (2) a preponderance of two-variable research designs examining the relationship between a stressor and a stress response using correlational analyses. This design does not make it possible to determine causality and ignores the role of intervening variables; (3) the designs are almost always cross-sectional or retrospective with no longitudinal or prospective feature; (4) the populations studied have been small and/or organizationally or occupationally specific rather than large and representative of a general population, (5) when moderator variables have been included, they have been few in number, (6) valid psychological and physical health data are rarely included; (7) the respondents are almost always men, with little attention given to the effects of work stress on women; and (8) persisting confusion about what is being measured. Are researchers measuring stress, work and organizational characteristics causing stress, or a process which includes both stressors and stress response? There is still disagreement among researchers in definition and conceptualization of work stress in organizations. In summary, most of the research on work stress has involved small scale studies (limited samples, few variables, self report data) which replicate earlier studies.

These factors, taken together, suggest that the research findings observed to date should be treated conservatively (Beehr & Schuler, 1982). The data are "fragmentary . . . difficult to replicate and subject to multiple etiological interpretations" (Kasl, 1981, p. 682).

We had earlier expressed the optimistic belief that stress researchers would begin to standardize their measures (Payne, Jick & Burke, 1982). Movement in this direction has begun to occur. Thus, particular occupational stressors are likely to be examined using a given measure (Ivancevich & Matteson, 1980; Caplan et al., 1975). Type A behavior is likely to be measured by the Jenkins Activity Survey (Jenkins, Zyzanski & Rosenman, 1979), the structured interview (Friedman & Rosenman, 1974) or the Framingham Type A scale (Haynes et al., 1978, 1980). Psychological burnout is likely to be measured by the Maslach Burnout Inventory (Maslach & Jackson, 1981).

Another positive sign is the inclusion of organizational consequences of stress such as absenteeism and performance (Matteson, Ivancevich & Smith, 1984; Bhagat, 1983), along with the initial emphasis on individual well-being and health outcomes.

FUTURE STRESS RESEARCH CONTENT

Future work stress research must fill some obvious gaps in knowledge. These include: respondents (women, sex differences, blue collar workers), content (coping behaviors, work, family and societal interface) and the conceptualization of work stress itself (process). Let us briefly consider each of these areas.

Work Stress of Women

Studies of work stress have almost exclusively focussed on men. However, with the dramatic rise in women's employment in recent years and their increasing visibility in non-traditional areas such as management, there is a growing need for the systematic investigation of factors related to women's work stress. Moreover, evidence suggests that even in the same employment situation, men and women may experience different stressors (Greenglass, 1982; Jick & Mitz, 1985). In addition to the occupational demands faced by men, women may experience stressors unique to their gender such as token status, sex-discrimination and sexual harassment (Terborg, 1985).

A movement in this direction raises some questions about the measures that are used to assess work stressors. The Jenkins Activity Survey (Jenkins, Zyzanski & Rosenman, 1979) is frequently used with female respondents though it was developed and validated on primarily white middle class males. It will be important to develop Type A behavior measures and validate them on women. This is necessary since women exhibit different degrees of particular Type A characteristics than men as a result of different socialization experiences (Price, 1982). Measures of work stress unique to women (e.g., minor status, sexual harassment) need to be developed and systematically explored.

Sex Differences in Stress Dynamics

It is well recognized that individual differences play an important moderating role in the experience of work stress. Many researchers have proposed sex differences in stress dynamics. However, relatively little attention has been given to the role of sex as a moderator of stressor-strain relationships (Jick & Mitz, 1985). In addition it appears to be important to consider both sex and sex roles since these may be different. Gender may be viewed either as a moderator between stressors and strain or as predictor of stressors, strain and coping responses. It may be that men and women are exposed to different stressors, and the relationship between stressors and appraisal, appraisal and coping, and coping and strain may be moderated by gender.

Based on a review of 19 studies, Jick and Mitz concluded that women tended to report higher rates of psychological distress and that men were more prone to physical illness. Although several explanations of these findings were proposed (structural, social psychological) several questions remain unanswered.

Blue and Pink Collar Workers

Work stress researchers have devoted little research attention to blue collar workers and workers in lower level clerical positions (e.g., secretaries). There are some notable exceptions such as Shostak (1980), House, McMichael, Wells, Kaplan and Landerman (1979) and Karasek (1979). But these stand out as exceptions. Much more research attention needs to be focussed here.

Coping Behaviors

Most comprehensive work stress models include coping behaviors. Unfortunately this variable is only generally spelled out (Cherniss, 1980), under researched, or examined separately from the overall stress paradigm (Burke & Weir, 1980). Some measures of coping responses are now available (Folkman, 1982; Pearlin & Schooler, 1978). Apart from the need to refine and validate these measures, it would be useful to relate them to cognitive styles such as attributional preferences and to behavioral styles such as Type A, which has an underlying cognitive component. Recent work on social class and occupational differences in health (Shostak, 1980) suggest that attributional processes may play a key role in coping with stress. Much more research is needed on the effectiveness of various stress management techniques. It will also be important to include a measure of group coping (social support) and organizational coping strategies since some research (Shinn, Rosario, Morch & Chestnut, 1984) have suggested that *individual* coping responses do not reduce strain produced by work stress.

Work, Family and Societal Interface

Most models or frameworks for the study of occupational stress tack on a panel of variables after termed "extraorganizational" (Cooper & Marshall, 1976) to capture the influence of family or life stress on the already occupational stressed individual. I earlier wrote (Payne, Jick & Burke, 1982) that this panel of variables is almost never examined. Instead each life domain is treated as a closed system and the interaction of work and family has been largely ignored.

This picture appears to be changing. We are beginning to understand the sources of conflict between work and family roles (Greenhaus & Beutell, 1985). But few studies have examined sources of stressors in work and family simultaneously while also considering manifestations of stress in both work and family.

A potentially fruitful avenue for research in this area involves incorporating stressful life events research into the mainstream of occupational stress (Bhagat, 1985). In fact it is somewhat surprising that the vast literature spurred by the development of the Holmes and Rahe (1967) scale of life change events has had so little impact on the field of work stress. The incorporation of the role of stressful life events into frameworks for understanding individuals at work would extend our knowledge of how individuals respond to stressful experiences in their work and family lives. There is already evidence that this might prove useful (Cooke & Rousseau, 1983; Bhagat, 1983; Bhagat et al., 1985; Vicino & Bass, 1978; Kobassa, 1979; Kobassa & Puccetti, 1983; Kobassa, Maddi & Puccetti, 1983). The potentially stressful effect of daily hassles (Kanner, Coyne, Schaefer & Lazarus, 1981; Delongis, Coyne, Dakof, Folkman & Lazarus, 1982) might be included as well. Researchers should be aware of some methodological concerns (Dohrenwend & Shrout, 1985; Lazarus, Delongis, Folkman & Gruen, 1985).

There has been relatively little work addressing sources of more pervasive societal on environmental stress. The Three Mile Island incident precipitated a score of articles in the early 1980s (Chisholm & Kasl, 1982). We may expect research on the consequences of the recent Chernobyl disaster. The economic recession of the late 1970s and early 1980s highlighted the stressful effects of unemployment (Fryer & Payne, 1986; Fineman, 1979) and job future insecurity (Jick, 1985). More research is needed in these areas.

Stress as a Process

Stress is, as Pearlin and his colleagues (1981) have argued, a process in which individuals confront sources of stress, attempt to adapt to them using their personal and social resources, and develop more or less enduring health problems as a result of this process. If we are to understand the impact of stress on health and disease variables which take a long time to develop, we must move beyond both cross-sectional studies and prospective studies which measure stress at only a single point in time toward studies which measure both objective potential stressors and perceived stressors at several points in time (House et al., 1986).

House and his colleagues found that none of the job characteristics and stresses measured in 1967-69 predicted mortality by 1979 in the Tecumseh Community Health Study. However, in a subsample of men that also provided data on job characteristics and stressors in 1970, those reporting moderate to high levels of job stressors or tension at *both* times were three times as likely to die between 1970 and 1979 as those whose level of job stressors were low at one or both times. Thus future research must measure experienced stress over time if we expect to find a relationship with outcome variables (morbidity, mortality) having a long etiology (House, 1985).

Work Stress — Is There Less There Than Meets the Eye?

When one examines the stressful effects of such events as job loss on individual well-being, one inevitably raises questions about the relative severity of the effects of work stress on individual well-being. One can make the case, based on available research findings, that though work stress may be momentarily unpleasant, it accounts for only a small amount of the variance in a worker's quality of life. An examination of the correlations reported by Jackson and Schuler (1985) suggests that role conflict and ambiguity (two widely examined work stressors) explain slightly more than 5 percent of the variance in job satisfaction. Job satisfaction, in turn, tends to be a relatively unimportant contributor to one's quality of life (Brief & Hollenbeck, 1985).

It is legitimate that work stress researchers identify harmful work events and work conditions that exist in organizations. An impressive body of empirical research findings on the correlates and consequences of work stress have been accumulated over the past decade. But the important question that must be eventually asked is how significant are these events and conditions to the quality of life and quality of health of workers?

FUTURE STRESS RESEARCH METHODOLOGY

Kasl (1978, 1984a, 1984b) has been a voice in the wilderness raising various methodological issues and challenges for stress researchers. His concerns have gone largely unheeded. I would encourage any individual undertaking work stress research to pay attention to Kasl's guidance and suggestions.

There are two methodological trends that are critical if our understanding of work stress is to be advanced significantly. One involves an increase in the use of longitudinal research designs; the other involves increasing utilization of physiological measurements of work stress.

We have suggested that work stress must be conceptualized as a process. This notion is embedded in much of the available writing (Cherniss, 1980; Folkman & Lazarus, 1985). Unfortunately, the vast majority of research designs use static one-shot methodologies. There are, however, beginning to be published the results of longitudinal research (Eden, 1982; House, Robbins & Metzner, 1982; Fisher, 1985). This trend must be expanded if stress researchers are to establish causal relationships.

It is also important to include a wider array of measures in work stress research. Too many studies involve questionnaire measures of all variables. This makes interpretation of results problematic. Some researchers (see Fried, Rowland & Ferris, 1984) have employed physiological measures of work stress but these measures have often been unrelated to the self-report measures. But as Fried and his colleagues observe, inadequate procedures for measuring such symptoms have often been employed. Thus the results and conclusions of these studies are often invalid or at best questionable. Future stress researchers are encouraged to include physiological measures paying special attention to the procedures for measuring such symptoms. Researchers need to improve their measurement of physiological factors if we are to develop a more complete understanding of not only physiological manifestation of work stress, but to increase the external validity of work stress research in general.

RESEARCH AND PRACTICE—
TWO CULTURES AGAIN?

There is a large gap between work stress researchers and practitioners—the producers and consumers of stress research findings. This can be seen most clearly between work stress researchers and clinicians or applied psychologists, but it also exists between work stress researchers and organizational consultants. The most obvious illustrations of this gap can be seen in: little awareness of research findings by practitioners, little intervention activity being undertaken at the organizational level, little research being undertaken to determine the effectiveness of individual-level interventions, and an increasing irrelevance of work stress research for intervention and policy development. Bridging this gap would appear to be an important concern for readers of this special issue. The result would be better informed research and practice.

This gap is not unique to the area of work stress however (Kilman, 1983). The field of organizational behavior is currently engaged in an examination of ways of doing research that are useful for both theory and practice (see *Administrative Science Quarterly,* 27, 1982; *Administrative Science Quarterly,* 28, 1983; Lawler et al., 1985). Both researchers and consumers of research findings would benefit from an examination of this literature. It is possible to combine research and intervention in the area of work stress (Gardell, 1982) to produce findings of value for policy formulation.

I agree with Beehr and Schuler (1982) where innovative work stress research is likely to result. The ideal research study would involve a large sample of respondents representing the general population, be interdisciplinary in nature, combine both psychological and medical data, be longitudinal in design, involve several different methods of collecting data, assess both objective and subjective work conditions and utilize complex and sophisticated data analysis techniques. These conditions are likely to be found at the larger, more experienced and better funded research institutes (ISR, NIOSH).

CONCLUSION

The quantity of organizational stress research has grown markedly in recent years as has general interest in the subject. Yet in spite of this larger volume, our understanding of the stress phenomenon remains quite limited. This results from the complexity of the stress process as well as a variety of dilemmas and ambiguities facing stress researchers. The latter involve issues of definition, inferences from data collected at one point in time, small and often non-representative samples and a wide variety of different measures of the same concepts.

I expect a continuing commitment to stress research. The magnitude and complexity of the problem warrants this investment. The number of researchers now interested in stress has grown. Some advances in conceptualization and methodology have already taken place. But much more systematic research is needed to elucidate the factors and processes involved in the experience and manifestations of stress. It appears that increases in our understanding of work stress will only come slowly.

REFERENCES

Addison-Wesley Series on Occupational Stress. Reading, MA: Addison-Wesley, 1979.
Administrative Science Quarterly, Special Issue, Part I, The utilization of organizational research, 1982, 27, 588–685.
Administrative Science Quarterly, Special Issue, Part II, The utilization of organizational research, 1983, 28, 63–144.
Beehr, T.A. & Schuler, R.S. Stress in organizations. In Rowland, K.M. & Ferris, G.R. *Personnel Management*. Boston: Allyn & Bacon, Inc., 1982, 390–419.
Beehr, T.A. & Bhagat, R.S. *Stress and cognition in organizations: An integrated perspective*. New York: John Wiley, 1985.
Bhagat, R.S. The role of stressful life events in organizational behavior and human performances. In T.A. Beehr & R.S. Bhagat (eds). *Human Stress and Cognition in Organizations*. New York: John Wiley, 1985.

Bhagat, R.S. Effects of stressful life events on individual performance effectiveness and work adjustment processes within organizational settings: A research model. *Academy of Management Review*, 1983, 8, 660–671.

Bhagat, R.S., McQuaid, S.J., Lindholm, H. & Segovis, J. Total life stress: A multimethod validation of the construct and its effects on organizationally valued outcomes and withdrawal behaviors. *Journal of Applied Psychology*, 1985, 70, 202–214.

Brief, A.P. & Hollenbeck, J.R. Work and the quality of life. *International Journal of Psychology*, 1985, 20, 199–206.

Burke, R.J. Correlates of psychological burnout phases among police officers. *Human Relations*, 1986, 39, 487–502.

Burke, R.J. & Bradshaw, P. Occupational and life stress and the family. *Small Group Behavior*, 1981, 12, 329–375.

Burke, R.J., Shearer, J. & Deszca, G. Correlates of burnout phases among police officers. *Group and Organization Studies*, 1984b, 9, 451– 466.

Burke, R.J., Deszca, G. & Shearer, J. Career orientations and burnout in police officers. *Canadian Journal of Administrative Sciences*, 1984, 1, 179–194.

Burke, R.J. & Greenglass, E.R. Work and family. In C.L. Cooper & I. Robertson (eds). *International Review of Industrial and Organizational Psychology*. New York: John Wiley, 1987, in press.

Burke, R.J., Shearer, J. & Deszca, G. Burnout among men and women in police work: An examination of the Cherniss model. *Journal of Health and Human Resources Administration*, 1984a, 7, 162–188.

Burke, R.J. & Weir, T. Coping with the stress of managerial occupations. In C.L. Cooper & R. Payne (eds). *Current concerns in occupational stress*. New York: Wiley, 1980, 11, 209–335.

Caplan, R.D., Cobb, S., French, J.R.P. Jr., Harrison, R. Van & Pinneau, S.R. Jr. *Job demands and worker health*. U.S. Government Printing Office, Washington, DC, 1975.

Cherniss, C. *Professional burnout in human service organizations*. New York: Praeger, 1980.

Chesney, M.A. & Rosenman, R.H. Type A behavior in the work setting. In C.L. Cooper & R. Payne (eds). *Current concerns in occupational stress*. New York: John Wiley, 1980, 187–212.

Chisholm, R.F. & Kasl, S.V. The effects of work site, supervisory status and job function on nuclear workers' responses to the TMI accident. *Journal of Occupational Behavior*, 1982, 3, 39–62.

Cooke, R.A. & Rousseau, D.M. Relationship of life events and personal orientations to symptoms of strain. *Journal of Applied Psychology*, 1983, 68, 446–458.

Cooper, C.L. *Stress research: Issues for the Eighties*. New York: John Wiley, 1983.

Cooper, C.L. & Payne, R. *Stress at work*. New York: John Wiley, 1978.

Cooper, C.L. & Payne, R. *Current concerns in occupational stress*. New York: John Wiley, 1980.

Cooper, C.L. & Marshall, J. Occupational sources of stress: A review of the literature relating to coronary heart disease and mental ill health. *Journal of Occupational Psychology*, 1976, 49, 11–28.

Delongis, A., Coyne, J.C., Dakof, G., Folkman, S. & Lazarus, R.S. Relationship of daily hassles, uplifts and major life events to health status. *Health Psychology*, 1982, 1, 119–136.

Dohrenwend, B.P. & Shrout, P.E. "Hassles" in the conceptualization and measurement of life stress variables. *American Psychologist*, 1985, 40, 780–785.

Eden, D. Critical job events, acute stress, and strain: A multiple interpreted time series. *Organizational Behavior and Human Performance*, 1982, 30, 312–329.

Fineman, S. A psychological model of stress and its application to managerial unemployment. *Human Relations*, 1979, 32, 323–345.

Fisher, C.D. Social support and adjustment to work: A longitudinal study. *Journal of Management*, 1985, 11, 39–53.

Folkman, S. An approach to the measurement of coping. *Journal of Occupational Behavior*, 1982, 3, 95–108.

Folkman, S. & Lazarus, R.S. If it changes it must be a process: Study of emotion and coping during three stages of a college examination. *Journal of Personality and Social Psychology*, 1985, 48, 150–170.

Ford, D.L. Jr. Facets of work support and employee work outcomes: An exploratory analysis. *Journal of Management*, 1985, 11, 5–20.

Ford, D.L. Jr. An examination of work environment support — work outcome relationships for black professionals. *Journal of Applied Behavioral Science*, 1983, 29, 7–14.

French, J.R.P. Jr., Kahn, R.L. & Mann, F.C. Work, health and satisfaction. *Journal of Social Issues*, 1962, 18, 1–129.

French, J.R.P. Jr. & Caplan, R.D. Occupational stress and individual strain. In Marrow, A.J. (ed). *The Failure of Success*. New York: AMACOM, 1972.

Freudenberger, H.J. *Burnout: The high cost of human achievement*. Garden City, NY: Anchor Press, 1980.

Fried, Y., Rowland, K.M. & Fernis, G.R. The Physiological Measurement of Work Stress: A Critique. *Personnel Psychology*, 1984, 37, 583–615.

Fryer, D. & Payne, R. Being unemployed: A review of the literature on the psychological experience of unemployment. In C.L. Cooper & I. Robertson (eds). *International Review of Industrial and Organizational Psychology*. New York: John Wiley, 1986, in press.

Friedman, M. & Rosenman, R.H. *Type A behavior and your heart*. New York: Alfred Knopf, 1974.

Ganster, D.C., Fusilier, M.R. & Mayes, B.T. Role of social support in the experience of stress at work. *Journal of Applied Psychology*, 1986, 71, 102–110.

Gardell, B. Scandinavian research on stress in working life. *International Journal of Health Services*, 1982, 9, 31–40.

Golembiewski, R.T. An orientation to psychological burnout: Probably something old, definitely something new. *Journal of Health and Human Resources Administration*, 1984, 7, 153–161.

Golembiewski, R.T. & Munzenrider, R. Active and passive reactions to psychological burnout? Toward greater specificity in a phase model. *Journal of Health and Human Resources Administration*, 1984, 7, 260–289.

Golembiewski, R.T. & Munzenrider, R. Efficacy of three versions of one burn-out measure. *Journal of Health and Human Resources Administration*, 1981, 4, 208–244.

Golembiewski, R.T., Munzenrider, R.F. & Stevenson, J.G. *Stress in organizations: Toward a phase model of burnout*. New York: Praeger, 1986.

Golembiewski, R.T., Munzenrider, R. & Carter, D. Phases of progressive burnout and their work-site covariants. *Journal of Applied Behavioral Science*, 1983, 19, 461–482.

Greenglass, E.R. *A world of difference: Gender roles in perspective*. New York: John Wiley, 1982.

Greenhaus, J.H. & Beutell, N.J. Sources of conflict between work and family roles. *Academy of Management Review*, 1985, 10, 76–88.

Gupta, N. & Jenkins, G.D. Jr. Dual career couples: Stress, stressors, strains, and strategies. In T.A. Beehr and R.S. Bhagat (eds). *Human stress and cognition in organizations*. New York: Wiley, 1985, 141–176.

Hall, D.T. & Hall, F.S. Stress and the two-career couple. In G.L. Cooper & R. Payne (eds). *Current concerns in occupational stress*. New York: Wiley, 1980, 243–268.

Haynes, S.G., Feinleib, M. & Kannel, W.B. The relationship of psychosocial factors to coronary heart disease in the Framingham Study. III. Eight-year incidence of coronary heart disease. *American Journal of Epidemiology*, 1980, 111, 37–58.

Haynes, S.G., Feinleib, M., Levine, S., Scotch, N. & Kanall, W.B. The relationship of psychosocial factors to coronary heart disease in the Framingham study. II. Prevalence of coronary heart disease. *American Journal of Epidemiology*, 1978, 107, 384–402.

Holmes, T.H. & Rahe, R.H. The social readjustment rating scale. *Journal of Psychosomatic Research*, 1967, 11, 213–218.

House, J.S. Chronic life situations and life change events: Content discussion. In Ostfeld, A.M. & Eaker, E.D. (eds). *Measuring psychological variables in epidemiologic studies of cardiovascular disease*. Proceedings of a workshop. U.S. Department of Health and Human Services, 1985, NIH Publication No. 85–2270, 129–135.

House, J.S. *Work stress and social support*. Reading, MA: Addison-Wesley, 1980.

House, J.S., Robbins, C. & Metzner, H.M. The association of social relationships and activities with mortality: Prospective evidence from the Tecumseh Community Health Study. *American Journal of Epidemiology*, 1982, 116, 123–140.

House, J.S., Strecher, V., Metzner, H.L. & Robbins, C. Occupational stress and health among men and women in The Tecumseh Community Health Study. *Journal of Health and Social Behavior*, 1986, 27, in press.

House, J.S., McMichael, A.J., Wells, J.A., Kaplan, B.N. & Landerman, L.R. Occupational stress and health among factory workers. *Journal of Health and Social Behavior*, 1979, 20, 139–160.

Ivancevich, J.M. & Matteson, M.T. *Stress and Work: A Managerial Perspective*. Glenview, IL: Scott, Foresman & Company, 1980.

Jackson, S.E. & Schuler, R.S. A meta-analysis and conceptual critique of research on role ambiguity and role conflict in work settings. *Organizational Behavior and Human Performance*, 1985, 36, 16–78.

Jenkins, C.D., Zyzanski, S.J. & Rosenman, R.H. *Jenkins Activity Survey Manual*. New York: Psychological Corporation, 1979.

Jick, T.D. As the ax falls: Budget cuts and the experience of stress in organizations. In Beehr, T.A. & Bhagat, R.S. (eds). *Human stress and cognition in organizations: An integrated perspective*. New York: John Wiley, 1985, 83–114.

Jick, T.D. & Mitz, L.F. Sex differences in work stress. *Academy of Management Review*, 1985, 10, 408–420.

Jick, T.D. & Burke, R.J. Occupational stress: Recent findings and new directions. *Journal of Occupational Behavior*, 1982, 3, 1–4.

Kahn, R.L., Wolfe, D.M., Quinn, R.P., Snoek, J.D. & Rosenthal, R.A. *Organizational stress: Studies in role conflict and ambiguity*. New York: John Wiley, 1964.

Kanner, A.D., Coyne, J.C., Schaefer, C. & Lazarus, R.S. Comparison of two modes of stress measurement: Daily hassles and uplifts versus major life events. *Journal of Behavioural Medicine*, 1981, 4, 1–39.

Kanter, R.M. *Work and family in the United States: A critical review and agenda for research and policy*. New York: Russell Sage, 1977.

Kasl, S.V. Stress and health. *Annual Review of Public Health*, 1984a, 5, 319–341.

Kasl, S.V. Chronic life stress and health. *Health Care and Human Behavior*, 1984b, 41–55.

Kasl, S.V. Epidemiological contributions to the study of work stress. In C.L. Cooper & R. Payne (eds). *Stress and Work*. New York: Wiley, 1978.

Kasl, S.V. The challenge of studying the disease effects of stressful work conditions. *American Journal of Public Health*, 1981, 71, 682–684.

Karasek, R.A. Job demands, job decision latitude, and mental strain: Implications for job redesign. *Administrative Science Quarterly*, 1979, 24, 285–308.

Karasek, R.A., Triantis, K.P. & Chaudry, S.S. Coworker and supervisory support as moderators of associations between task characteristics and mental strain. *Journal of Occupational Behavior*, 1982, 3, 181–200.

Kilman, R.H. (ed). *Producing useful knowledge for organizations*. New York: Praeger, 1983.

Kobassa, S.C. Stressful life events, personality and health: An inquiry into hardiness. *Journal of Personality and Social Psychology*, 1979, 37, 1–11.

Kobassa, S.C. & Puccetti, M.C. Personality and social resources in stress resistance. *Personality and Social Psychology*, 1983, 45, 839–850.

Kobassa, S.C., Maddi, S.R. & Puccetti, M.C. Personality and exercise as buffers in the stress-illness relationship. *Journal of Behavioral Medicine*, 1982, 5, 391–404.

LaRocco, J.M. & Jones, A.P. Coworker and leader support as moderators of stress strain relationships in work situations. *Journal of Applied Psychology*, 1978, 63, 629–634.

LaRocco, J.M., House, J.S. & French, J.R.P. Jr. Social support, occupational stress, and health. *Journal of Health and Social Behavior*, 1980, 21, 202–218.

Larwood, L., Stromberg, A.H. & Gutek, B.A. *Women and work: An annual review*. Beverly Hills, CA: Sage Publications, 1985. Volume 1.

Lazarus, R.S., Delongis, A., Folkman, S. & Gruen, R. Stress and adaptational outcomes: The problem of confounded measures. *American Psychologist*, 1985, 40, 770–779.

Lawler, E.E., Mohrman, A.M., Mohrman, S.A., Ledford, G.E. & Cummings, T.G. *Doing research that is useful for theory and practice*. San Francisco: Jossey-Bass, 1985.

Lee, M.D. & Kanungo, R.N. *Management of work and personal life*. New York: Praeger, 1984.

Maddi, S.R. & Kobasa, S.C. *The hardy executive: Health under stress*. Homewood, IL: Dow Jones-Irwin, 1984.

Maslach, C. *Burnout: The cost of caring*. Englewood Cliffs, NJ: Prentice-Hall, 1982.

Maslach, C. & Jackson, S.W. Measurement of experienced burnout. *Journal of Occupational Behavior*, 1981, 2, 99–113.

Matteson, M.T., Ivancevich, J.M. & Smith, S.V. Relation of Type A behavior to performance and satisfaction among sales personnel. *Journal of Vocational Behavior*, 1984, 25, 203–214.

McLean, A. Occupational mental health: Review of an emerging art. *The American Journal of Psychiatry*, 1966, 61, 961–976.

Newman, J.E. & Beehr, T.A. Personal and organizational strategies for handling job stress: A review of research and opinion. *Personnel Psychology*, 1979, 32, 1–43.

Nieva, V.F. Work and family roles. In Lee, M.D. & Kanungo, R.N. (eds). *Management of work and personal life*. New York: Praeger, 1984, 15–40.

Nieva, V.F. & Gutek, B.A. *Women and work: A psychological perspective*. New York: Praeger, 1981.

Payne, R. Organizational strain and social support. In Cooper, C.L. & Payne, R. (eds). *Current concerns in occupational stress*. New York: John Wiley, 1980, 269–298.

Payne, R., Jick, T.D. & Burke, R.J. Whither stress research? An agenda for the 1980s. *Journal of Occupational Behavior*, 1982, 3, 131–145.

Pearlin, L.L., Liberman, M.A., Managhan, E.G. & Mullan, J.T. The stress process. *Journal of Health and Social Behavior*, 1981, 22, 337–356.

Pearlin, L.I. & Schooler, C. The structure of coping. *Journal of Health and Social Behavior*, 1978, 19, 2–21.

Pines, A., Aronson, E. & Kafry, D. *Burnout: From tedium to personal growth*. New York: Free Press, 1981.

Price, V.A. *Type A behavior pattern: A model for research and practice*. New York: Academic Press, 1982.

Quick, J.C. & Quick, J.D. *Organizational stress and preventive management*. New York: McGraw-Hill, 1984.

Shinn, M., Rosario, M., March, H. & Chestnut, D.E. Coping with job stress and burnout in the human services. *Journal of Personality and Social Psychology*, 1984, 46, 864–876.

Shostak, A.B. *Blue-collar stress*. Reading, MA: Addison Wesley, 1980.

Staw, B.M. Organizational behavior: A review and reformulation of the fields outcome variables. In Rosenzweig, M.R. & Porter, L.W. (eds). *Annual Review of Psychology*, Palo Alto, CA: Annual Reviews Inc., 1984, 35, 627–666.

Terborg, J.R. Working women and stress. In Beehr, T.A. & Bhagat, R.S. (eds). *Human Stress and Cognition in Organizations*. New York: John Wiley, 1985, 245–286.

Vicino, F.L. & Bass, B.M. Life space variables and managerial sources. *Journal of Applied Psychology*, 1978, 63, 81–88.

Wells, J.A. The role of social support groups in stress coping in organizational settings. In
Sethi, A.S. & Schuler, R.S. (eds). *Handbook of organizational stress coping strategies*.
Cambridge, MA: Ballinger, 1984, 113–143.